Getting Unscrewed and Staying That Way

The Sourcebook of Consumer Protection

David Klein, Marymae E. Klein, and Douglas D. Walsh

Henry Holt and Company
New York

Henry Holt and Company, Inc.
Publishers since 1866
115 West 18th Street
New York, New York 10011

Henry Holt® is a registered trademark of Henry Holt and Company, Inc.

Library of Congress Cataloging-in-Publication Data
Klein, David.
Getting unscrewed and staying that way: the sourcebook of consumer protection /
David Klein, Marymae E. Klein, and Douglas D. Walsh.—1st ed.
p.   cm.
Includes index.
1. Consumer protection—United States. 2. Consumer protection—Law and
legislation—United States.   I. Klein, Marymae. II. Walsh, Douglas D.   III.
Title.
HC110.C63K58   1993
381.3′4′0973—dc20   92-37110
                                                                CIP

ISBN 0-8050-2590-1

First Edition—1993

Printed in the United States of America
All first editions are printed on acid-free paper. ∞
10 9 8 7 6 5 4 3 2 1

*To attorneys general and
assistant attorneys general
who protect consumers everywhere*

Contents

Note to the Reader

IN ADDITION TO Ralph Nader and his colleagues Sidney Wolfe and Joan Claybrook, we regard two people as heroes of consumerism. Both of them are unnamed and their efforts have gone unsung, but each of them can teach us a useful lesson.

Back in the early 1960s, long before the Lemon Law had been invented, a middle-aged Michigan man fulfilled his lifelong dream of buying a Cadillac. After purchasing it, however, he discovered to his dismay that "it went thunk" every time he put it in reverse.

He immediately took the car back to the dealer, who was either unwilling or unable to make repairs. He wrote to General Motors and got no response. Then his campaign got under way. He wrote to GM's president and asked whether he wasn't ashamed to be the head of a corporation whose flagship product "went thunk every time it was shifted to reverse."

Receiving no reply, he wrote personal letters to each of the corporation's directors asking them whether they were aware that their company was producing a luxury car that "went thunk every time it was shifted to reverse." Again no response.

He then sent special-delivery letters and telegrams (timed to arrive at inconvenient hours) to the wife, children, relatives, and friends of GM's president asking them whether they were not ashamed to be related to or associated with a corporate executive responsible for a car that "went thunk every time it was shifted to reverse."

The campaign took several months and cost him a fair amount of time, postage, and telegram charges, but one morning there was a knock on his door—a brand new Cadillac was delivered and the old one driven away. The new one did not go "thunk" every time it was shifted to reverse.

Our second hero is a university professor who late one night checked in to Montreal's Queen Elizabeth hotel to attend an international pediatrics meeting. The desk clerk looked at the professor's confirmed reservation slip, shook his head, and told him that "there must be some mistake. We simply don't have a room for you."

The professor glanced at his watch and said, in civil tones, "Look, I've had a lousy flight and I'm dead tired. So if you don't get me a room within the next three minutes I'm going to take my clothes off right here, get into my pajamas, and go to sleep on that sofa near the elevator."

Needless to say, he got his room before he had time to loosen his necktie.

The lesson is obvious. If you are persistent, and if you have some ingenuity and the courage of your convictions, you can— most of the time if not always—stick up for your rights as a consumer and have your grievance redressed. *Getting Unscrewed and Staying That Way* is devoted to showing you the various ways of doing this. It can also help you stay out of trouble in the first place.

But some words of caution are in order. This book is *not* a lawyer in book form, and you cannot use its contents as irrefutable arguments in a dispute or a lawsuit. For one thing, although we have been careful to provide information and listings that are up-to-date for all fifty states, we have no way of knowing whether, after publication, state and federal laws will change, if the policies of regulatory agencies will be revised, or if the exigencies of budgeting will limit or eliminate any services that now inform or protect the consumer.

Another reason is that we know nothing about you or the specific details of your complaint or their validity in a dispute. When consumer advocates first enter the field, many instinctively side with the consumer and take it for granted that the complaint is justified. It takes them little time, however, to discover that complaining consumers are not always right—that they sometimes neglect to mention documents they've signed or letters they've received or conciliatory offers made by the supplier, or that they're unaware of the state laws governing the transaction.

Despite these limitations, the general guidelines we offer should help you analyze and respond to situations in which you feel you've been ripped off. If, however, the transaction involves significant rights or property, or any degree of legal complexity, you would do well, after reading the advice we offer, to consult a lawyer.

1

It Takes Two . . .

1

Sins of the Sellers

UNTIL WE STOP to think about it, or until we've been badly ripped off, most of us feel moderately satisfied with what's called the "market economy." As socialist economies around the world struggle or collapse and as most of us continue to enjoy a comparatively high standard of living, it's easy to feel that we live in the best of all possible worlds.

And American business continues to reinforce this notion. Advertisements for banks stress the friendliness of their tellers and the helpfulness of their loan officers. Major corporations, by sponsoring public television programs, community improvement projects, museum programs, scholarships, and other worthy causes, convince us that they are "good guys" and divert out attention from their continuous lobbying against regulation, their massive contributions to pollution and unbridled materialism, and their oligopolistic practices. Meanwhile, at the face-to-face level, every seller—from the airline ticket agent to the neighborhood pharmacist and supermarket checkout clerk—tells us to "have a nice day."

But a moment's thought makes it clear to us that, despite the carefully orchestrated "good guy" image, the relationship between buyer and seller is basically adversarial. The seller, understandably, wants to reap as high a profit as possible on the car or the airline seat or the toaster. The buyer, on the other hand, seeks to acquire high-quality goods and services for as few dollars as possible. And so, although we may have learned in our high school economics course that the laws of supply and demand make the consumer king and that the supplier dances for the buyer's dollar, in reality the consumer confronting the supplier is like a boxer—a boxer who, in almost every bout, faces an opponent who outmatches him in weight, skill, and stamina.

This is not to say that every transaction ends up with the consumer flat on the floor. On the contrary, most of us, especially if we are reasonably smart shoppers, are moderately satisfied with—or at least resigned about—what we buy, be it a refrigerator, a video camera, or a shopping cart full of groceries. Yet a substantial proportion of consumers report that they've been badly disappointed with at least one major purchase, and a large number of them feel bitter and humiliated about being ripped off. When the consumer protection division of the attorney general's office in a relatively small state receives more than 220,000 telephone complaints and inquiries and more than 18,000 written complaints from its citizens each year, one can hardly conclude that all goes smoothly in the marketplace.

WHO'S TO BLAME?

It's easy, of course, to blame all these rip-offs, real or perceived, on the suppliers—car dealers, travel agents, mail-order firms, and others. After all, even those who are scrupulously ethical have the upper hand, whether through the seductiveness of their glossy advertising and sophisticated sales pitch or because of the consumer's inability to judge accurately the quality of the product. But the consumer is not always an entirely innocent victim. Every transaction in which the consumer feels ripped off involves two parties—the ripper and the rippee. To understand the dynamics of consumer abuse we need to look more closely at the behavior of each party. In this chapter, we'll deal with the supplier; in the next, with the consumer.

YESTERDAY AND TODAY

A backward look at the marketplace in the "good old days" early in this century can make all of us nostalgic, whatever our age. Back then, buyers tended to deal with sole proprietors: the local grocer, butcher, or hardware store owner. Most transactions took place between people who knew each other as neighbors, fellow church members, or even distant relatives. The relationship was personal, and cheating was discouraged by the seller's realization that "word would get around." The small-town grocer would extend credit to customers who were temporarily hard up, and even the biggest business in town—the early department store—was owned or managed locally by a family or a group of businessmen who felt some commitment to the community as well as concern over their personal reputations. In short, integrity and customer service were intimately linked with business success and profitability.

This is not to say that the early years of this century were a consumer's paradise. Because government food and drug regulation was nonexistent or primitive at best, thousands of people died from botulism and other kinds of food poisoning. Lydia Pinkham's Compound, a tonic sold for the alleviation of "female problems," turned countless women into closet alcoholics with its 19 percent alcohol content. The snake oil sold by peddlers at county fairs earned a permanent place in dictionaries as a synonym for fraud. And career con artists plied their trade with even more abandon and profit than they do today.

Nevertheless, most transactions in earlier days took place between people who knew each other. Even today, consumer protection agencies receive relatively few complaints against suppliers in small towns, where reputation and word-of-mouth advertising can make or break a business.

In today's urban society, by contrast, virtually all transactions take place between strangers, many of whom are the agents of large, impersonal businesses. We know nothing about the salesperson from whom we buy our car, the clerk in a department store, or even the proprietor of a local boutique. And this impersonality is not much tempered by the supermarket clerk's programmed "Hi, how are you today?" or the dry cleaner's posted assurance, "We love our customers." Hence, our comfort in any transaction must be based on what we know about the supplier itself—which is often precious little—or on our assumption that the seller complies with normal business practices—an assumption that all too frequently turns out to be invalid.

THE EQUAL OPPORTUNITY EXPLOITERS

As we discuss in the next chapter, some consumers are more vulnerable than others to various forms of exploitation. But some large corporations might well be called "equal opportunity exploiters," because they injure all individuals no matter their race, creed, or general sophistication. Air pollution and oil spills, for example, harm all of us, rich or poor, educated or not. Industrial accidents harm not only workers but often bystanders and the community as a whole. The reluctance of manufacturers to produce truly fuel-efficient cars affects not only individual pocketbooks but the national economy as well. And the airlines' arbitrary follow-the-leader fare increases affect every traveler.

What aggravates this situation is the increasing concentration of American business. As the takeovers and mergers continue to build conglomerations and reduce the number of companies—whether automobile manufacturers, banks, or airlines—competition diminishes, and the consumer is left with fewer choices. The system is governed by corporate officers who must produce short-term profits and who are far more concerned with pleasing the shareholders than with satisfying the customers.

The consequences are easy enough to identify. To begin with, there's the matter of price-fixing—or, to use the more polite term, "price leadership." Whether we are shopping for a compact sedan or an airline ticket from San Francisco to New York, we are likely to find prices remarkably consistent. When one automobile manufacturer offers incentives, the others follow suit, and when one airline announces a ticket sale, the others follow in a matter of hours.

Our choice, then, is limited to what economists call "product differentiation"—that is, our decision that one car is better than another, or that one airline's meals are less inedible than what its competitors serve, or that one brand of gasoline cleans our intake valves more effectively than another. Of course, most of us don't know how to determine which car is better in terms of economy and reliability; we can determine that one airline meal is better only after having consumed some poorer ones; and we are unlikely to dismantle our engines to inspect the intake valves.

Moreover, because the market for basic appliances, from potato peelers to refrigerators, has been saturated, manufacturers have had to channel their efforts in two directions: creating demand for new products (whether they are useful or not) and making certain that their products don't last too long. This is why we are seduced by automobile ads that stress gadgetry, the pleasures of outpacing the Joneses, and other psychic gratifications rather than the durability or price of the car; and by such items as cigarette lighters that (unlike the classic guaranteed-for-life Zippo) are guaranteed *not* to last longer than the brief lifetime of their butane charge. And, as one reader of kitchen mail-order catalogues remarked, "These gadgets promise to solve problems that you never knew existed." Small wonder, then, that few consumers are truly delighted with what they buy, that most are resigned, and that a great many are disappointed.

Let the Customer Do It

Another trend among large corporations is to reduce their costs by burdening the consumer with tasks that were formerly performed by the companies themselves. This shifting of responsibility may be legitimate when the savings benefits the consumer, as it does when the customer pumps the gas or direct-dials a long-distance call, but in most cases the profits go to the corporation. Examples are easy enough to come by:

- By building weaker automobile bumpers that can only withstand impact at less than 2.5 miles per hour, a number of manufacturers are saving a few dollars per car. But car owners have been forced to spend thousands of dollars to repair damages sustained at very low speeds.
- By forcing the user to provide ZIP codes, the U.S. Postal Service saves huge amounts of time and work, yet postage rates continue to escalate.
- By using hub systems, airlines improve their revenues, but the lack of nonstop flights forces passengers to fly thousands of miles out of their way.
- By making baggage-checking both risky and time-consuming, the airlines force many passengers to buy compact luggage and carry it themselves, which contributes to congestion in boarding and deplaning.
- In order to reduce the number of switchboard operators, companies instruct callers to "press 1, 2" or whatever in order to reach a further menu of "press 1, etc." before they can reach their parties, obtain information, or get operator assistance.
- Supermarkets have abandoned the use of price labels on items in favor of "shelf-pricing," a considerable savings in time and work but a physical hardship for customers who wear bifocals and a financial inconvenience for those who want to keep track of prices.
- Fast-food restaurants package their condiments in cost-effective but user-resistant plastic pouches, offering many customers a choice between breaking a fingernail and doing without.
- When an American automobile manufacturer discovered that only 1 percent of the Japanese radios it inspected before installation in its cars were defective, it

decided to save money by not inspecting them. This forced
1 percent of its customers to return to the dealer for
replacement of a defective radio.

Cost-saving tactics might be acceptable if they benefit the consumer through better service or lower prices. But the cost of groceries, fast foods, and other products and services goes up steadily,
and the quality seems no better, even though the changes are invariably introduced by the supplier as being "new and improved"
or "for your convenience."

Where's the Referee?

Outmatched as the consumer is by the giant corporations, one
would think that there ought to be a referee to ensure a minimum
of fairness. And in theory, various referees exist. But although the
antitrust laws and other fair-trade regulations, as well as such regulatory agencies as the Federal Trade Commission and the Food
and Drug Administration, purport to protect the consumer, their
effectiveness depends on the extent to which they are funded and
politically motivated. And this depends, in turn, on the current
ideology of Congress and the administration, neither of which, in
recent years, has shown much substantive dedication to consumer
welfare. Still other agencies, such as the Interstate Commerce
Commission, the Federal Aviation Administration, and the National Highway Traffic Safety Administration, have been accused
of favoring the regulated industries rather than the consumer (see
Chapter 16).

The influence of industry on regulation can be seen at two levels. By making substantial campaign contributions, lobbyists can
inhibit lawmakers from passing regulatory legislation. But even if
public outcry makes regulation politically inevitable, the lobbyists
are able to participate in the rule-making sessions of the regulatory
agency to ensure that the final regulations are as toothless as possible.

Nevertheless, gross malfeasance by major corporations generally does get corrected, though often belatedly and after much damage has been done. The Federal Trade Commission and the U.S. Postal Service do prosecute flagrant mail fraud (after enough complaints accumulate), and the Securities and Exchange Commission functions as a watchdog over the stock markets, as does the Federal Communications Commission over the media. Individual cabinet officers—notably Secretaries of Health and Human Services—have also taken an aggressive stand in the banning of harmful products and in requiring truth in labeling.

As for dangerous or defective products, the National Highway Traffic Safety Administration has ordered numerous recalls of defective vehicles, and the Consumer Product Safety Commission has recalled hazardous products, though neither of these agencies goes into action until complaints pile up or a mishap of tragic or near tragic proportions attracts national attention. The Food and Drug Administration does bar dangerous and ineffective drugs from the market and can recall those that prove harmful. And although some manufacturers, such as the firms that produced the silicone breast implant and the Dalkon Shield, have shown themselves to be extremely irresponsible, many others recall faulty products voluntarily, as Johnson & Johnson did at enormous expense when tampered containers of Tylenol were found to be responsible for a few deaths.

Occasionally, even state governments, either unilaterally or through cooperation among their attorneys general, can influence federal regulation or the behavior of large corporations. The Attorneys' General Multistate Task Force on Environmental Marketing, for example, has vigorously policed the national marketplace for deceptive and fraudulent "green" claims about biodegradable, recyclable plastic packaging and "earth-friendly" aerosol sprays. And a coalition of state attorneys general has forced major credit-reporting bureaus to end a wide array of consumer abuses—an action that seems likely to produce general reform in an industry whose widespread negligence has created serious problems for thousands of consumers.

The state of California, because its citizens buy vast numbers of cars, has been able to set its own antipollution standards, forcing manufacturers to produce a less polluting "California" model for sale in that state and petroleum refiners to produce a cleaner gasoline.

The Lemon Laws of several states have saved millions of dollars for consumers who bought new but seriously defective vehicles. And, as we shall see in Chapter 11, the state attorneys general, by analyzing individual complaints filed with their consumer protection divisions, often discern patterns of gross abuse that lead to legislative remedies.

Even county governments can make a difference. Several county legislatures in New York, responding to consumer complaints that supermarket shelf-pricing was inconvenient and confusing, have prohibited the practice within their jurisdictions and now require supermarkets to label each item with its price, despite the supermarkets' protestations on grounds of cost.

But the remedies against the abuses we've noted are essentially political and, because they are often legislative responses to loud public outcry, they are easily misdirected. In the 1950s, after the deaths of six children who were trapped in discarded refrigerators, new legislation required that all refrigerators be openable from the inside, a change that required considerable retooling across the industry. In the same year, more than seven hundred children were "accidentally" killed by firearms, but Congress did nothing in response to this much higher death toll. Presumably the appliance manufacturers' lobbyists were less effective than the National Rifle Association.

Similarly, in an effort to reduce childhood poisoning, new legislation required companies to package medication in the almost universal childproof drug containers. In fact, the vast majority of childhood poisonings are caused by petroleum products and household chemicals, but the politically popular childproof caps continue to inconvenience thousands of childless users, especially the arthritic elderly.

Often, too, a popular uproar subsides and nothing results from it. The gas shortages and the increase of the federal deficit over the past two decades led Congress to pass legislation aimed at increasing the fuel efficiency of motor vehicles. But industry lobbying has weakened this legislation critically. Partly as a consequence of campaign financing by political action committees (PACs), legislators tend to favor the interests of business rather than those of the consumer and only if the consumer takes an aggressive stand against corporate abuses are they likely to be eliminated.

Although the individual may feel powerless in these situations, such citizen groups as the Center for Automotive Safety, the Center for Science in the Public Interest, the Sierra Club, Greenpeace, and other voluntary organizations have had significant impact on both the corporate offenders and the bureaucratic regulatory agencies. Supporting them can offer the consumer considerable satisfaction and empowerment, even though such support will not remedy an individual problem.

SNIPERS AND SHARPSHOOTERS

The vast majority of consumer complaints involve not the major corporations but smaller companies—some of them local and some of them, such as mail-order firms and telemarketers, who do business interstate. Many of these firms apparently believe that the occasional sharp practice is essential if they are to remain profitable. But others are set up for the sole purpose of exploiting the consumer and disappear with their ill-gotten gains before the regulatory agencies can take action against them. What these companies have in common is that, unlike the equal opportunity exploiters, they target specific groups of consumers who are in some way particularly vulnerable.

Until the Federal Trade Commission established the Funeral Rule in 1984, funeral homes were notorious for selling expensive and unnecessary services to bereaved survivors who were too distraught emotionally to realize that they were being cheated. Today the consumer shopping for funeral services is well protected, and the level of compliance by funeral homes is high. Similarly, unsophisticated homeowners were widely defrauded by itinerant roofing, siding, and driveway-resurfacing salespeople until the passage of the three-day cancellation rule, although violations remain widespread.

But abuses of vulnerable consumers persist. Throughout the country, classified advertisements promise the unemployed "work at home" opportunities (if they buy a worthless kit), a listing of "jobs overseas" (if they make an expensive call to a [900] number), or a "business seminar" that will teach them, for a fee of several hundred dollars, how to earn "more than $50,000 a year by working in your home for just a few hours a day."

People who have poor credit are offered bogus credit cards in return for a substantial fee, or they are saddled with usurious loans for "as is" cars by used-car dealers who assure them that "your job is your credit."

Parents with low levels of education, who are understandably concerned about their children's educational progress, are frequently the victims of door-to-door sellers of thousand-dollar encyclopedias, which more sophisticated consumers would reject out of hand.

The elderly are also a prime target—for poor-value medigap insurance policies and for living trusts, which are often sold to people who are close to indigence. And, if they live in older housing, they are especially vulnerable to "home improvement" salespeople.

But perhaps the largest group of victims is composed of people who are not skeptical enough to question the "Congratulations! You have just won a . . ." postcard that has been mailed to thousands of people, or the "miraculous" new labor-saving gadget that turns out not to work, or the investment scheme that promises a rate of return 50 percent higher than what they could earn from the best legitimate investment, or even the state lottery, in which the odds *against* winning are far higher than the million-to-one payoff.

WHERE ARE THE COPS?

Given this prevalence of crime against the consumer, one might well ask about a police presence. As we shall see in Part Three, there are, fortunately, numerous police forces, although their effectiveness varies. The basic problem stems less from the absence or ineffectiveness of these forces than from the reluctance of the bilked consumer to cry "Help!"

Although the consumer protection agencies across the country log many thousands of calls each day, their staffs are aware that these calls represent only the tip of the iceberg of consumer abuse. Consumers in the huge submerged section have varied explanations for their apathy. Some are unaware that the agencies exist. Others are too embarrassed to admit that they have been victimized. Still others cynically believe that they will get no more action on their behalf than they get from a big-city police force when they report a robbery.

What these silent victims fail to realize is that, whether or not their individual complaint is resolved, it is only when the agencies can compile enough data to reveal a pervasive and consistent pattern of abuse that they can take aggressive enforcement or legislative action to eliminate it.

Chapters 3 through 9 deal with a wide range of transactions that persistently generate a high volume of consumer complaints, and they suggest ways in which the consumer can avoid abuse. Chapters 10 through 16 identify channels through which the abused consumer can seek redress.

2

Blunders
of the Buyer

SOME CONSUMERS COPE with the marketplace competently, and they emerge from thousands of transactions more or less unscathed. This is not to say that they have never had a problem—with a coat that shrank at the dry cleaners, for example, or with a car that rusted out prematurely. But despite occasional disappointments, they derive reasonable satisfaction from what they buy.

Other consumers, by contrast, seem to be "accident-prone." They first experience trouble when their health club goes bankrupt and then get into more serious difficulties when they default on the bank loan they negotiated to pay the health club fees. This leads, of course, to problems with their credit rating. Or they buy a defective used car, get no satisfaction from the seller, and then run into further problems with the mechanic they hired to fix it.

Is there any way to distinguish between the "smart" consumer and the "dumb" one? One might think that income has something to do with it, since well-to-do consumers rarely buy terminally defective used cars and don't fall for fraudulent offers of credit repair, work-at-home opportunities, or get-rich-quick schemes. Yet the well-to-do seem to be victimized often enough by financial advisers, realtors, architects, and other experts they consult. And they frequently overpay for goods and services because they don't take the time to shop around.

Do intelligence and education count? To some extent they do. Well-educated and well-informed consumers usually avoid "hard sell" door-to-door salespeople and fraudulent investment schemes. They are not taken in by the blatant scams advertised in the supermarket tabloids, and they are more likely to do some research before buying a big-ticket item. But they may be easy prey for a persuasive stockbroker or the status appeal of an Acura or an Infiniti.

What about experience? The adage "Once bitten, twice shy" has some relevance here, but the "bite" can be extremely painful, and it doesn't necessarily immunize the victim against other animals. The consumer who has been disappointed with a mail-order purchase may have learned something from the experience but may go on to have a more costly run-in with a realtor or an auto mechanic.

Since there seem to be no personal characteristics that immunize the consumer—and no vaccine either—what may be helpful is an analysis of consumer complaints that flood consumer protection agencies. Although these range from the trivial (a faulty can opener) to the very serious (a $15,000 car that turns out to be a lemon), they have enough in common to reveal some of the behaviors that lead consumers, rich or poor, smart or dumb, into trouble. And from these examples we can derive some fairly reliable rules for protecting all kinds of buyers of all kinds of goods and services.

READ IT OR WEEP

Even though mortgage notes, insurance policies, warranties, or installment contracts have no redeeming literary value and are hardly written in elegant prose, the most effective tactics for consumer protection are reading these documents, asking blunt questions, and demanding understandable answers. A significant proportion of consumer complaints are made simply because before signing the documents covering a transaction—the receipt for earnest money in a real estate transaction, the prospectus of a mutual fund, the exclusions on an insurance policy, the window sticker on a used car, the agreement covering the issue of a credit card—the consumer did not take time to read and understand them.

Read Before Shopping

But reading—especially when a substantial purchase is involved—should begin long before the buyer confronts the seller. Because most of us can't assess the quality of such high-tech products as automobiles or VCRs and often can't determine a fair price, we are forced to rely on experts—and expert advice is often available in print.

As we will note in Chapter 3, buyers of both new and used cars can consult an extensive literature that offers evaluations and price guidelines. The April "auto" issue of *Consumer Reports,* for example, offers a digest of its unbiased evaluations of virtually any car—both new and used—and careful reading can protect buyers against serious errors, provided, of course, that they don't lose their heads in the dealer's showroom.

Consumer Reports also evaluates other merchandise—from major appliances to dishwasher detergents. The evaluations don't cover every brand, and often the models evaluated are discontinued before the ratings appear, but for objectivity and accuracy, it's the only game in town.

There are, of course, other sources for other products: Standard and Poor's *Stock Guide* and the financial columns in major newspapers for investments, the product reviews in computer magazines for machines and accessories, the automotive magazines and the newspaper automobile columns for further information on new cars, and the boating journals for boats. The extent to which some of these sources are influenced by advertisers can never be known, nor is the technical competence of the writers a known quantity, but consulting several sources on the same product is likely to produce some consensus.

Advertisements, although intended to entice purchasers, can

also educate them about specifications and prices. The mail-order catalogues that seasonally clog our mailboxes may be a nuisance, but the reputable ones usually describe an item in more specific detail than do department store ads. And real estate ads, despite their hyperbole, can give house hunters a general notion of how much to pay for a house or an apartment of a certain size in a desired neighborhood.

A warning about promises made in television commercials: the information in these ads deserves a careful reading. The phrase "not sold in stores" should make viewers wonder why, and the fact that the legally required "disclosure" lines at the bottom of the screen are illegible should automatically warn viewers that the seductive promise made has a catch to it.

Read Before Signing

Reading and comparing before buying can prevent the purchase of an inferior product—for example, a car that is likely to give trouble or a computer that isn't as versatile as a competing brand. But failure to read and understand the *terms* of the transaction (whether it's a credit card application, the extended service warranty on a used car, a layaway deposit, or an order for a custom-made bridal gown or a special-order recreational vehicle) can cause far more serious problems. Yet some of us are so eager to get the paperwork over with that we neglect to scrutinize the terms of the purchase document. Impetuously in love with the product or the service, we fail to think or ask about what happens if things should go wrong.

Neglecting to read the purchase contract on a car has caused many buyers to be unaware that the value of their trade-in may be subject to last-minute change. By scanning instead of reading an auto-financing agreement many buyers overlook the paragraph that allows the lender to repossess their new purchase moments after a single payment is in default by even one day. Ignoring the fine print of a real estate binder can result in the loss of earnest money if the buyer should change his mind or fail to get financing.

By only glancing over the terms of a mortgage application, many buyers miss the fact that the appraisal fee is not refundable or that late payments can subject them to heavy penalties.

None of us enjoys reading paragraph after paragraph of dense legalese set in almost illegible type. And so we rely on the assurance of the seemingly sincere salesperson. Only when we complain of some inequity do we discover that oral assurances have no legal validity and that our signature has bound us irrevocably to the agreement that we now find unfair.

The most valuable consumer protection laws are those that require boilerplate contracts to include information on the consumer's cancellation rights and how they can be exercised. Buyers who fail to read the contract before buying stand to miss this critical information.

GET IT IN WRITING

Many of us have such nostalgic admiration for the stereotypical small-town transaction, which allegedly involved nothing more than a handshake with someone "whose word was as good as his bond," that we fail to realize the importance, in *every* major transaction, of "getting it in writing."

Many buyers of used cars, for example, rely on the dealer's oral assurance that the car is "in fine shape," only to discover a few miles down the road a major or even fatal defect for which, according to the contract of sale, the dealer accepts no responsibility.

Buyers of rebuilt automobile engines who are satisfied with the word *guaranteed* on their bill of sale do not realize until after they have had the defective engine installed that the guarantee did not cover the labor involved in installing and then removing it when it proved defective.

Many buyers of custom-made products—wedding gowns, pickup truck cabs, or furniture—willingly make a nonrefundable deposit but forget to specify a delivery date and find themselves, months later, with neither their money nor the product. Many applicants for health club memberships fail to get in writing some assurance about their rights and obligations should the club move, reduce its services, or go out of business.

Confronted with a contract, a lease, or other form of agreement—which almost invariably is written in language that protects the interests of the supplier—many consumers seem to feel that the printed word is sacrosanct and hesitate to use a pen to clarify, amend, or even remove some parts of it. They fail to realize that unless every one of its sentences is crystal clear and acceptable, they may be headed for trouble.

Another "failure to write" problem can arise when a major item is paid for with cash or money order instead of a check or a credit card. A cleared check constitutes immediate and irrefutable evidence of payment. A money order stub provides no evidence until the issuer can trace payment—a process that can take months. Payment in cash constitutes no proof unless the consumer gets a *genuine* receipt. Credit cards establish the chain of payment and, in addition, provide charge-back protection (see p. 141).

One would think that only drug dealers pay for major items in cash, but the practice extends to all sorts of noncriminal types. Some mechanics and contractors, on completing a job, ask the customer for cash on the grounds that they need the money immediately, and in some cases the obliging customer has gone to his or her own bank to get it. One customer, for example, paid $800 in cash for an auto repair—the attendant accepted the payment, handed him his car keys, and promptly absconded with the money, leaving the customer to be hounded for payment by the proprietor. A widow paid $500 in cash to a bogus insurance agent and received as a receipt his initials on an equally bogus business card.

READ IT AND KEEP

One of the most severe frustrations reported by lawyers and by consumer protection agencies involves complaints that appear completely legitimate but lack any kind of supporting documentation. For example, many consumers pursued by collection agencies claim to have paid the debt but cannot produce canceled checks, money order stubs, or receipts to prove their claim. Consumers who charge that they have been cheated by automobile dealers are unable to provide the window sticker or signed agreement that would support their complaint. Consumers who complain about a defective product are unable to produce the warranty that accompanied it. Many consumers who argue that their credit card statement is incorrect are unable to locate their copy of the disputed charge slip. And some consumers who complain about undelivered mail orders cannot even remember the name of the company from which they ordered.

In today's marketplace, the active consumer is forced to keep sometimes bulky files of documentation: contractors' estimates; sales slips, canceled checks, and warranties for each major transaction; catalogue tearsheets for mail-order items; newspaper ads that led to an automobile purchase; tax assessments; copies of complaint letters; and a miscellany of other papers. Some of these can, of course, be discarded once the transaction proves to be completely satisfactory, but even the residue is likely to require more than a shoebox for storage. Failure to keep such files often results in the disallowance of perfectly legitimate complaints.

JUST SAY "NO!"

Many consumers who have overpaid for something or who find themselves stuck with a bad buy owe their plight to their reluctance to walk away from a transaction at the last moment. Some car buyers, for example, develop so lustful an attachment to the model they're about to purchase that they are undeterred by a last-minute drop in the allowance for their trade-in or an unexpected "finance charge" on their bill of sale. Home buyers who fall in love with a piece of real estate may fail to inspect it thoroughly themselves or have it inspected by a professional or obtain an independent appraisal. And some consumers, after taking up a lot of an accommodating salesperson's time, feel too embarrassed to walk away even though they have serious reservations about the transaction.

It is at the moment before commitment that the consumer truly is an omnipotent king. But competent monarchs make decisions that are not influenced by impulsive, irrational desires or by feelings of embarrassment.

The urge to buy something new—whether it be the latest electronic marvel, the latest model of a sports car, or a "revolutionary" kitchen gadget—leads to two kinds of problems. To begin with, new models often turn out to be dismal failures or—at best—to have bugs that are eliminated in later production runs. And if they are successful and popular, the price drops sharply in a matter of months. VCRs, for example, are now selling at one-fifth the price of their primitive forebears, and the same holds true for personal computers.

ASK QUESTIONS

Both print advertisements and salespeople naturally stress the great features of what they sell but often deliberately omit important details. And to avoid serious disappointment, the consumer must ask the appropriate questions. Mail-order offers, for example, often omit the dimensions of items. (One purchaser of a "bargain" spa, for example, received a small package containing a plastic inflatable tub.) Ads for fountain pens rarely describe the filling mechanism or mention whether the pen uses liquid ink, cartridges, or both. Display ads for VCRs often fail to mention the number of programs that can be scheduled or whether the features include on-screen programming.

When an item is described as made of "genuine leather" or "real fur," the unquestioning consumer has no way of knowing whether the leather is sleazy goatskin or top-grain cowhide, or whether the fur is rabbit or something more durable.

Asking the right questions involves, of course, knowing something about the product and being clear about its uses. But many advertisements and sales pitches are designed to entice the consumer who doesn't ask. In addition to asking questions of the seller, consumers should also, at the point of purchase, ask some questions of themselves:

- What is it about this product that makes it important to me?
- How much use will I actually get out of it?
- Is this the best model at the lowest price?
- Is this an impulse purchase?
- Am I being pressured by the seller?

Only if these questions can be answered honestly and positively should the consumer go ahead with the purchase.

AVOID THE FREE LUNCH

In a society that judges people largely by their wealth and their fiscal acumen, all of us are eager to show that we are not only smart consumers but also smart investors—smart enough to "get something for nothing," or for close to nothing. Some of us hunt for bargains because our budgets force us to cut costs, but many of us see successful shopping and investing as a source of dinner party braggadocio. Whatever our motives, our zeal to get bargains or to get something for nothing—whether in durable goods or investments—can easily cloud our judgment and make us forget the laws of probability.

It is this zeal that leads unsophisticated consumers to respond to postcards informing them that they have won a luxury car or that they have unclaimed funds waiting for them, or to classified advertisements promising them high earnings for a few hours of unskilled work at home or a well-paying job in Kuwait or Alaska.

Even more sophisticated consumers are not immune. Many middle-class people—especially those in blind-alley jobs—participate in "business seminars" that promise them high income in return for an investment in instructional materials and supplies. Others spend money on investment advisory services or books on winning big in the stock market without realizing that if these advisers were really financially omniscient, they could earn more by following their own advice than by publishing and selling it. Still others follow "hot tips" for stock market investments from friends, neighbors, or office mates.

Many of these consumers fall for investment solicitations without asking two questions: (1) Is the proposal too good to be true? and (2) Why me? Proposals that are too good to be true include investment schemes that promise a return substantially higher than what is generally available: for example, investment in a mortgage pool that promises a return rate two or three times higher than the going rate for mortgages, or investment in a shopping mall development at a time when existing malls show a high vacancy rate, or investment in a new "miracle" technology.

The investor who asks "Why me?" may decide that in one way or another his or her name was added to a sucker list. One should also ask, "With banks, mutual funds, and professional venture capitalists all eager to maximize their return, why am *I* being solicited? Are these more traditional sources restrained by realistic caution? Is the person soliciting me offering me a golden opportunity or does he suspect that I am greedy, gullible, and unaware of the 90 percent annual mortality rate of new ventures? Is the stock market tip offered as a generous gesture or is it part of an organized attempt to increase demand for the stock—and hence its price?"

The reason that we can be easily misled is that negative results are rarely reported. Lottery winners get high exposure in the media, but none of the accounts enumerate the losers. Our dinner party companion or tennis partner will readily tell us about the stock he bought two months ago at 3 and sold yesterday at 14, but he is less likely to mention the one he bought at 32 that is now selling at 7⁄8. And thus we get the impression that lottery tickets are a promising investment or that stock market trading is likely to be profitable. On a probability scale, the former is always a bad investment and the latter a highly questionable one.

KEEP AN EYE ON THE FAMILY

In the context of consumerism, the admonition to parents "It's ten o'clock. Do you know where your children are?" might well be changed to "Never mind what time it is. Do you know what your children are buying?" A significant number of calls received by consumer protection agencies are from parents attempting to cancel unauthorized, and usually ill-advised, purchases made by children.

These purchases include charges of hundreds of dollars for telephone calls made to pornographic (900) numbers by adolescent sons and their friends, and billings for mail-order "beauty kits," enrollment fees for "modeling agencies" or private vocational schools, rock fan magazines, or fraudulent dieting books ordered by their daughters. Many parents pay the bills, unaware that, because minors cannot legally enter into contracts, parents are not responsible for their minor's debts unless they countersigned the order. Otherwise these bills are not legally collectible.

Even children who legally are adults get into trouble because they lack supervision. Perhaps the most pitiable complaints come from parents seeking to undo an impulsive car purchase by their 18-year-old who discovered, just hours after signing the contract, that he could not possibly afford the scheduled payments.

Elderly people who are not in full possession of their faculties can also get into trouble, and their adult children are not legally responsible. Door-to-door salespeople can make their way into nursing homes to sell expensive "therapeutic" beds (claiming, falsely, that they are custom-fitted and comfortable and that "Medicare will pay for it") or living trusts and other estate plans to residents whose incomes are low enough to qualify them for Medicaid. And some nursing home residents who have credit cards and bank accounts and who suffer an intolerable level of loneliness and boredom spend much of their time on the telephone ordering goods and services that they can neither use nor afford.

COMPLAIN! COMPLAIN! COMPLAIN!

Although Better Business Bureaus, state attorney generals' offices, and the federal regulatory agencies log many thousands of consumer complaints each year, their staffs can only guess at the number of abuses and frauds that go unreported. Most believe that their load of complaints represents only a small fraction—this despite the fact that the United States is widely known as the world's most litigious society.

Many consumers fail to complain because they are simply not aware of the resources available to them. The consumers who are the most likely victims of blatant scams rarely use consumer information offered by the media and are generally not aware of government agencies that may be able to get them restitution. This is why the sophisticated consumer should complain on their behalf. But many sophisticated consumers apparently feel too embarrassed to expose their own greed, naiveté, or gullibility. Even those who eventually complain to consumer protection agencies often open their narratives with "Gee, I feel really stupid, but let me tell you what's happened."

Another factor that inhibits potential complainants is the assumption that the system is rigged against them—that the regulatory agency either won't or can't help them. (This attitude also explains why only a very small percentage of metropolitan robberies and burglaries are reported to the police.) This cynicism may, in fact, be justified. Most regulatory agencies are too limited in staff and budget to chase down the $15 that a consumer sent to a mail-order firm without ever receiving the goods ordered. But consumers who decide to "forget it" instead of filing a complaint fail to realize that if their complaints, *together with many others,* show a pattern of abuse or fraud perpetrated by the same company, the regulatory agencies *will* take action—action that will, at worst, put a stop to the offending practice or put the offending firm out of business and may, at best, get restitution for the victims. Similarly, victims who, despite their cynicism, report robberies and burglaries occasionally *do* recover their property and, in any event, contribute to statistics that result in more effective crime prevention.

In general, then, abused consumers should complain—often and early—to as many regulatory agencies as have jurisdiction over the complaint. Even if they don't recover their individual losses, their cumulative complaints play an important role in cleaning up the marketplace.

2

Buying
Goods and Services

3

Cars, New and Used

I T'S EASY ENOUGH to understand why buying a car—new or used—is the leading source of consumer dissatisfaction, emotional distress, and complaints to consumer protection agencies.

To begin with, if you are a typical car shopper, you probably know very little about the technical workings of the complex piece of machinery that you are about to buy—and the usual test drive, with a voluble salesperson* in the passenger seat, will tell you nothing whatever about possible future problems.

Worse yet, although the price of a car, like the price of a home, is completely negotiable, you may be at a disadvantage for two reasons. First, because our culture seems to denigrate hard bargaining, you may feel that haggling will make you look like a "cheapskate." But even if you're determined to bargain hard, you are likely to be, when confronted with the sophisticated negotiating tactics of a seasoned car salesperson, truly a babe in the woods.

But the bargaining process should occur only after you have

---

* Although car selling has been a male-dominated field in the past, women are entering this field in increasing numbers. Indeed, anecdotal evidence indicates that they adapt to high-pressure negotiation very readily and although—or perhaps because—they do not conform to the used-car-salesman stereotype, they may be even more hazardous to the customer's checkbook.

made a sound decision about what you intend to buy, and this decision can be as crucial to your ultimate satisfaction as success in negotiating the price.

DECISIONS, DECISIONS, DECISIONS

The Rational Approach

Rational car buyers begin the process of buying a car at home or in the local library. Their first step is to decide how much they can spend and whether they can afford a new car or only a used one. Then they decide on the type of car they want: sedan, van, station wagon, and so forth.

These decisions require the kind of introspection that isn't easy for most of us, because almost every car provides its buyer not only with transportation but also with an opportunity to fulfill emotional needs and present a certain image to acquaintances and even to the general public. This is not to say that you should want only the car that gets you from point A to point B as safely and as cheaply as possible. But you should recognize ahead of time the intangibles that enter into the decision and assess as accurately as possible your actual costs over the life of the car.

The next step is a careful reading of the April automobile issue of *Consumer Reports* to find out which of the new cars that meet your specifications are desirable and which of the used models are likely to be reliable. This publication evaluates the current models individually and specifies the best buys in each category.

Another very useful source is Jack Gillis's *The Car Book*, published annually by HarperCollins. Unlike the *Consumer Reports* issue, this book does not evaluate individual makes and models. Instead, it deals with factors such as safety, fuel economy, maintenance costs, complaint record, and insurance costs and ranks specific makes and models with respect to each.* Gillis's *The Used Car Book* is an equally useful guide.

---

* The origins of this book are interesting. Originally, the data were gathered and published annually by the federal government. But the Reagan administration, deciding that the in-

Whether you are buying a used car or trading one in, you can be prepared in advance with price information from several sources. The current regional editions of the *Official Used Car Guide,* published by the National Automobile Dealers Association, and the *Kelley Blue Book,* both available in most banks and credit unions, can tell you how much money to expect for your trade-in or how much you should expect to pay for the used car you've decided to buy. And a computer printout showing the dealer's cost of a specific new car with your precise choice of equipment is available at a reasonable cost from Consumers Union and other sources. Not until you have prices clearly in mind should you leave home to go shopping.

Lastly, if you know exactly what you want, you can avoid the stresses of negotiating by enlisting the services of an automobile broker. The computer network used by these brokers tells them immediately which dealers have the exact car the customer wants and which are likely to offer the lowest price because of low overhead and advertising budgets or in return for volume business. Not all brokers are equally efficient, but many buyers report savings of perhaps 5 percent over the best price they found locally, and even those who don't realize a significant saving are happy to avoid the time and stress involved in shopping among local dealers. For fees ranging from a few to several hundred dollars, these brokers can save you a significant amount of money on medium-priced and expensive cars but less on low-priced models, where there is less room for haggling.

Irrationalities

Unfortunately, not all car buyers are rational, and even the rational ones are known to lose their heads over the first pretty hood they see at the dealership or on the used-car lot. Even before the salesperson has begun the sales pitch, they sign the sales agreement

---

formation might harm the industry, terminated its publication. Mr. Gillis, however, obtains the data under the Freedom of Information Act and makes it available to the public.

without so much as a second thought, assuming (incorrectly) that they have a three-day "cooling-off" period during which they can cancel the transaction. Their morning-after regrets involve over-payment and burdensome or unaffordable financing arrangements and often, in the case of used cars, serious and costly mechanical problems.

THE NEGOTIATION PROCESS

There is abundant literature on "how to buy a car"—some of it excellent, some of it banal, much of it contradictory. Some "ex-perts," for example, advise buyers to present the salesperson with a fair, bottom-line price (derived from data they've obtained on dealer's cost) and allow him or her five minutes to take it or leave it. Others, however, recommend exhausting the salesperson with hours of negotiation and then making a "take it or leave it" offer after a substantial amount of time has been invested. Whichever tactic you choose, you need to be aware of the several negotiable factors that make up the price you finally pay.

Negotiations on the price of a car always involve the following distinctly separate elements, which the salesperson keeps moving around like a shell-game operator to mystify, confuse, and ulti-mately exploit the customer:

1. The value of the trade-in
2. The cost and terms of financing
3. Warranty or extended-service contract
4. "Extras" such as undercoating, rustproofing, fabric treatment
5. The number and types of options
6. The price of the car

Each of these elements is negotiable, but the skillful salesperson is likely to combine them in various ways to make you feel that you are getting a bargain. You yourself, however, can eliminate some of these elements, thus simplifying the transaction by reducing it to a matter of price and options.

Trade-in

The trade-in value can be eliminated from the negotiation process if you sell your current car independently. The price you can receive from a private party or a used-car dealer is likely to be so much higher than the trade-in value offered by the dealer that the cost of a classified ad and the time spent in dealing with potential customers will be justified.

Making a trade-in part of the negotiation creates two possible problems. First, a generous trade-in offer (often amounting to hundreds of dollars more than what the dealer expects to recover by selling your trade-in) can camouflage an excessively high price or oppressive financing terms for the new car. In addition, an overly generous trade-in offer may make it easier for buyers with marginal credit to get financing on an expensive model and then find themselves unable to meet the installments.

Financing

Dealer financing can be eliminated if you begin your shopping trip with a preapproved loan for a specified amount from a bank or a credit union. Unless the manufacturer is offering as an incentive low-interest financing for a reasonable length of time, the convenience of dealer financing is invariably expensive, and at the end of the negotiation process buyers often end up uncertain as to how much of the monthly payment goes for the car, how much for interest, and how long the monthly payments will continue. Although both federal and state laws require full disclosure of financing terms, many buyers sign the sales contract and credit documents without taking time to read and understand them.

On the other hand, if a bank or a credit union turns down your loan application, the dealer is likely to offer financing at a higher interest rate or for a longer term. In such circumstances you may not be able to afford the payments—which was why legitimate lenders turned you down—or you may continue making payments long after the car has become worthless junk.

Extended-service Contracts

The extended warranty or service contract is unnecessary on a new car because the manufacturer's "bumper to bumper" warranty will cover almost any problems that show up during its lifetime, and extended warranties have proved to be of very poor value (see Chapter 4). The same holds true for extended warranties on used cars, which often carry exorbitant price tags and provide extremely limited coverage. If you are tempted to buy one, however, bear in mind that the price is (1) highly inflated and (2) fully negotiable.

"Extras"

The "extras" can be eliminated simply because they add to the dealer's profit without benefiting you in any way. The manufacturer's undercoating on new cars is adequate under most conditions, and the new-car warranty on rust-through eliminates the need for additional rustproofing. And you yourself can make the upholstery stain-repellent with a can of spray available for less than ten dollars from any auto supply store or upholstery shop.

If you've managed to eliminate the foregoing four items, you're left with a considerably simpler situation consisting of only two elements: options and price.

Options

The price of a car advertised in television commercials sponsored by the manufacturer usually applies to the basic model—which in some cases is basic indeed—and the buyer who wants even minimal options can expect to pay a significantly higher price. Because American manufacturers tend to regard as optional some features that foreign manufacturers include as standard equipment, it's important to compare various makes in terms of which "options" are included in the price. The difficulty is that some desirable options (air-conditioning, for example) are available only as part of a package that may contain a number of unnecessary or actually undesirable options, such as special wheel trim or power seats. But because a single desirable option, if available, may cost you almost as much as the package, you should carefully compare the cost of what you want with what you get in the package.

A common manager's-office scam involves the offer of "free" options—free because they will not raise the stipulated monthly payment. What the manager does not disclose is the fact that the number of payments will increase substantially or that some other aspect of the deal will be changed to your detriment.

In connection with options, it's important to recognize that dealers are much more eager to sell a car from their stock (which they have already paid for or are paying bank interest on) than to order one with your exact specifications. For this reason, you may be able to drive a harder bargain for a "loaded" car whether or not you want the extras. In fact, one buyer—a lover of classical music—who told the dealer, "I can't stand sound systems in cars. Take this one out and cut the price accordingly," was able to buy the car complete with sound system because the dealer didn't want to assume the cost of removing it and the problem of what to do with it. Similarly, you can bargain for a car in the dealer's inventory by objecting to the color or trim but indicating a willingness to buy it at a lowered price.

In choosing options, you may also want to consider the car's resale value. *You* may not want air-conditioning, but future buyers may. And a future buyer may not share your affection for the color purple.

Price

A growing number of new-car dealers have dismissed their sales staffs and labeled each car with a nonnegotiable price that they claim reflects their savings of the salaries and commissions of the salespeople. In such transactions, the trade-in value remains negotiable, but if you've disposed of your trade-in, you can avoid the stress of negotiating if the fixed price strikes you as fair.

But, except for extremely popular models for which many dealers add a "supplement" to the sticker price, the vast majority of car prices remain entirely negotiable. Because competition among manufacturers generates rebates and other buyer incentives and because competition among dealers generates discounts and special offers, even unsophisticated buyers don't take the sticker price seriously, and most salespeople open negotiations with an immediate offer of discount.

But disregard the first offer. Even when the salesperson produces the alleged manufacturer's invoice and offers the car at "just a couple of hundred bucks above our cost," you should recognize that the invoice does not reflect the dealer's true cost because of various bonuses and incentive payments that the dealer receives from the manufacturer, often amounting to as much as 3 percent of the sticker price. At this juncture further bargaining is still possible.

COPING WITH THE PAPERWORK

Although dealing with the salesperson may be tiring or stressful, the most serious hazards in car buying await you when you confront the last step—signing the final sales documents in the manager's office. All too often this "moment of truth" turns out to be a moment of *un*truth. If you are fatigued by the negotiation process and impatient to get behind the wheel of your new car, you may not take the time to read all the figures. But it is at this point that your attentiveness is most important, because the finance person can easily alter the credit terms or add charges you did not authorize. When this happens, many buyers find themselves indebted for considerably more than the agreed-upon price for the car.

It is extremely important, therefore, to scrutinize the sales contract to make sure that the total price matches the final figures quoted by the salesperson and that it contains in writing any promises made. The FTC window sticker, a model of understatement, points out that "verbal promises are difficult to enforce." You will inevitably regret the failure to get any dealer promises in writing.

To judge by the complaints received by consumer protection agencies, a great many car buyers believe that they have a three-day (or longer) cooling-off period in which to change their minds and cancel the transaction. Although a cooling-off period is required by federal law for a very limited number of transactions (door-to-door sales, for example), it does *not* apply to cars, new or used.

Once the contract has been signed the sale is final, and if the used car you buy should break in two as you drive it off the dealer's lot, you will be the unhappy owner of both halves. This is why you must satisfy yourself completely about the price, the safety and mechanical condition, and the presence of emission controls and such accessories as a spare tire and a jack before signing a single piece of paper, including the "offer sheet," often presented with the refrain "If I can get this price, will you buy it today?"

But the condition of the car is only one element that you need to consider before signing any document. It is important to bear in mind that your signature signifies a commitment for which you will be held fully responsible. Often, for example, the dealer will pressure a hesitant customer to pay a deposit on a car so that it will be held until a specified date. You should understand that by making the deposit you are entering into a binding contract to buy the car and that, unless you have put in writing the circumstances under which a refund will be made, you may forfeit part or all of the deposit if you fail to complete the deal.

All contingencies in a contract of sale should have a time limit of two or three business days, after which the contract becomes void. Otherwise the dealer can manipulate you mercilessly for a higher down payment or a lower trade-in value and attempt to hold you accountable for the original price even after the contingency falls through.

If you sign a purchase agreement "subject to financing," you must make certain that an acceptable interest rate and acceptable monthly payments are specified and that you can cancel the contract and get a refund and the return of your trade-in if the dealer fails to obtain financing at the agreed-upon terms within a specified period of time *even if the dealer gave you possession of the car.*

Occasionally the buyer, after having signed the contract and taken possession of the car, gets an apologetic call from the dealer demanding "another $800" because "the bank won't lend you the full amount we asked for" or because "our used-car manager found that the rear end is shot on your trade-in." This practice, known as "bushing," is illegal in many states, and the dealer is obligated to honor the original contract or renegotiate the contract from scratch, returning all deposits and the traded-in vehicle.

If the deposit involves future delivery of a car to be ordered from the factory, the purchase order should specify return of the deposit in full if delivery is not made by a specified date or with the equipment ordered. And the contract should be very specific with respect to charges for title and registration. Overcharges on these items are frequently not refunded because of "oversight."

In general you should avoid signing any document until you are convinced that the deal, as represented in writing, is fully acceptable. The salesperson's statement that the quoted price "is good only if you buy now" is a high-pressure tactic that should be disregarded, and taking a day or two to think it over is invariably sensible. If the car for which you are negotiating gets sold to another customer, you can be quite sure that there are other, similar cars on the market on the same or even better terms.

Title Problems

The dealer who sells any car—new or used—is obligated to provide the buyer with a clear title and registration. Although the dealer has a reasonable period—usually thirty days—in which to file the necessary papers with the state department of motor vehicles, delays sometimes occur. In such circumstances, you should complain to the department promptly and should hold back any installment payments owed to the dealer (but not to a bank or credit union) until the title is received.

In some cases, the delay may signal a failing dealership that has not acquired ownership of the car from the prior owner or the manufacturer. In used-car cases, it may mean that the vehicle was stolen, that it was repurchased as a result of Lemon Law proceedings, that there is a lien against it, that it was written off as a total loss by an insurance company, or that it was pieced together from two junked or totaled cars and is therefore unlicensable.

NEW-CAR REPAIR PROBLEMS

"Won't-fix" Problems

Aside from exploitative dealer financing (about which nothing can be done once the papers have been signed), most consumer complaints about new cars involve mechanical defects that the dealer either won't or can't fix. To anticipate and avoid "won't-fix" problems, you should read the new-car warranty with the greatest care and distrust any oral information offered by the seller. It is only by a careful reading of the warranty that you can determine whether the dealer will refuse to repair a defect on the grounds that "it's not covered."

Because warranty work is paid for by the manufacturer, it is a source of profit for the dealer. But some dealers attempt to maximize this profit by disclaiming warranty obligation, because the rate paid by the manufacturer is lower than the rate paid by the customer.

In some cases, the dealer responds to a customer's warranty problem by insisting that "there's nothing wrong with the car," in the hope that a repair can be delayed until the warranty expires. It is important to understand, therefore, that after warranty expiration the dealer is required to repair problems that were reported during the lifetime of the warranty. You should obtain a repair order *every* time you bring the vehicle in for service, because warranty repair orders are the best evidence for enforcing your warranty rights under the law.

If you are unsatisfied with the dealer's "nothing wrong" response, you can get a diagnosis of the problem from another dealer (who may be more cooperative) or from an independent mechanic, but you should not permit this mechanic to do the necessary repair work because this may invalidate the warranty, and you will not be reimbursed by the manufacturer.

Conflicts over warranty coverage can be settled at several levels. Many large dealerships designate one of their employees as a "consumer representative," and this person, who is presumably more concerned with public relations than with mechanical details, may well overrule the service manager.

If the consumer representative cannot or will not resolve your complaint, the next level in the appeal process is the manufacturer's zone office. As with all complaints, a detailed, objective letter is far more effective than an angry telephone call. The zone office, if it cannot resolve the complaint by telephone or letter, may dispatch a representative for on-site inspection or mediation.

If the zone office offers no satisfaction, a direct appeal to the manufacturer's head office (see Table 3.1) may be effective. Several of the manufacturers have either established their own arbitration panels (Ford and Chrysler) or support arbitration programs administered by independent groups, such as the American Automobile Association (AUTOSOLVE), the Better Business Bureau (AUTOLINE), and the National Automobile Dealers Association (AUTOCAP). In addition, the dealer-licensing departments or the attorney general's offices of many states have units that focus specifically on the problems of car owners.

Generally speaking, however, both the manufacturers' arbitration programs and those administered by independent organizations tend to reflect the perspectives of the industry rather than the concerns of the consumer, and they are helpful only in cases of serious and obviously valid complaints that the industry clearly wants to go no further. They seem to be most effective in states that have especially strong and well-administered Lemon Laws (see p. 45) and vigorous consumer protection agencies. Even rela-

TABLE 3.1
Automobile Manufacturers' Company Headquarters

Many, but not all, manufacturers have zone offices. Space does not permit a complete listing, but the headquarters office will provide the address of the nearest one.

ACURA
1919 Torrance Blvd.
Torrance, CA 90501
(800) 382-2238

AMC
See Chrysler

AUDI
888 W. Big Beaver
  Rd.
Troy, MI 48007
(800) 822-AUDI

BMW
P.O. Box 1227
Westwood, NJ
  07675
(201) 307-4000

BUICK
902 E. Hamilton
  Ave.
Flint, MI 48550
(800) 521-7300

CADILLAC
2860 Clark St.
Detroit, MI 48232
(800) 458-8006

CHEVROLET/GEO
P.O. Box 7047
Troy, MI 48007
(800) 222-1020

CHRYSLER
P.O. Box 1086
Detroit, MI 48288
(800) 992-1997

FORD
P.O. Box 43360
Detroit, MI 48243
(800) 392-3673

GEO
See Chevrolet

GM
See specific make

HONDA
1919 Torrance Blvd.
Torrance, CA 90501
(213) 783-3260

HYUNDAI
P.O. Box 20850
Fountain Valley, CA
(800) 633-5151

ISUZU
P.O. Box 2480
City of Industry, CA
(800) 255-6727

JAGUAR
555 MacArthur
  Blvd.
Mahwah, NJ 07430
(201) 818-8500

MAZDA
P.O. Box 19734
Irvine, CA 92718
(800) 222-5500

MERCEDES-BENZ
1 Mercedes Dr.
Montvale, NJ
  07645
(201) 573-0600

MITSUBISHI
6400 W. Katella
  Ave.
Cypress, CA 90630
(800) 227-0037

NISSAN
P.O. Box 191
Gardena, CA 90248
(800) 647-7261

OLDSMOBILE
P.O. Box 30095
Lansing, MI 48909
(800) 442-6537

PEUGEOT
1 Peugeot Plaza
Lyndhurst, NJ
  07071
(800) 345-5549

TABLE 3.1 (continued)

PONTIAC
1 Pontiac Plaza
Pontiac, MI 48340
(800) 762-2737

SUBARU
P.O. Box 6000
Cherry Hill, NJ
    08034
(609) 488-3278

VOLVO
P.O. Box 914
Rockleigh, NJ
    07647
(201) 767-4737

PORSCHE
P.O. Box 30911
Reno, NV 89520
(702) 348-3154

TOYOTA
19001 S. Western
    Ave.
Torrance, CA 90509
(800) 331-4331

YUGO
120 Pleasant Ave.
Upper Saddle River,
    NJ 07458
(800) 872-9846

SAAB
P.O. Box 697
Orange, CT 06477
(800) 955-9007

VOLKSWAGEN
888 W. Big Beaver
    Rd.
Troy, MI 48007
(800) 822-8987

tively weak Lemon Laws provide the consumer with a basis for legal action, and the awareness of this can motivate the arbitrators to provide redress when the complaint is justified.

Although the Lemon Law is the owner's best resource, assertive owners can seek reparation in other ways. A threat to report the situation to the local television consumer program may be effective. And an inquiry to the Center for Auto Safety (2001 S St., NW, Washington, DC 20009) may disclose a "secret warranty," under which manufacturers instruct dealers to remedy defects for "squeaky wheel" customers but not for more passive types.

"Can't-fix" Problems

In terms of the buyer's frustration and inconvenience, "won't-fix" problems are less serious than "can't-fix" problems. Some of these are solved when the National Highway Traffic Safety Administration (or the manufacturer on its own initiative) orders a recall, under which a widespread defect—usually one that is related to safety—will be repaired by any authorized dealer free of charge.

A recall order requires that the manufacturer notify all registered owners of affected vehicles, but this does not always happen. Owners of defective vehicles can call the NHTSA hotline—(800) 424-9393—to find out whether their vehicle has been recalled and, if no recall has been issued, can at the same time report a defect that may justify a recall—especially if it is related to safety.

Lemon Laws

Most "can't-fix" problems, however, involve a dealer who may be thoroughly cooperative but is unable to repair a defect despite repeated attempts. In such a situation, you have substantial recourse in Lemon Laws, which provide compensation for buyers of new cars with persistent defects that the dealer cannot correct after a certain number of attempts or within a specified time period. (Of course, you must have bought the car in a state that has enacted such a law.) In some cases, the buyer is offered a rebate; in others, the manufacturer is required to buy back the car.

With the exception of Alabama, Arkansas, Georgia, and South Dakota (which offer the buyer protection under state and federal warranty laws), all states have Lemon Laws. As Table 3.2 indicates, the specific terms of the laws vary widely, but even the weakest give the consumer what lawyers call "statutory causes of action"—that is, the unquestionable right to sue a recalcitrant manufacturer for compensation for a "lemon."

USED-CAR PROBLEMS

Although some new-car problems are serious, they are insignificant in terms of prevalence, severity, and cost to the buyer compared to the problems encountered by the buyer of a used car. Most consumer protection agencies report that the highest proportion of complaints they receive involve mechanical defects in

TABLE 3.2
State Repair/Replace (Lemon) Laws

State	Vehicles Covered	Repair Attempts	Days out of Service*	Coverage Periods
Alaska	Four-wheel vehicles normally used for personal, family, or household purposes, requiring registration, except tractors, farm vehicles, or off-road vehicles.	3	30b	Express warranty period or one year, whichever occurs earlier.
Arizona	Vehicles under 10,000 lbs. GVW, used to transport persons or property over public highways.	4	30c	Express warranty period or one year, whichever occurs earlier.
California	Vehicles used primarily for personal, family, or household purposes, except motorcycles, portions of motor homes used primarily for habitation, or off-road vehicles. Includes the chassis, chassis cab, and that portion of a motor home devoted to its propulsion.	4	30c	One year or 12,000 miles, whichever occurs earlier.
Colorado	Four-wheel passenger motor vehicles, normally used for personal, family, or household purposes, sold within the state, including pickups, vans; excluding motor homes.	4	30b	Express warranty period or one year, whichever occurs earlier.
Connecticut	Passenger or passenger and commercial motor vehicles sold or leased within the state. Exceptions listed under 14-1 include agricultural tractors.	4	30c	Two years or 18,000 miles, whichever period occurs first.
Delaware	Passenger motor vehicles, except motorcycles and living facilities of motor homes, bought, leased, or registered in the state.	4	30b	Express warranty period or one year, whichever occurs earlier.
District of Columbia	Vehicles sold or registered in D.C. and designed for transporting persons, except buses, motorcycles, motor homes, and recreational vehicles.	4	30	Two years or 18,000 miles, whichever occurs earlier.
Florida	Vehicles sold or leased in the state and used primarily for personal, family, or household purposes, excluding off-road vehicles, mopeds, trucks over 10,000 lbs., the living facilities of recreation vehicles, and motorcycles.	3	30c	One year or 12,000 miles, whichever occurs earlier.
Hawaii	Vehicles used or bought for use primarily for personal, family, or household purposes. Includes dealer-owned vehicles and "demonstrators" or other motor vehicles sold with a manufacturer's new warranty. Excludes vehicles over 10,000 lbs.	3	30b	Express warranty period.

*c = calendar days, b = business days.

State	Vehicles Covered	Repair Attempts	Days out of Service*	Coverage Periods
Idaho	New motor vehicles normally used for personal, family, or household purposes, excluding motorcycles, farm tractors, house trailers, or any motor vehicle with a gross laden weight over 12,000 lbs.	4	30b	One year or 12,000 miles, whichever occurs earlier.
Illinois	Passenger cars and vehicles under 8,000 lbs., used primarily for personal, household, or family purposes, excluding motor homes and van campers.	4	30b	One year or 12,000 miles, whichever occurs earlier.
Indiana	Motor vehicles sold, leased, transferred, or replaced by a dealer and registered in Indiana having a GVW of less than 10,000 lbs., intended primarily for use and operation on public highways, excluding conversion vans, motor homes, farm tractors, road building equipment, truck tractors, road tractors, motorcycles, mopeds, snowmobiles, or vehicles designed primarily for off-road use.	4	30b	18 months or 18,000 miles, whichever occurs earlier.
Iowa	Cars and pickups, as defined under 321.1, purchased for a personal, family, household, or agricultural purpose.	4	30c	Express warranty period or one year, whichever occurs earlier.
Kansas	Vehicles sold in the state and registered for a gross weight of 12,000 lbs. or less.	4	30c[1]	Any warranty period or one year, whichever occurs earlier.
Kentucky	All vehicles owned by a Kentucky resident and purchased in Kentucky and required to be registered or licensed in the state, except conversion vans, motor homes, mopeds, motorcycles, farm equipment, and vehicles with more than two axles.	4	30	12 months or 12,000 miles, whichever occurs earlier.
Louisiana	Vehicles under 10,000 lbs. sold in this state and excluding motor homes, motorcycles, and vehicles used for commercial purposes only.	4	30c	Express warranty period or one year, whichever occurs earlier.
Maine	All vehicles sold in Maine except commercial vehicles over 8,500 lbs. or business or commercial enterprise registering three or more motor vehicles. Includes leased vehicles.	3	15b	Two years or 18,000 miles, whichever occurs earlier.
Maryland	Purchased or leased passenger vehicles, trucks with a ¾ ton or less rated capacity, and multipurpose vehicles registered in the state, excluding fleets of five or more motor vehicles and excluding motor homes as defined under the Motor Vehicle Administration regulations.	4[2]	30	15 months or 15,000 miles, whichever occurs earlier or one year/12,000 miles, whichever occurs earlier for leased vehicles.

[1]for same nonconformity
[2]or 1 unsuccessful repair of braking or steering system

TABLE 3.2 (continued)

State	Vehicles Covered	Repair Attempts	Days out of Service[*]	Coverage Periods
Massachusetts	All vehicles, except those used primarily for business purposes, off-road vehicles, auto homes, and motorized bicycles.	3	15b	One year or 15,000 miles, whichever occurs earlier.
Michigan	Four-wheel vehicles used for personal, family, or household use, or fleets of less than ten, including pickups and vans, excluding buses, trucks, and motor homes.	4	30b	Express warranty period or one year, whichever is earlier.
Minnesota	Passenger automobiles, pickup trucks, vans, and recreational equipment chassis, sold or leased to a consumer in this state, used at least 40 percent for personal, family, or household purposes.	4[3]	30b	Express warranty period or two years, whichever occurs earlier or three years following the delivery if nonconformity is first reported during express warranty.
Mississippi	Vehicles sold in this state, used primarily for personal, family, or household purposes, excluding off-road vehicles, mopeds, motorcycles, and parts of a motor home added by the manufacturer of the motor home.	3	15b	Express warranty period or one year, whichever occurs earlier.
Missouri	All vehicles used primarily for personal, family, or household purposes, excluding commercial vehicles, mopeds, motorcycles, and RVs, except for the chassis, engine, powertrain, and component parts of RVs.	4	30b	Express warranty period or one year, whichever occurs earlier.
Montana	All vehicles sold in this state except motor homes, trucks of 10,000 lbs. GVWR or more, and motorcycles.	4	30b	Two years or 18,000 miles, whichever occurs earlier.
Nebraska	All vehicles sold in this state, normally used for personal, family, household, or business purposes, except mobile homes.	4	40	Express warranty period or one year, whichever occurs earlier.
Nevada	Motor vehicles normally used for personal, family, or household purposes, except motor homes or off-road vehicles.	4	30c	Express warranty period or one year, whichever occurs earlier.
New Hampshire	Four-wheel private passenger vehicles, motorcycles, and other vehicles under 9,000 lbs. GVW, excluding tractors, mopeds, and RVs.	4	30b	Express warranty period or one year, whichever occurs earlier.
New Jersey	Leased or purchased passenger automobiles or motorcycles registered in New Jersey.	3	30c	Two years or 18,000 miles, whichever occurs earlier.

[3]or 1 unsuccessful repair of completely failed braking or steering system likely to cause death or substantial bodily injury

TABLE 3.2 (continued)

State	Vehicles Covered	Repair Attempts	Days out of Service*	Coverage Periods
New Mexico	Passenger motor vehicles, pickups, motorcycles, and vans, under 10,000 lbs. GVW, sold and registered in New Mexico, normally used for personal, family, or household purposes.	4	30b	Express warranty period or one year, whichever occurs earlier.
New York	Passenger vehicles sold and registered in New York, including leased vehicles, excluding motor homes, motorcycles, and off-road vehicles.	4	30c[4]	Two years or 18,000 miles, whichever occurs earlier.
North Carolina	Motor vehicles sold or leased in North Carolina, under 10,000 lbs. GVW, except house trailers.	4	20[5]	One year/12,000 miles; one year or express warranty, whichever is greater; or 24 months/24,000 miles.
North Dakota	Passenger motor vehicles and trucks 10,000 lbs. GVW or less, normally used for personal, family, or household purposes and sold in North Dakota, excluding house cars.	3	30b[6]	Express warranty period or one year, whichever occurs earlier.
Ohio	Passenger vehicles and noncommercial motor vehicles, motor homes (except cooking and sleeping facilities), manufactured homes, and recreational vehicles, but excluding vehicles of government entities and vehicles of business or commercial enterprises registering three or more motor vehicles.	3[7]	30c	One year or 18,000 miles, whichever occurs earlier.
Oklahoma	Vehicles registered in the state and under 10,000 lbs. GVW, excluding the living facilities of motor homes.	4	45	Express warranty period or one year, whichever occurs earlier.
Oregon	Passenger motor vehicles normally used for personal, family, or household purposes, sold in Oregon, including leased vehicles and motorcycles.	4	30b	One year or 12,000 miles, whichever occurs earlier.
Pennsylvania	Vehicles purchased and registered in Pennsylvania used primarily for personal, family, or household purposes except motor homes, motorcycles, and off-road vehicles.	3	30c	One year, 12,000 miles, or duration of warranty, whichever occurs earlier.

[4]or for a substantial defect within 20 days of receipt of notice given by the consumer using certified mail
[5]during any 12-month period
[6]during one year or express warranty term, whichever is less
[7]for same defect, eight total repair attempts, one attempt to repair condition likely to cause death or serious bodily injury

TABLE 3.2 (continued)

State	Vehicles Covered	Repair Attempts	Days out of Service*	Coverage Periods
Rhode Island	Automobiles, trucks, and vans under 10,000 lbs. GVW, excluding motorized campers.	4	30c	One year or 15,000 miles, whichever occurs earlier.
South Carolina	Passenger motor vehicles, trailers, semitrailers, sold and registered in the state, which are designed, used, and maintained for the transportation of persons but not operated for the transportation of persons for compensation, except to schools, religion affiliated programs, or other prearranged excursions. Excludes motorcycles, living portions of recreational vehicles, trucks with a GVW over 6,000 lbs., and off-road vehicles.	3	30c	One year or 12,000 miles, whichever occurs earlier.
Tennessee	Class "C" vehicles sold and required to be registered in state, used for personal, family, or household purposes, including leased vehicles, excluding motor homes, motor and garden tractors, RVs, off-road vehicles, motorized bicycles, and vehicles over 10,000 lbs.	4	30c	Express warranty period or one year, whichever occurs earlier.
Texas	Motor vehicles.	4	30	Express warranty period or one year, whichever occurs earlier.
Utah	Vehicles sold in this state excluding motorcycles, truck tractors, farm tractors, road tractors, motor or mobile homes, or any motor vehicle with a gross laden weight of over 12,000 lbs.	4	30b	Express warranty period or one year, whichever occurs earlier.
Vermont	Passenger motor vehicles purchased or registered in Vermont, excluding tractors, motorized highway building equipment, roadmaking appliances, snowmobiles, motorcycles, mopeds, trucks over 6,000 lbs., or the living portion of RVs.	3	30c	Express warranty period.
Virginia	Passenger cars, pickups, panel trucks, motorcycles, self-propelled motorized chassis of motor homes, mopeds, demonstrators, and lease-purchased vehicles used in substantial part for personal, family, or household purposes.	3	30c	18 months
Washington	Self-propelled vehicles leased or purchased and registered in this state, excluding buses, vehicles in fleets of ten or more, living portions of motor homes, motorcycles, or trucks with GVW of 19,000 lbs. or more.	2[8]	30c[9]	Two years/24,000 miles, whichever occurs first.

[8]for same serious safety defect; or four attempts for same defect (at least one of which is during manufacturer's warranty)
[9]at least fifteen of which occur during the manufacturer's warranty
[10]one unsuccessful repair of condition likely to cause death or serious bodily injury

TABLE 3.2 (continued)

State	Vehicles Covered	Repair Attempts	Days out of Service*	Coverage Periods
West Virginia	Passenger motor vehicles, pickup trucks, vans, and motor vehicles chassis of motor homes purchased in this state on or after 1/1/84, used primarily for personal, family, or household purposes.	3[10]	30c	Express warranty period or one year, whichever occurs earlier.
Wisconsin	All vehicles, registered (or transferred) in this state, including demonstrators, non-resident or foreign registered vehicles purchased, leased or transferred in this state, except mopeds, semitrailers or trailers designed for use in combination with a truck or truck tractor.	4	30	Express warranty period or one year, whichever occurs earlier.
Wyoming	All vehicles under 10,000 lbs. GVW, sold or registered in the state.	3	30b	One year.

used cars, that most of these defects show up within a few days of the purchase, and that a substantial proportion are so serious as to render the purchase valueless. These complaints have led to the conclusion that shameless misrepresentation of quality and safety is widespread in the used-car business. But many problems can be avoided by the consumer whose expectations are realistic and who goes to the used-car market fully aware of its perils.

The reason for the preeminence of used-car complaints is easy to understand. With the exception of houses and garage-sale items, most of us are unaccustomed to buying used products. Most serious defects in a house are likely to be obvious and, because of the gravity of such a purchase, buyers often pay for a professional inspection to reveal those that are not. As for garage-sale items, their cost is usually trivial and the buyer's expectations are not high. But serious (and often fatal) defects in a used car are not necessarily apparent even after a short test drive, because dealers are skilled at camouflaging them temporarily. And, although condemned shanties rarely appear in real estate ads, their automotive equivalents abound on the used-car lots. Buyers of these automotive "shanties" usually can't afford the cost of an independent mechanic's evaluation and, having spent every last penny on the car itself, they are usually unable to pay for the repairs that become necessary almost immediately.

It is important to understand that new-car owners can, with conscientious maintenance, get about 100,000 miles or more out of their vehicle. But eventually they realize that it is no longer worth repairing, at which point it shows up on a used-car lot. It is far more likely, however, that the high-mileage vehicle has been through several owners, none of whom was able to afford necessary repairs. In fact, one dealer who was investigated by a state attorney general sold the same high-mileage car six times—repossessing it each time from customers who could not afford the major repairs in addition to the monthly payments.

Where to Buy

Most used cars are bought from private parties, either through word of mouth or through classified ads. There are no reliable data on buyer satisfaction in private transactions because consumer protection agencies are not permitted to take action against private sellers. But those who buy from private parties need to be aware that they have no implied-warranty protection whatever. Although they may file a lawsuit against the seller on grounds of gross misrepresentation—a statement, for example, that a car is "in perfect running order" when the seller knows, in fact, that the engine block is cracked—this is extremely difficult to prove and impossible to prove in the absence of a witness.

Moreover, the "private" seller may, in fact, be an unlicensed "curbstone" dealer—that is, a backyard mechanic or a transient (gypsy) dealer who buys one or two cars at a time, does some minimal or purely cosmetic repairs, perhaps turns back the odometers, and presents the cars for sale as his or her personal vehicles or tells the prospective buyer, "I'm selling it for my mother."

If you know the seller (and the seller's driving habits), or if he or she is recommended by a friend, chances are you will do better than by buying from a dealer. Otherwise you need to recognize that there may be as many dishonest private parties as there are dishonest dealers.

Authorized Dealers

Judging from consumer complaints, it is probably safer to buy a used car from a franchised dealer who sells new cars of the make in which you are interested. Such dealers are more likely to get well-maintained trade-ins with a detailed service history from regular new-car customers and to siphon off the "dogs" to used-car dealers, wholesalers, or automobile auctioneers. In addition, their service departments are likely to be familiar with any generic weaknesses of specific models and able to correct them promptly, whether or not the car is warranted. A used car bought from a dealer may be somewhat more expensive than one bought on a used-car lot, but your peace of mind may be well worth the difference.

Used-Car Dealers

The very low esteem in which used-car dealers are held seems to be well earned. But whether this is due to character flaws or the nature of the industry is hard to determine. The business is highly competitive on the issue of price, and most dealers have a large inventory of old and defective vehicles to unload on customers who need transportation and can't afford anything better. Thus, although some dealers specialize in "preowned" luxury cars, the inventory of most consists of bottom-of-the-barrel vehicles that were "someone else's problem"—repossessions, unrepairable cars, cars bought at used-car auctions, and, often, cars that have been involved in serious crashes and have been restored only cosmetically.

Even low-mileage cars can be hazardous to the buyer. So-called program cars—which are variously described by dealers as "brass hat specials" or "executive" or "demonstrator" cars—are, in fact, cars that the manufacturers buy back from auto rental companies as part of a fleet deal and then distribute to used-car dealers for resale through closed auctions.

These cars have been driven by numerous strangers, often under unfavorable conditions. A "program" car offered in North Carolina, for example, may have spent its rental life in the "rust belt"—so called because the salt used on winter roads eats away at the undercarriage and fenders. Rental cars driven on the rough roads of Alaska age prematurely, despite their cosmetic appearance. Although they may have received regular maintenance, these cars are likely to have been driven by people who had no interest in their longevity or their resale value. To make matters worse, "program" cars are frequently ineligible for Lemon Law protection.

Financing

By charging high interest rates for low-quality cars, dealers who advertise "easy payments" or proclaim that "Your job is your credit!" or promise financing "even if you are bankrupt, unemployed, divorced, or disabled," exploit buyers who are unable to obtain credit through legitimate sources. In general, buyers with low or irregular incomes who need a car for travel to and from work or school should not spend every last cent on the car. Instead, they should save at least 20 to 30 percent of their car budget to pay for repairs that will be inevitable when they buy a low-priced car.

Checking Out the Used Car

Consumer Reports and a number of books provide advice on checking out a used car, but some of the recommended techniques are difficult to perform correctly by a buyer who is not a mechanic.

A test drive, if it is done carefully, can reveal some defects but not others, such as a cracked block, excessive oil consumption, compression problems, a faulty cooling system, intermittent electrical problems, or the condition of the emission-control system. Moreover, as mentioned earlier, unscrupulous used-car dealers are quite proficient at temporarily covering up major defects in the transmission and other expensive-to-replace components.

Your best protection against buying a car with serious mechanical faults is a thorough inspection and road test by a competent independent mechanic. In many urban areas franchised operations have been set up whose sole purpose is to perform computerized diagnostic tests on prospective purchases. As evidence of their independence, these organizations will never advise you to buy a car and do not make repairs. Their role is limited to identifying defects and estimating for you the cost of correcting them. If the dealer does not give you a reasonable opportunity for an independent inspection, your best response is to walk away.

Another—and probably the best—source of information about the condition of a used car is the previous owner. Previous owners, having no more interest in the car, are likely to be quite candid about its condition, especially if they feel that they were paid less for it than seemed fair or, on the other hand, were happy to have got rid of it. Although many used-car dealers refuse to disclose who the previous owner was, citing the right to privacy, the information is on public record with the state department of licensing, and the law in many states requires such disclosure. The dealer's refusal to supply this information should serve as a warning.

It is especially important to find out whether the vehicle has been involved in a wreck, because this may have produced frame damage, alignment problems, and other defects that are impossible to correct. Because dealers are understandably reluctant to disclose this information, a signed statement from the dealer denying that the vehicle has been wrecked can serve as good grounds for a lawsuit if it proves to be false.

One item often overlooked by the used-car buyer is the presence and functioning of the emission control system. Buyers in states that require emission inspection have arrived at the inspection station only to discover that the entire emission control system was missing and that their car was therefore unlicensable. Some states require that a vehicle pass inspection before it can be transferred, but in others you can protect yourself by getting a signed statement from the dealer attesting that the emission system is operational and will pass the state emissions test.

Odometer Readings

A false odometer reading can lead to unexpected and serious problems, but it can be easily checked before purchase. Although odometer tampering is a violation of state and federal law and provides buyers with grounds for a lawsuit if they can present proof, it still occurs in 5 to 40 percent of used cars. Perhaps more important, because most odometers register only five digits, cars that are only a few years old but have traveled, say, 135,000 miles are sometimes sold with the odometer showing only 35,000. In general, if the odometer on a ten-year-old car shows less than 50,000 miles, it should probably be rejected unless it has a thoroughly reliable history of ownership and maintenance.

"As Is" Purchases

When used cars are sold "as is," the Federal Trade Commission requires the display of a window sticker that clearly informs the buyer of the warranty status of the vehicle and spells out his or her rights or—more commonly—the lack of them. But this sticker does nothing more than specify the warranty status. It does not alert the buyer to the implications of an "as is" purchase—namely that the buyer, who may have paid several thousand dollars for the vehicle, has no come-back should it break down two or three hours after the purchase.

All too often, the prospective buyer of a used car listens attentively to the salesperson's oral assurances that the car is "in fine condition" and the promise that "we'll take care of any problems that may come up." Meanwhile the salesperson checks off the "as is" box on the sales contract and the FTC window sticker, leaving the buyer with no legal recourse whatever. Of course, the buyer who can persuade the salesperson to commit any assurances to writing and to make them part of the sales agreement will be afforded some degree of protection, but few salespeople will agree to this.

As a result, many thousands of "as is" buyers have found themselves with a vehicle that, within a day or two of purchase, manifests a defect (e.g., an inoperative transmission, faulty brakes, or a cracked engine block), the repair of which can cost as much as one-half of the price paid for the car or, worse yet, an undisclosed defect (a broken frame resulting from an earlier crash) that is not repairable at all. And, as mentioned earlier, some vehicles have been stripped of their emission controls and are therefore unlicensable in some states.

Some states prohibit the sale of motor vehicles "as is." A few states (Connecticut, Maryland, Massachusetts, Minnesota, New York, and Rhode Island) have used-car Lemon Laws covering vehicles sold above a minimum price or below a maximum age or mileage, and some require certain measures that inform consumers of the risks they run. But in most states the buyer is left with no protection whatever from the often deceptive oral assurances of the salesperson. Although the principle of implied warranty may apply, enforcing it may require the buyer to sue the dealer in court.

Under most dealer-licensing statutes, personal-injury laws, and the principle of implied warranty, a dealer may not sell "as is" a car that is unsafe—that is, one with seriously defective brakes, inoperative lights, or a cracked or clouded windshield—but this law is frequently disregarded, and the buyer discovers the defect only after the purchase.

In such circumstances, the buyer who cannot get immediate cost-free repair from the dealer should point out that if the car is subsequently involved in an accident attributable to the defect, the dealer may be held responsible by a court of law, even though the driver is always primarily responsible for the safe condition and operation of the vehicle. Moreover, a court may find a dealer's disclaimer of certain safety defects to be unconscionable.

In negotiating a purchase, one protective tactic that the buyer may be able to use is to point out to the salesperson that the "as is" car may have a major defect and to suggest that the risk of such a defect be split between the seller and the buyer. If this tactic produces a significant reduction in the price (below the "blue book" price for the vehicle's make, year, and mileage) the "as is" risk may be worth taking. Since buying a car "as is" requires you to assume all risks of defect, it seems only reasonable to make a lower offer unless the seller is willing to provide at least some form of written warranty.

Extended Warranties, Service Contracts, Breakdown Insurance

Dealers who sell cars on an "as is" basis are usually quick to offer hesitant customers—often at prices two or three times the dealer's cost—an extended warranty that purportedly protects them against failure of the major components. Consumer protection agencies, however, have been so inundated by complaints about these warranties that they generally advise consumers not to buy them. One problem is that many of the underwriters of these warranties have gone bankrupt and, although the seller of the warranty (the dealer) may have some residual responsibility for honoring it, this obligation has been difficult to establish and enforce.

Regardless of the solvency of the underwriter, many of these warranties are written deceptively with respect to coverage. One such warranty, for example, provides for repair of the engine but excludes from this coverage the valves and pistons on the grounds that they are subject to "normal wear and tear," even though a faulty valve or connecting rod can severely damage or completely destroy an entire engine.

An extended warranty does, however, offer the buyer one possible advantage. If the extended warranty is bought from the dealer, the dealer cannot waive the implied warranty on the car. But because the duration and coverage of implied warranty is variable (perhaps one to three months) and may require resolution by a court, this advantage is questionable.

The purchaser of an extended warranty should look carefully at its provisions for cancellation, which in some states are controlled by law. Some warranties may be canceled on a pro rata basis; others carry a penalty charge.

Complaints

Of the six states that have used-car Lemon Laws, only two have compulsory arbitration programs, and even in these states dealer failure to comply with arbitration decisions favoring the buyer runs as high as 37 percent. And, given the power of the used-car dealers' lobbies, the prospects for widespread adoption of effective used-car Lemon Laws are rather dim.

If you find yourself with a defective purchase, you should, as a first step, complain to the dealer. Low-cost defects related to safety are likely to be repaired—especially if you remind the dealer of his legal liability should an accident occur. But some dealers, in order to preserve customer good will, voluntarily correct other defects. Dealers who are recalcitrant may be motivated by your threat to file a lawsuit and/or a complaint with the attorney general's office or the dealer division of the state licensing department.

Some buyers have the defect corrected at their own expense and then attempt to recover the cost by filing suit against the dealer. A favorable verdict is more likely if the buyer can prove that the dealer offered specific oral assurances (which were known to be false) about the condition of the vehicle in order to promote the sale.

Whether a complaint to the attorney general or other state agency will be resolved depends on a number of factors, among them the aggressiveness and the budget of the agency and the attitude of the dealer. Some dealers, feeling threatened by a letter from a regulatory agency, readily adjust the complaint. Others, aware that the agency may have a limited staff or limited enforcement powers, simply ignore it. It is only when a specific dealer is the target of numerous complaints about defective vehicles or deceptive sales tactics that regulatory agencies are likely to take legal action. And even if such action forces the dealer out of business, the customers are unlikely to get redress.

4

Products, Refunds, Prices, and Warranties

A RETAIL TRANSACTION can involve a 58-cent can of beans or a $12,000 set of custom living-room furniture, but the major consumer complaints are much the same. Most of them center on refunds, overpricing, deceptive advertising, and bad service, especially from mail-order firms.

RETAIL TRANSACTIONS

"I Want My Money Back"

Because major department stores generally offer "no questions asked" refunds on purchases that customers decide, for whatever reason, they regret buying, there is a widespread belief that *all* retailers follow this same liberal policy. But the fact is that a seller is *not* obliged to refund your money unless your purchase is demonstrably defective.

Some retailers—notably the sellers of computers and software—charge a sometimes substantial "restocking fee" on merchandise returned for refund. This, too, is legal provided that the customer was informed of the practice at the time of purchase.

Normally, a defective item must be replaced under the principle of implied warranty (see p. 72), but this does not apply to "scratch-and-dent" sales used by some retailers to dispose of damaged or returned merchandise. If this merchandise is clearly labeled "sold as is," the consumer has no right to expect a refund. For refunds on mail-order purchases, see p. 70.

Form of Payment

Retailers have the right to specify the form or forms of acceptable payment. They are not obliged to accept checks or credit cards, and they have the right to limit the use of credit cards to purchases above a specified minimum. Although retailers can specify "cash only" prices, it is illegal for them to impose a surcharge for the use of credit cards. On the other hand, where credit cards are acceptable, some consumers have been able to get a discount of 3 to 5 percent by offering to pay cash instead of using a credit card.

Rain Checks

When the supply of an advertised product is exhausted, many retailers offer the customer a "rain check" unless the advertisement for the item specifies "limited to the supply on hand," or "no rain checks." But, as is true of refunds, rain checks are not required by law. Retailers who advertise an item at a very low price are required to have on hand a supply adequate to meet "reasonable" demand, but this policy is difficult to enforce unless the violation is blatant or persistent—that is, when the eighth customer in a long line is told that the supply is exhausted or when the customer experiences the same problem repeatedly. In such circumstances a complaint to the Better Business Bureau or the state attorney general's office may get immediate results or may at least put a stop to the practice.

"Bait and Switch" Tactics

Some merchants use the "out of stock" ploy on an attractively priced and prominently advertised item to steer the customer to a more expensive alternative. But "bait and switch" can also be used by a salesperson who denigrates the bargain item by pointing out deficiencies or telling the customer that "we're just trying to get rid of it."

If you are certain that the advertised item is suitable for your needs, you should insist on buying it and, if you are told that the item is not available, you should threaten to file a complaint with the attorney general's office, because "bait and switch" selling is an unfair and deceptive practice that violates the law.

Layaway and Special-Order Items

Before making a deposit on layaway merchandise, you can protect yourself against a possible dispute by getting, in writing, the conditions under which the deposit is refundable. If you are buying an item involving a special order—for example, furniture upholstered in a custom fabric, a wedding dress, or jewelry—you should, in addition, specify a delivery date, beyond which a refund is guaranteed if the merchandise has not been delivered.

Because a sales agreement for special-order merchandise is binding on both the buyer and the seller, it should specify as clearly as possible all the details—size, materials, color, finish—and should, where practical, be accompanied by fabric swatches, paint samples, monogram samples, or anything else involved in the order.

Custom-ordered merchandise may, of course, be rejected by the customer if it is obviously defective or does not conform to the specifications on the order, but if buyer and seller disagree—if, for example, the wedding gown does not fit and the seller argues that the buyer has gained weight since placing the order—a dispute is inevitable. To the extent possible, such circumstances should be anticipated and provided for in the initial agreement. A woman ordering a bridal gown, for example, might note her weight and measurements on the order form.

Since in such disputes time is often of the essence, the buyer might make the best of the matter by accepting the merchandise, paying for alterations if possible, and immediately lodging a complaint against the seller with the attorney general's office or filing suit in small-claims court. In these circumstances, the wronged party must take reasonable steps to mitigate the damages. As in other disputes, stopping payment on a check or refusing to pay the balance is likely to worsen matters rather than improve them (see pp. 135–36).

Is the Price Right?

Many print advertisements that quote the price of an item use such comparisons as "original price," "retail value," "comparable value," "manufacturer's suggested list price," and "20 percent off" to persuade readers that the current advertised price is an irresistible bargain. Because each of these phrases is frequently used deceptively, they need careful scrutiny.

Original price is often set at an artificially high level in anticipation of discounting it. On the other hand, it may well have been the price of the item several years ago, and over time the item has been superseded by better (and possibly cheaper) items. This practice of reference pricing is especially prevalent in the sale of electronics, window coverings, furniture, automobiles, carpeting, kitchen cabinets, and clothing, where new styles or improved models appear on the market frequently.

Retail value is legitimate only when other retailers in the community are actually charging the alleged retail value. It is not legitimate when the retailer's competitors are selling the item at a similar price.

Comparable value lies strictly in the eyes of the retailer, since it applies to a supposedly similar but not identical (and perhaps superior) product. The consumer should ask, "Comparable to what?" The phrase is legitimate when the consumer can actually compare prices, as when a firm advertises the identical item as "20 percent below _____'s price."

Manufacturer's suggested list price is virtually meaningless. Some manufacturers do suggest "list" prices, but most of their products are sold for less. The comparison is legitimate only if the item has, in fact, been sold in the retailer's area at the list price for a significant length of time.

"20 percent off" should alert the consumer to ask, "Off what?" The laws of most states require that the retailer must have sold the item at full price for a reasonable length of time immediately prior to the "20 percent off" sale.

Although all of the preceding practices may constitute deceptive advertising, which is illegal, most consumers don't take the trouble to complain to the authorities, especially if the amount that they may have overpaid is small, because the likelihood of obtaining redress is not great and the practices are so widespread. This is unfortunate, because attorneys general have found that firms using these tactics do so persistently and thus bilk large numbers of consumers. These firms are vulnerable to court actions that can impose fines and order them to cease deceptive advertising. If each consumer were to complain against a firm, the emerging pattern would lead to legal action.

The critical issue in all cases of reference pricing is whether the offer constitutes a genuine bargain or an illusory one. Unless the retailer has actually sold a significant number of items at the higher price, the offer is false and deceptive.

"How Deep Is the Discount?"

Since there is no law prohibiting a retailer from using the words "discount" or "factory outlet" in its name, the careful consumer will not assume that stores using these terms abound with bargains. "Discount" pharmacies, for example, have been shown to charge higher prices than some of their competitors, and the same is true of other "off price" firms. If you intend to buy an expensive item or expect to buy a prescription drug for a period of years, careful comparison shopping will save you more money than blind faith in such words and phrases as "discount," "clearance," "liquidation, "close out," or "fire damaged."

Recently, many parts of the country have seen the emergence of "buying clubs" or "wholesale warehouses" that, in return for an annual membership fee, promise consumers a wide variety of merchandise—from produce and toilet paper to computers and cars—at close-to-wholesale prices. Some of their prices are clearly competitive, but others just as clearly are not. Here, too, comparison shopping is in order, not only among "buying clubs" but also on specific items.

One problem with these organizations is that they sell only in bulk, requiring the consumer to buy, for example, twenty-four rolls of toilet paper, fifty pounds of kitty litter, or gallon jugs of olive oil. The careful consumer should consider whether hauling home such quantities is worth the saving, which may not, in fact, be very significant.

"Going out of Business"—But When?

When a branch of a reputable chain of stores or an established local retailer goes out of business, a clearance sale of remaining inventory may be a source of genuine bargains. But some retailers, especially in metropolitan areas, have found it highly profitable to hold "going out of business" sales for a period of years. And the gullible customers come away with no bargains at all.

Perpetual "going out of business" sellers practice "backdooring"—that is, they bring new merchandise in through the back door, offer it as the "last remaining inventory," and never seem to close down.

To curb this fraudulent practice, some cities require these sales to be licensed and conducted for only a limited time. But often the offending firm goes out of business, resurfaces under a new name, and immediately proceeds to "go out of business." When a firm that is "going out of business" becomes a familiar part of the scenery, the sophisticated consumer will avoid it. The consumer who is tempted by such a sale should ask the manager to specify on the bill of sale precisely how long the sale has been going on. Should the merchandise prove unsatisfactory, the manager's false statement is prima facie evidence of fraud.

Filing a Complaint

Complaints involving defective goods or the delay or nondelivery of merchandise should be addressed to the Better Business Bureau or the attorney general's office, where they will be taken seriously. But many of the complaints are groundless. The fact is that, unless the merchandise is defective, a purchase is a binding transaction, and the fact that a consumer finds the same item at a lower price elsewhere does not ensure a refund on the original transaction. Yet valid complaints against abusive or misleading pricing practices should be registered since it is the accumulation of these complaints that gives the regulatory authorities grounds to clean up such abuses.

MAIL ORDERS

According to opinion surveys of their customers, mail-order firms seem to resemble the little girl who had a little curl: when they are good they are very, very good, but when they are bad they are horrid.

In terms of merchandise quality, promptness of delivery, guarantees, and refunds, the top-of-the-line mail-order firms—most of them specializing in clothing, outdoor gear, and hard-to-find tools—receive high marks. But the bottom-of-the-line and fledgling firms, especially those that promote their wares through television commercials, classified advertisements, or display advertisements in the media that appeal to unsophisticated consumers, are generally either unsatisfactory or downright fraudulent. The same holds true of mail orders that are actively solicited by telephone (see Chapter 9).

In addition to being less fatiguing and more convenient than mall shopping, shopping the specialized mail-order firms may offer you a wider selection of merchandise and a wider range of sizes than your local shops can carry. But before opting for a catalogue item of any kind, you should check to see whether the same item is available locally. If it is, the local price will almost certainly be lower—in some cases by 60 percent or more. You'll probably have to pay sales tax on the local purchase, but you avoid shipping charges.

Furthermore, if your local community offers good shopping resources, you might well ask why the local retailers *don't* carry an item featured in a mail-order catalogue. It may be, of course, that the item's appeal is too limited, but it is also possible that the retailer, having appraised the item, feels that too many customers will be dissatisfied with it and hence return it for refunds.

Because the term "mail order" may be used loosely to cover virtually any purchase not made face-to-face in a retail establishment, a somewhat stricter definition is in order. A purchase made by telephone with a credit card and delivered by United Parcel Service is *not* a mail order, and this fact exempts the supplier from surveillance and possible legal action for fraud or deception by the U.S. Postal Inspection Service. This distinction is not important when you know that the seller is reputable, but it becomes crucial when the purchase is not initiated by you but is solicited by an unfamiliar seller.

On all telephone orders made from a catalogue, you should make a note of the date of the order, the name of the order-taker or a confirmation number, and a catalogue tearsheet or other clear description of the merchandise ordered, including its price and the shipping charges.

Late Delivery or Nondelivery

Federal law requires that mail-ordered merchandise be delivered within 30 days unless the seller specifies a later date ("delivery in 5 to 8 weeks"). The seller unable to meet this deadline must offer you the choice of waiting until a specified date or receiving a full and prompt refund or credit to your credit card.

When an order is delayed beyond the 30-day limit, you should first query the seller. Nondelivery may be the result of a clerical error, but all too often it is due to shoddy practice or even bankruptcy on the part of the seller. If a response is not forthcoming or is unsatisfactory, you should file a complaint with the Direct Marketing Association (6 East 43rd St., New York, NY 10017), which monitors its own membership but can do little about fly-by-night companies.

At the same time, complaints should be filed with the state attorneys general in both your own state and the state of the offending firm. Filing a complaint in the firm's state may lead to prompter and more effective action because complaints from all over the country are likely to accumulate there. The concentration of fraudulent mail-order and telemarketing schemes in certain states casts some doubt on the effectiveness of their attorneys general. On the other hand, some attorneys general have driven hordes of unscrupulous mail-order firms and telemarketers out of their states by creating a hostile environment for consumer fraud, whether out-of-state or home-grown.

If the firm is located out of your own state, a complaint should also be filed with the Federal Trade Commission and, if the transaction was truly a mail order, with the U.S. Postal Inspector. If the seller is in bankruptcy, a claim can be filed with the seller's local bankruptcy court, but this is unlikely to yield results because the seller's secured creditors' claims have priority.

In general, mail orders should be paid for by credit card whenever possible because, in the event of bankruptcy, nondelivery, or failure to respond to a customer's complaint, the credit card issuer may cancel the customer's indebtedness for the transaction (see p. 141).

Refunds

The best of the mail-order firms offer very liberal guarantees, some of them beginning with "If you are *ever* dissatisfied with the item . . ." Other firms are somewhat more restrictive but offer satisfaction or your money back if you return the item in its original condition within 30 days."

A general problem with mail-order guarantees is that, although the purchase price of the item is refunded—cheerfully or otherwise—the shipping charges, both to receive and return the item, are not. Because these unrefundable charges may come close to the value of the item, the customer may well decide to take a loss on the merchandise instead of investing money to return it.

Even the reputable mail-order firms do not automatically refund shipping charges, but customers who ask will generally receive the refund if the return was motivated not by a change of the buyer's mind but by some defect in the merchandise, such as a wrong size, unsatisfactory tailoring, or a color that differed significantly from the catalogue illustration.

Shipping Charges

Many customers use mail order to avoid state sales taxes (see below), but in some cases the shipping charges may cancel out this saving. Some mail-order firms calculate the shipping charges on the basis of weight; others on the value of the merchandise; still others impose a flat shipping charge regardless of the value of the order. If the shipping charges seem unreasonably high, you may well suspect that they are intended to discourage returns.

Some mail-order firms, in addition to "shipping and handling" charges, add a charge for "insurance." Although this charge is not illegal, the mail-order seller is always legally responsible for getting the merchandise to the customer in perfect condition. Hence, the "insurance" charge should be seen as nothing more than a price increase. Some consumers who have refused to pay it have received the merchandise anyhow.

Sales Tax

Although there have been sporadic legislative efforts to force mail-order firms to collect sales tax from out-of-state customers and remit the tax to the customer's state, and although these efforts are likely to persist, the most recent U.S. Supreme Court decision has passed the issue to the state legislatures, which are not likely to act either promptly or consistently.

Currently a mail-order firm is required to collect taxes from out-of-state customers only if the firm has a "physical presence" in the customer's state. Thus, a mail order to a Sears catalogue center is taxable because Sears has stores in every state. An order from a New York customer to the Nature Company's California mail-order center would be taxable because the Nature Company has a store in New York, but a Utah customer would not be taxed. But this issue is currently under Supreme Court review.

Mailing Lists

Virtually every mail-order firm derives part of its income from selling its customer list to other mail-order firms. This is why active mail-order customers receive mailings from companies with which they have never done business and whose merchandise may be of no interest to them.

Most firms offer their customers the option of not having their names sold, but you can have your name removed from the lists of all national companies by addressing a request to Mail Preference Service, Direct Marketing Association, P.O. Box 3861 Grand Central Station, New York, NY 10163. The disadvantage of this total proscription is, of course, that it will deprive you of catalogues that may be genuinely interesting.

WARRANTIES

When buying a mechanical product—a refrigerator, a VCR, or a food processor, for example—most of us assume that it carries some sort of warranty. But, although the retailer is required by federal law to have a copy of the warranty on file (and available to consumers) for every warranted item offered for sale for $15 or more, few of us take the trouble to look at it before making our purchase. Even when buying big-ticket items, such as a car, many consumers tend to rely on the salesperson's oral (and often unduly favorable) summary of the warranty instead of reading it line by line to comprehend its terms. Yet only a clear understanding of warranties can alert you to some of the fine-print limitations that can leave you without recourse if your purchase breaks down.

Implied Warranties

Probably the least understood warranties—even though they apply, unless validly waived, to virtually every manufactured produce sold by merchants—are the implied warranties. These warranties do not appear in printed form and are almost never mentioned in the course of a transaction (hence the term *implied*), but they are embodied in federal law and in the laws of all but a few states, and they can offer you significant protection.

Implied warranties offer buyers protection if their purchase is not in "merchantable condition" at the time of sale—that is, if it does not function properly (1) *for its intended purpose or in ordinary use* or (2) for a *reasonable length of time* compared to a substantially similar product. "Merchantable condition" means, simply, that the product is in working order. It means, for example, that a toaster must toast bread properly and that a used car must be reasonably safe, in running order, and in a general mechanical condition similar to that of other cars of similar price, age, make, and mileage.

The phrase "intended purpose or use" means that implied warranty will cover a noncommercial-grade kitchen blender used in a household kitchen but not if it's used in a restaurant. A low-priced electric screwdriver may be covered for normal use by homeowners but not by professional carpenters, who would, of course, be protected if they were to buy an industrial-grade power screwdriver. On the other hand, a vehicle sold for use by a paraplegic must be not only in safe mechanical condition but must also be able to accommodate the buyer's physical limitations, and a vehicle sold with the understanding that it will be used to haul a boat trailer must prove able to do so under normal operating and road conditions.

The "reasonable length of time" limitation is flexible and therefore more difficult to specify. Obviously a clock radio that proves defective when first plugged in is covered under implied warranty, but in this situation the buyer is usually also protected by the retailer's refund policy or by the manufacturer's written warranty. The problem arises when the product fails shortly after the manufacturer's warranty has expired or for a reason not covered by the written warranty. Although there are data on the life expectancies of such major appliances as refrigerators and kitchen ranges, the length of time a VCR, a telephone answering machine, or a used car should continue to function is not easy to determine. Moreover, federal law permits manufacturers to limit implied warranty to the duration of their written warranties provided that such limitation is not "unconscionable."

Nevertheless, if a product breaks down shortly after its written warranty has expired, or if the seller claims that the defect is not covered by the written warranty, or if complaints to the manufacturer or the dealer go unanswered, you may be able to get satisfaction by filing a complaint with the attorney general's office or, if the value and the expected normal durability of the defective item justifies it, taking legal action on the basis of implied warranty.

Although implied warranties are broadly covered by the federal Magnuson-Moss Act, state law may specify conditions that augment or limit implied warranties. In most, but not all, states, a manufacturer or retailer can disclaim implied warranties simply by embodying a conspicuous statement to that effect on the purchase agreement or on whatever printed warranty is offered. Most written warranties contain wording informing the consumer that "certain state laws" may provide him with additional protection. They are referring to the more liberal interpretation of implied warranty offered by some states, which prohibit or limit disclaimers in warranties or sales contracts.

This liberal interpretation can occasionally help you. The express warranty on one brand of electronic wrist watch, for example, specifically excludes coverage of the watchband (apparently the most vulnerable part). Nevertheless, the manufacturer agreed to replace a defective band when a buyer cited his state's implied warranty law.

Express Warranties

Express warranties are printed manufacturers' warranties that accompany the product at the time of sale. Although many such warranties instruct you to return a postcard to "register" your purchase of the product, you will not lose your warranty rights if you fail to do so in the case of a full (as opposed to limited) warranty. All you need do is retain proof of purchase in the form of a dated sales slip. Generally speaking, however, it is advisable to return all such registration cards so that the manufacturer can notify you in case of a recall and to verify your right to warranty protection.

Some warranties specify that the defective item need only be returned to the dealer; others require returning the item to an authorized repair service or the manufacturer. Express warranties are of two types: full and limited.

Full Warranties. A full, or unlimited, warranty is extremely liberal, which is why it is not very common, although it is a reliable indicator of the manufacturer's confidence in its product. A full warranty must comply with the following conditions:

- it must be transferrable to anyone who purchases the item while the warranty is in force;

- it must offer to remedy defects in the product within a reasonable time and at no cost to the purchaser;
- unless it specifically excludes them, it cannot limit the duration of any implied warranties;
- it must take responsibility for "consequential" damages—that is, if a guaranteed battery leaks and thus damages a portable radio, the battery manufacturer must repair or replace the radio;
- it must provide for a refund or replacement of the product after a number of unsuccessful attempts at repair;
- it must require no additional actions by the consumer aside from notifying the manufacturer of the defect and returning it to the manufacturer or to an authorized repair service.

Given these strict conditions, it is hardly surprising that full warranties are very rarely offered. Nevertheless, some reputable mail-order companies promise a replacement or a refund "at any time" that a product fails to satisfy the customer "for any reason." And some department stores offer return policies that are almost as liberal.

Limited Warranties. Under federal law, virtually any warranty that does not meet the requirements for a full warranty must be described as a *limited* warranty. But, because limited warranties range from excellent to worthless, you should scrutinize the terms of every warranty with the following questions in mind:

How long does it last? The duration of warranties on different brands of the same product may vary widely. On different makes of VCR, for example, warranties range from 90 days to two years. Other things being equal, the brand offering the longest warranty is obviously the better buy.

A "lifetime" guarantee can be meaningless. Does it cover the lifetime of the original buyer, or a reasonable life expectancy of the product, or does it imply Judgment Day or the demise of the manufacturer, whichever occurs first?

What does it cover? On new cars and trucks, a "bumper-to-bumper" warranty usually excludes items subject to normal wear and consumables, such as tires, batteries, filters, and windshield wipers, some of which may be covered by a separate warranty. A "power-train" warranty, which usually runs longer than the bumper-to-bumper warranty, needs very careful scrutiny to ascertain whether it covers such items as the clutch in manual-transmission vehicles, the head gasket, and other parts that tend to break down and can cause significant consequential damage. New-car buyers (and in some states used-car buyers) are further protected by the state's Lemon Law (see Chapter 3).

Many consumers are attracted to franchised shops that offer "lifetime" warranties on mufflers, transmissions, and other automobile components. When they return to demand replacement of the defective or worn-out muffler under the warranty, they are told that the entire tailpipe assembly needs replacement—often at a higher price than their local garage would charge. Mufflers are cheap. Tailpipe assemblies are not. Nevertheless, in some situations these warranties can prove useful—if, for example, you don't plan to keep the car for several years. And if you use your car only to drive the mile or two to and from work, you are likely to need muffler replacement as frequently as once a year because driving short distances does not allow the engine to warm up sufficiently to dry out the tailpipe assembly and hence the muffler will corrode more rapidly.

On electronic products and major appliances, does the warranty cover the entire product or only major components (such as the tube on television sets or the compressor on refrigerators and freezers)? And does it cover parts and labor or only parts? With few exceptions, the labor on repairs is far more expensive than the cost of parts and cannot be estimated by the buyer. Hence, the exclusion of labor costs may render the warranty virtually worthless.

What do I have to do? Some warranties require you simply to return the defective item to the retailer for "in store" exchange. Others require you to return the product to the manufacturer or an often remote authorized repair facility at your expense, and still others bill you for a "service charge" or for return shipment. If you consider the difficulty and cost of packing and shipping a computer or a 60-pound television set back to the manufacturer, you may decide that paying for the repair locally is the better alternative. Many manufacturers of small appliances have authorized repair facilities in major cities that handle warranty work on a walk-in basis. And a few warranties—especially for computers and other expensive and large items—provide for on-site repairs, but this service may not be available in isolated areas.

Will the warrantor remain in business? The most generous warranty is worthless if its issuer goes out of business before you need to exercise it. And, of course, the shoddier the product, the more likely the manufacturer's demise. Some courts have held that the retailer who sells the product is responsible for honoring the warranty or for correcting the defect under implied-warranty law if this has not been validly disclaimed, but this obligation has been difficult to establish and enforce.

Prorated Warranties. Warranties for automobile tires and batteries are "prorated"—that is, the item may be fully guaranteed for 30 or 90 days, but beyond that period the credit offered for replacement of the defective item decreases with time or use. For example, if a battery that is guaranteed for 60 months fails at the end of 48 months, you will be credited with only 20 percent of its purchase price, and by that time the price of batteries may have increased substantially, making this kind of warranty almost valueless.

When the same kind of warranty is offered for tires, the credit is prorated on the basis of tread wear and mileage. Here again, you can anticipate a higher price for the replacement than you paid for the original tires.

Extended-service Contracts. Many retailers (Sears, for example) offer, for a fee, extended-service contracts that provide warranty protection on major appliances and electronic equipment for a given period after the basic warranty expires.

Most authorities on consumer affairs question the value of such contracts on two grounds. First, defects on these products tend to show up within the limits of the manufacturer's basic warranty. Second, the fact that these extended-service contracts are actively promoted by the seller makes it clear that they are profitable—that is, that far less will be paid out for repairs than will be earned in premiums. Applying this statistic to your own case, you may conclude that your odds of benefiting from such a contract are not high, despite the "peace of mind" pitch.

The most consumer-abusive extended-service contracts are those offered by automobile dealers, usually at an exorbitant price, in the form of a policy written and backed by an independent underwriter—that is, a third party. Ironically, despite the profitability of these policies (especially for the dealer who retails them) their underwriters go bankrupt in alarming numbers, leaving the consumer with no protection and no refund.

Complaints to regulatory agencies about these contracts focus on several issues: bankruptcy of the warranty's underwriter, vagueness or severe limitations of their coverage, refusal of repair facilities to honor them, and delays in approval of or payment for work done. Although the automobile dealer who sells such a contract may have some responsibility to honor it if the underwriter has gone bankrupt, here, too, the obligation has been very difficult to establish and enforce.

Cancellation rights in connection with an extended-service contract are governed by state law or by the conditions spelled out in the contract itself. In some cases the contract can be canceled for a full refund within 90 days; in others, the underwriter of the contract is permitted to retain a cancellation fee. Some service contracts are transferable to a subsequent buyer; others are not.

Despite these limitations, however, a service contract in connection with a used car purchased "as is" offers you one important advantage: if you buy the contract within 90 days of your car purchase, the dealer cannot waive his obligations under implied warranty. In these circumstances, a service contract, whatever its limitations, can serve to protect you by restoring your implied-warranty rights, which for a limited time require the vehicle to be mechanically operational and reasonably safe.

Buying "As Is"

Although, in order to be competitive, most manufacturers offer some kind of express (and therefore implied) warranty, and most department stores will accept the return of defective merchandise, there is nevertheless a substantial market in which products are offered "as is"—that is, without either implied or express warranty.

Regardless of any oral reassurances by the seller, the buyer of an item "as is" gives up all rights to *any* remedies should the purchase prove defective or worthless. Unfortunately, studies show that more than half of American consumers, accustomed to ubiquitous limited warranties and the liberal return policies of some retailers, do not understand the implications of buying an item "as is."

"As is" sales are, of course, the rule at flea markets and thrift shops. Here the buyer of a second-hand radio or clock understands that the item may or may not work but assumes the risk because of the very low price. The "as is" principle also may apply when retailers clear their old inventories or when appliance dealers hold "scratch and dent" sales and indicate clearly that "all sales are final." But it predominates in the selling of used merchandise—especially cars (see Chapter 3).

Credit Card Warranties

In their aggressive competition for new customers, some issuers of credit cards offer extended warranty coverage (plus coverage for loss or damage) on items that the buyer charges to the card. Although these warranties were rather liberal when first introduced, they have become extremely restrictive with respect to both the amount of coverage and the exclusions, and significant numbers of claims have been disallowed. But since credit card warranties cost you nothing, you may as well take advantage of them if the issuer's interest rates and annual fee are otherwise competitive.

Complaints

Problems with both implied and express warranties should be addressed initially to the seller or the manufacturer. If the problem is not resolved, a complaint should be filed with the Federal Trade Commission, the Better Business Bureau, and the state attorney general. In addition, if the value of the item or the cost of repairing it falls below the maximum permitted in the small-claims court, a suit against the seller or the manufacturer can be filed. Often the mere threat of these several actions can persuade a recalcitrant seller or manufacturer to resolve the problem.

5

Services: Professional, Commercial, and Governmental

THERE ARE SEVERAL reasons why consumer complaints about services—ranging from medical care and auto repair to pool maintenance and carpet cleaning—far outstrip complaints about retailing. Because most retailers—department stores, mail-order firms, or chain discount retailers—are large companies, their bureaucratic structure serves to prevent sharp practices, either by individual employees or by management. The salesclerk is unlikely to cheat the customer because he or she stands to gain little or nothing from it personally. And management may be deterred by the possibility of whistle-blowing by a disgruntled employee or the threat of regulatory action.

In general, these firms tend to be reasonably concerned about their image and devote some effort to maintaining good customer relations. In any event, their operations are governed by federal and state laws such as the Uniform Commercial Code, the Truth in Lending Act, and other fair-trade laws, all of which specify in considerable detail unacceptable business practices and the obligations of retail merchants and franchises.

Services, by contrast, tend to be small operations—often sole proprietorships. Because many services are subject to no regulation other than routine business licensing, and because the cost of entry is often low, they can attract individuals who are incompetent, inexperienced, or not above sharp practices, in an effort to recoup their initial investment quickly. In addition, small firms tend to have a high rate of bankruptcy, sometimes vanishing with an oriental rug they promised to clean or a computer left for repairs.

Even when services are strictly regulated, the regulators tend to protect the occupation or profession rather than the consumer. The regulation of medical practice, for example, by restricting entry into the profession, effectively maintains the high salaries of the practitioners. The record of medical regulation that protects the consumer from negligence or exploitation, however, is far from impressive.

In addition, small, unestablished firms tend to be less responsive to consumer complaints, whether brought to the firm's attention or filed with a regulatory agency. Large retailers have complaint departments that respond quickly to consumer or government-agency complaints. The sole proprietor may not even have a typewriter on which to generate a response or may refuse to adjust complaints because they threaten an already narrow profit margin.

This is not to suggest that all consumer transactions should be conducted with large, well-established firms. There are, undoubtedly, many neighborhood enterprises that provide better (and possibly less expensive) services than the large firms or their franchisees. But before using a small and newly established firm for a major transaction, it makes sense to check its reputation carefully.

The sequence in which the services are listed in this chapter is neither alphabetical nor random. It represents a ranking based either on frequency of complaints received by regulatory agencies or on the seriousness of the charges. You may prefer to scan the chapter in search of entries that are immediately relevant to you, but a reading of other entries may immunize you against future problems.

AUTOMOBILE REPAIR AND MAINTENANCE

Getting a car repaired is, all too often, such a horrendous experience that many people who can afford to pay for peace of mind buy a new car shortly after the manufacturer's warranty on their current car expires. This practice is costly, because depreciation on a car is highest during the first three years, and it doesn't guarantee tranquility, because getting repairs under the manufacturer's warranty is not always a simple process (see Chapter 3). But, although some new cars turn out to be lemons, most of them run well during their early years, and their owners can avoid the tension, frustration, and costs so frequently involved in getting a car repaired.

Another—and very important—safeguard is to adhere religiously to a maintenance schedule on the grounds that an ounce of prevention is worth a pound of cure. With very few exceptions, the modern automobile is quite capable of running well for 100,000 miles or more provided that its owner monitors and replaces regularly all filters and fluids (not only oil but also antifreeze and brake and transmission fluids) and has it checked and tuned regularly. Except in old and unreliable cars, serious or fatal problems (such as a cracked cylinder head or a thrown connecting rod) are almost invariably the result of inadequate maintenance or abusive driving.

Repair Problems

Auto repairs persistently rank among the top three consumer complaints to regulatory agencies, and they are among the most difficult to resolve. A major reason is that most of us, knowing little or nothing about the workings of our car, find ourselves completely at the mercy of the repair shop, which all too often does not have our interests at heart. There is, unfortunately, no Hippocratic Oath for automobile mechanics.

Although many complaints involve overcharges—usually for work not specified in the initial estimate—most center on unsatisfactory work—that is, the persistence or recurrence of the problem that the repair service has allegedly corrected.

The most frequent complaints stem from the following practices:

> Underestimating the cost of repairs in order to persuade the customer to agree to them and later confronting the customer with a much higher figure. Thus, "All you need is a $50 tune-up" becomes "Sorry, we'll need to do a valve job, too—for $450."

> Misrepresenting the vehicle's safety or reliability in order to frighten the customer into authorizing needless repairs, as in "I wouldn't drive this car another mile without replacing . . ."

> Charging for parts and labor that are not necessary.

> Cleaning an existing part, reinstalling it, and charging the customer for its replacement.

> Charging for an unreplaced part and showing the customer a worn-out part taken from another vehicle.

> "Chasing" a problem by replacing several parts or systems before locating the problem, which might have been solved earlier and far less expensively.

Although all of these abuses have been extensively documented by regulatory agencies, enforcement is extremely difficult. It requires the enforcement agency to turn over to a suspected repair shop a vehicle that has been certified as perfectly operational by certified mechanics so that it can pounce when the shop's repair bill includes charges for unnecessary work, unperformed labor, and unreplaced parts. Although this tactic is obviously very expensive and, given the thousands of repair facilities in every state, not a practical cure for the problem, it has proved extremely effective. The California attorney general's discovery of persistent consumer deception by Sears automotive centers resulted in massive customer refunds not only in California but in other states as well.

Choosing a Mechanic

Some car owners are fortunate enough to have found a trustworthy dealer, independent repair shop, or service station that does good work at reasonable prices or makes reliable referrals for special problems. Others swear by a "backyard" mechanic who takes care of their maintenance and repairs at a bargain price and even makes house calls. But none of these sources is available when the car breaks down several hundred miles from home. Worse yet, as cars become increasingly sophisticated, the local service station or backyard mechanic simply cannot keep up with the technology or the diagnostic equipment and tools that are essential for competent troubleshooting and repair.

Lacking a reliable repair shop (or word-of-mouth recommendation), it's probably wise to use a dealer who sells your make of car or a repair facility that employs certified mechanics. This by no means guarantees satisfaction but, in return for the probably higher hourly rate, you are likely to encounter mechanics who are more familiar with your car and its problems than the general repair shop, and hence your repair may take less time and save you money despite the higher rate. In addition, in case of an unsatisfactory repair that can't be adjusted by the dealer, you can complain to the manufacturer's zone office or national headquarters (see p. 42 and Table 3.1) or the state authority that certifies mechanics or licenses dealers. Even the threat of this may persuade the repairer to resolve the problem. Another relatively reliable repair facility is an AAA-approved service station, since problems arising with these stations can be settled by AAA arbitration.

The franchised dealerships, certified mechanics, and AAA-approved stations may be your best bet if a breakdown occurs when you are far from home, but they are no substitute for conscientious maintenance and a pretrip checkup.

Getting an Estimate

Disputes arise most frequently because of poor communication between the shop and the customer. The repairer fails to provide a clear, *written* estimate of the cost of the repair and an under-standable *repair order* that specifies the work to be done and the parts to be replaced. Lacking these documents, you may fail to get a realistic notion of your final costs and thus be unhappily surprised if the problem turns out to be more serious than initially perceived. You should at this point specify that any deviation from this estimate will require your preapproval after you have been persuaded that additional work is needed. In addition, you should at this juncture ask to be shown all worn or defective parts that are in fact replaced.

If possible, you should obtain a firm, written promise that the work will be completed by a specified time, especially if you need the car for travel to and from work. Parts for most cars (even imported models) are available everywhere within 1 to 7 days. Parts for old models are readily obtainable from junkyards, many of which belong to a regional computer network, and repairers can get delivery within a few days. The shop's failure to complete the work when promised is a breach of contract but, if failure to meet your deadline seems excusable, you might ask for a loaner car or credit for a rental car to compensate for your loss of transportation.

In some states, if the estimate exceeds a specified amount (usually around $75), and you have not authorized work beyond the initial estimate, the repair facility is not entitled to more than a specified amount (usually about 10 percent) above the estimate and must release the car when you pay that amount. In these states, if there is no written estimate, the repair shop may not under any circumstances refuse to release the car until the bill is paid.

Repairers who do not have a valid lien and refuse to release your car are violating state law and should be reported to the attorney general's office or sued in small-claims court. But unless the attorney general's office is willing to persuade the repairer by telephone to release the car, the process is likely to take more time than you can afford, and consulting an attorney can usually produce quicker results.

Release of the car does not, of course, free you from the obligation to pay for the repair. Indeed, several states permit the repair shop to place a mechanic's lien against your vehicle, which prevents you from selling it until the lien is paid. It does, however, prevent the repair shop from holding your car hostage while you are disputing the bill.

If, as is often the case, your disabled vehicle is towed to a repair facility and, for one reason or another, you may have no face-to-face contact with its staff, you have three options:

1. You can request that no work be started before you approve a written estimate and that you be notified (by telephone if necessary) if the work will exceed the estimate by more than a certain percentage.
2. You can authorize repairs up to a specified limit and require your authorization if they exceed that limit.
3. You can give the repair shop carte blanche to proceed with the repairs.

A dispute is most likely to arise when the repair shop provides an initial estimate and then reports to you that "a lot more work needs to be done" before the car can be put back in working order. In some cases, this is legitimate, because not all problems can be diagnosed by superficial inspection. On the other hand, this "further work" ploy is often used by dishonest repair shops to make money for work that is unnecessary or that they in fact don't perform.

The difficulty is, of course, that you have no way of determining the facts. You may show up at the repair shop only to find your vehicle so thoroughly disassembled that it cannot be driven (or even towed) to another shop for a second opinion and that the shop demands an exorbitant price merely to put it back together again unrepaired. This situation can be avoided by specifying in advance that you will pay an agreed-upon charge for diagnosis and for complete reassembly of the car if you decide that the repair isn't worth doing or if you want to shop around for a second opinion.

"Let Me Tell You What's Wrong"

A common error made by consumers is to diagnose the malfunction and then instruct the repair shop to remedy it. All too often the repair shop follows the owner's instructions but the defect remains because its cause had nothing to do with the owner's diagnosis. It makes far more sense to tell the repair shop how the car has malfunctioned ("It stalls at traffic lights," for example, or "It won't start on cold mornings") than to pretend to some knowledge and instruct the repair shop to change the spark plugs or adjust the timing.

The Do-It-Yourselfer

Some enterprising owners, in an attempt to save themselves money, buy parts at an auto supply store or a junkyard and attempt to install them on their own. Although many owners are quite capable of replacing such simple consumables as air cleaners, spark plugs, and oil filters, some of them ambitiously attempt to install more expensive or more challenging components, such as radiators, alternators, and head gaskets. When the work turns out to be unsatisfactory, such owners tend to blame the supplier for selling them the wrong make or the wrong size, but these disputes are not likely to be resolved in favor of the amateur mechanic.

Other owners, in need of a replacement engine, shop around for the engine at several sources and then bring it to a backyard mechanic to install. Although the engine itself may carry a warranty of some kind, this warranty almost invariably covers only the engine and not the labor involved in installing or removing it. And so, if the engine fails within a week or two of installation, the owner faces a substantial labor bill for removing and replacing it. On large repairs, such as engine rebuild or transmission overhaul, the somewhat higher price charged by an established firm that guarantees the entire job may be money well spent.

Warranties

Generally speaking, reputable repair shops warrant their work for a limited period—typically 90 to 120 days—and will attempt to make good on any work that proves unsatisfactory. But some repair shops tell a dissatisfied owner that the current problem is unrelated to the warranted repair. And this argument is virtually impossible for the owner to rebut, since "smoking gun" evidence of shop fault is almost never available. It is occasionally possible to take a car that has been repaired improperly to another shop and have it repaired successfully. But even if the second shop provides you with a statement to use in a lawsuit against the first shop, the result will be a "swearing contest" with no guarantee of the outcome. Auto repair experts, like doctors and lawyers, can argue ad infinitum about cause and effect.

Complaints

Complaints that cannot be resolved with a repair shop should be addressed, if the repair shop is part of a new-car dealership, to the zone office and, if necessary, the corporate headquarters for the make of car involved (see p. 42 and Table 3.1). Unresolved complaints, as well as those against independent repair shops and service stations, can also be filed with the certifying agency or association, the Better Business Bureau, the AAA, the attorney general's office, and, in some states, with the department of licensing. And many complaints can be resolved by filing (or threatening to file) a suit in small-claims court.

CONTRACTORS

Contractors who do home building or remodeling, roofing, electrical work, painting, plumbing, and driveway paving make up the largest category of consumer complaints received by some regulatory agencies and rank second or third in most others. The reasons for this are easily understood. Unlike fuel-oil suppliers, telephone companies, and supermarkets, which absorb a significant part of the homeowner's money, contractors are small (and often undercapitalized) firms or individuals. Worse yet, the homeowner is likely to know little or nothing about what needs to be done, the materials involved, and the kind of workmanship required.

Choosing a Contractor

Unless they can get a word-of-mouth recommendation, homeowners often find a contractor through the *Yellow Pages* or the classified advertisements in a local newspaper. On calling the contractor's number, they are likely to be greeted by the contractor's spouse or an answering machine, either of which announces that the contractor is "out on a job" and will return the call.

This news often gratifies homeowners, who conclude that the contractor has low overhead (which should result in a low price) and, presumably, other customers. What they fail to realize are two possibilities:

1. that the contractor is operating on a shoestring, and hence will require a large deposit for materials, and
2. that the contractor probably uses casual (and perhaps unskilled) labor as needed and hence may require a deposit to pay wages while the job is in progress.

To guard against out-and-out incompetents, you should first check with the regulatory authorities (usually a division of the state's licensing department) to make sure that the contractor is licensed and bonded. The licensing may or may not offer reassurance. Some states require a rigorous written exam; others issue a license to anyone who is able to pay for bonding. (The bond, which is intended to reimburse the contractor's clients for incomplete or unsatisfactory work, offers only limited protection because it is too small to reimburse all the customers of a seriously delinquent or defaulting contractor.) The real purpose of the call is to enable you to reject as clearly unfit any contractor who is not licensed and bonded.

You should not rely on the contractor's personal assurances about licensing and bonding, and you should make certain that the contractor carries worker's compensation and insurance adequate to cover injury to employees and damage to your property.

Writing the Contract

Very often, contractors, most of whom offer a free estimate, will arrive on the premises, inspect the work to be done, and provide an oral estimate that specifies neither the materials to be used nor a starting or completion date. Nor will they guarantee that the completed job will be satisfactory—that the repaired roof or basement will not leak, that the paint will not peel, or that the driveway resurfacing will not crack for a specified length of time. These oral contracts are the source of a very large proportion of consumer complaints.

Unless you know precisely what the job involves—or unless you have consulted an architect or an engineer—you should not tell the contractor what to do. If you do, the job may turn out to be unsatisfactory because the contractor followed your inadequate or faulty instructions to the letter. Instead, you should describe the *problem* and let the contractor suggest the solution. Then, by inviting estimates from other contractors, you will get second opinions and will be able to award the contract on a more informed basis than merely the estimated price.

A written contract should cover every significant element mentioned above in very specific detail. In particular, materials should be clearly specified: not "a good-quality" paint, insulation, or roofing material but a specific brand of each. And, if you have consulted *Consumer Reports* or another source of information, you, rather than the contractor, should specify the brand of paint to be used. If new windows or kitchen cabinets are to be installed, their make and models should be clearly specified.

Not only is a starting and completion date essential but a clause should be negotiated that provides a stipulated penalty for each day that work continues beyond the completion date.

Most contractors demand a deposit on signing of the contract, and this is reasonable if it covers a substantial outlay for materials. But you should try to make certain that the deposit will actually be used to pay for materials and not for employee wages or last month's overhead. A further schedule of payments may be agreed upon, but a substantial proportion of the total should be withheld until the work is satisfactorily completed.

If you plan large-scale remodeling, a further safeguard is to establish an account with an escrow company. Under this arrangement you pay the full amount into the account, but the contractor can draw it out only in part payments as agreed-upon stages of the work are satisfactorily completed. This assures the contractor of full payment and assures you that your money is safe until work is actually performed. The fee charged by the escrow company is an inexpensive form of insurance.

A contract that embodies all the terms discussed here will offer you substantial protection, but it does not guarantee it. A contract is only as good as its signatory, and contractors have been known to go bankrupt, to fail to finish a job, to seriously damage the homeowner's property, or simply to disappear from the community.

Workmanship

The quality of the contractor's workmanship is impossible to specify in a contract, but it may be possible to buy a warranty from a third party that guarantees a standard of performance and is likely to remain in business even if the contractor does not. The Homeowners Warranty Corporation (P.O. Box 152087, Irving, TX 75015, 800-433-7657), which initially provided ten-year warranties on new homes, now offers similar warranties on work done by contractors on its approved list. But because the level of craftsmanship guaranteed by a HOW policy may not meet your own standards, you should scrutinize the policy carefully to understand the level of protection it offers.

Liens

One very unpleasant surprise encountered by some homeowners is the discovery that the employees or the suppliers of a contractor have placed a lien on the customer's property because they have not been paid by the contractor or a subcontractor. This procedure is fully supported by law, because it offers the employees and suppliers their only protection against a defaulting contractor. As a consequence, some homeowners, having paid the contractor the full price, have been forced to pay off liens against their property simply because the contractor disappeared with the payment. Of course, the homeowner who has to remove such a lien can sue the contractor for the amount of the lien plus any penalty fees—provided that he can be tracked down.

To avoid this situation, you may want to check with one or more of the contractor's suppliers as to his financial stability and personal integrity. Another protective tactic involves inserting in the contract a "hold harmless" or general indemnification clause stipulating that if you make all payments as scheduled, the contractor will satisfy all labor and materials costs in a timely manner.

Door-to-Door Contractors

The very worst problems are likely to be encountered with "door-to-door" contractors who approach the homeowner with a statement that they are doing work "in your neighborhood" and are thus able to offer a very low price for driveway paving or the installation of roofing, siding, or new windows. Others offer a special price "if you'll allow us to use your house as a model." Many of these contractors have been known to disappear with their customers' down payment. Others have abandoned a half-completed job, and those who complete the work are the target of numerous complaints. Door-to-door contractors who offer to begin work immediately are in clear violation of the three-day cooling-off requirement that governs door-to-door solicitations. Given the volume of complaints against such sales tactics, the homeowners' best protection is a firm "No, thanks."

Some Further Information

An indispensable source of advice for anyone contemplating a remodeling project, large or small, is Creed D. Jackson's *The Intelligent Remodeler* (American Homebuilders Publishing Co., 236 Huntington Ave., Boston, MA 02115). A cautionary horror story about building a house is Ruth S. Martin's *And They Built a Crooked House* (Lakeside Press, 5125 Mayfield Rd., Cleveland, OH 44124).

Complaints

The best way to avoid contractor problems is probably to get several word-of-mouth recommendations. If these are not available, it is useful to ask the contractor for the names of recent customers and to visit them to inspect the work or, at least, call them to ask whether the work was satisfactorily completed, on schedule, and within budget. A check with the local Better Business Bureau, the state attorney general, or the state contractor-licensing department is another way of determining whether any complaints have been made. Any unresolved complaints should be filed with all three.

If a contractor you used has declared bankruptcy, your only recourse is to file a creditor's claim with the bankruptcy court, but the likelihood of recovery is small. If the contractor is still in business, you or your lawyer should put him on notice with a request to complete or correct the work within a specified time. If the contractor fails to respond, you can have the work done by another contractor and sue the first one for damages and costs.

HEALTH SERVICES

Physicians and Dentists

Complaints against physicians and dentists range from personal incompatibility, through callousness in treatment, refusal to release records, excessive charges, sexual harassment or assault, to inappropriate treatment that causes irreversible damage. The channel for complaints often depends on the context in which the professional is working as well as the nature of the complaint.

Physicians

Many patients today receive their medical treatment from an "assigned" physician in a health maintenance organization or a group practice. Not all such patients realize that they have the right to ask for a change of physician if they are dissatisfied with the one assigned. The high-quality health maintenance organizations are generally zealous about patient satisfaction, and patient complaints to the organization's administration help it monitor the quality of the practitioners it employs as well as the care they deliver.

Medical Records. Although some patient complaints are frivolous, some are clearly legitimate. Both the release of medical records to the patient and their unauthorized release to third parties are frequent sources of contention. Although some physicians are willing to release the records directly to the patient, others are reluctant, arguing that a patient's record, couched as it is in medical terminology, is meant to be read only by professionals and would cause patients needless anxiety because they would not understand it.

In fact, physicians are required by law to release all medical records, including X rays, to all patients who request them except mental patients. A physician's reluctance to release records to a patient requesting them may indicate a basic attitude that the patient may find unacceptable.

Release of your records to any other party—an employer or an insurance company, for example—is illegal without your express authorization. If, however, you apply for a life insurance policy, the insurer will usually require you to permit access to your medical records. This information may then be filed in the Medical Information Insurance Bureau's data bank for use by other insurers with your authorization. You can obtain a copy of your current file by writing to the Bureau at P.O. Box 105, Essex Station, Boston, MA 02112.

Unnecessary Treatment. In recent years, an oversupply of surgeons has led to charges that a significant proportion of surgical procedures—hysterectomies prominent among them—are medically unnecessary and are performed for the financial benefit of the surgeon rather than the welfare of the patient. In addition, research has shown that many patients who undergo bypass surgery do not survive any longer than those who are treated more conservatively by medication.

Before undergoing any major surgery, therefore, you would do well to get a second opinion. The value of a second opinion is confirmed by the fact that medical insurers are increasingly willing to reimburse patients who seek them. Some even require a second opinion or a medical review prior to major surgery or any anticipated hospitalization.

Informed Consent. Whether or not you seek a second opinion, you need to understand the concept of "informed consent." Both the law and the principles of medical ethics require that before undertaking any treatment, whether it be surgery or the administration of a drug that has side effects, the physician must obtain your formal consent. But this consent must be "informed"—that is, you must be told, in clear and comprehensible language, not only the anticipated benefits of the treatment but also its risks, in terms of its possible failure and its side effects.

In theory, informed consent would seem to offer you significant protection. But in practice it can cause problems. How much detail, for example, should the physician provide? If operations under general anesthetic result in a death rate of less than 0.1 percent attributable to the anesthetic itself, should you be informed of this minuscule risk or would it merely increase your already high anxiety and perhaps lead you to reject needed treatment? And is the answer to this question the same if you face certain death unless the operation is performed, are having cosmetic surgery, or are having a tooth removed under general anesthetic?

On the other hand, many patients routinely sign a blanket "consent" form along with their hospital admission papers without reading or understanding it, and occasionally physicians use this form as a waiver of their responsibility to inform the patient more specifically. However, if you suffer adverse consequences from treatment and can prove that you did not provide "informed consent," you may have grounds for a complaint if not, indeed, a lawsuit based on medical malpractice.

Complaints. Complaints against physicians are not easy to file or to resolve. In general, although physicians are licensed by state governments, the licensing authorities have permitted the medical profession to be almost entirely self-regulating. Hence, the complaint should be filed with the county or state medical association, which has a disciplinary process specifically established to adjudicate complaints. The complaint should also be filed with the state's professional licensing board, especially if board membership includes a "public member"—that is, a layperson appointed for the specific purpose of protecting the interests of patients.

Whether patient complaints are handled fairly or whether the medical associations' fundamental aim is to protect their membership is not clear. It is true that associations dismiss the majority of complaints against their members as groundless or unsubstantiated and that penalties imposed on physicians found delinquent are usually limited to mild censure. On the other hand, when a medical association receives a number of similar complaints against a single physician, it is more likely to consider them seriously and to take action. The stated aim of professional associations is to rid the profession of the "few bad apples." Unfortunately, there is little information on the number of complaints needed to identify the "bad apple" or on the time involved in removal.

In general, the effectiveness of the complaint process is open to serious question because of pervasive professional secrecy. No information is available, for example, on the percentage of complaints filed that result in disciplinary action or the grounds on which complaints are dismissed. And the data on discipline are not encouraging. In 1990, according to the Public Citizens Health Research Group, only 1,437 serious disciplinary actions, including suspension, revocation of license, or probation, were taken against physicians—a rate of only 2.5 actions per 1,000 physicians—whereas several independent studies have found that at least 100,000 patients are injured or killed annually because of medical negligence.

In 1990, a national data bank was established to record all disciplinary actions against physicians, but it is open only to hospitals that are considering whether to allow a physician to practice there and to state licensing boards. It is not open to the public or even to other physicians.

If a serious complaint against a physician is dismissed or disregarded by a medical association, the state medical licensing or disciplinary board may help resolve it. But if the complaint involves significantly adverse consequences for the patient—for example, through obvious misdiagnosis, the administration of an inappropriate medication, or the failure to follow established surgical procedures—the patient has no alternative but to retain a lawyer to explore filing a lawsuit (see Chapter 14).

In recent years the escalation of malpractice insurance for physicians has received widespread publicity, implying that malpractice suits are increasingly successful. This impression is reinforced by news stories describing astronomical awards to a few plaintiffs. The fact is that astronomical awards are very often reduced on appeal or in out-of-court settlements. The increases in malpractice premiums are due largely to the insurers' obligation to defend the increasing number of lawsuits, and a substantial proportion of the premiums goes to attorneys and expert witnesses, not to "wronged" patients.

Many dissatisfied patients attempt to file a lawsuit on a contingency basis, assuming that it will cost them nothing unless they win. To begin with, this is a misconception because if they lose, their lawyer will charge them for the out-of-pocket costs incurred for expert witness fees, the taking of depositions, the buying of transcripts, and many other incidentals. Moreover, few lawyers will undertake a malpractice case unless they see clearly some opportunity for recovery of damages. Unlike many patients, lawyers know that winning a case requires clear-cut proof of negligence and that a treatment outcome that disappoints the patient is not by itself grounds for a verdict in the patient's favor.

Dentists

The oversupply of dentists in many parts of the country is the main cause of complaints made against them. Because fluoridation of the water supply and toothpastes has dramatically reduced the demand for cavity-filling and other maintenance work that was once the mainstay of most dentists' incomes, many dentists are persuading their patients to undergo rather expensive and not altogether necessary procedures—tooth implants rather than dental plates, for example, or periodontal or orthodontal work where it is not clearly necessary or even desirable.

As in the case of expensive or complicated proposed medical treatment, a second opinion is very useful, and this may be available at the clinic of a nearby college of dentistry. The procedures to follow when filing complaints and initiating malpractice suits against physicians apply equally to dentists.

Hospitals

Most complaints against hospitals involve overcharges. Although some overcharges stem from clerical errors or from double-billing the patient as well as the insurer, most result from the common practice of billing the patient several dollars for the administering of a pill that may cost only a few cents. Hospitals argue that such charges reflect their very high overhead costs and, unfortunately, the patient is in no position to rebut this argument.

Virtually every accredited hospital has a patient representative or ombudsman or a designated administrator whose duty is to straighten out billing and insurance problems and to mediate disputes between the patient and the hospital. This person may also be able to negotiate bill payment for uninsured patients, especially if their convalescence is likely to reduce their earning ability.

If an overcharge cannot be reduced through intervention of the patient representative, you should try to make arrangements to pay the bill, because hospitals, despite the humanitarian image they like to present, are notoriously quick to turn delinquent patient accounts over to collection agencies.

All hospitals are licensed by the state, and the better ones are accredited by the Joint Commission on Accreditation. Complaints about the quality of treatment should be filed with your attending physician, then with the department of health or other state agency that supervises hospital standards and practices, and, finally, with the U.S. Department of Health and Human Services' Inspector General's Hotline, P.O. Box 17303, Baltimore, MD 21203, (800) 368-5779. According to Walt Bogdanovich's *The Great White Lie* (Simon & Schuster, 1992), none of these regulatory agencies takes action until complaints pile up—a good reason for lodging a complaint, whether or not your personal case is resolved.

The federal government periodically publishes a "scoreboard" of mortality rates at various hospitals. Although this kind of comparison has been criticized on the grounds that the hospitals compared do not attract equally vulnerable patients, your local hospital's "score" may offer you some notion of the competence of its staff. Of course, hospital practices that have seriously injured you may be grounds for a negligent personal injury suit filed by your lawyer.

Ophthalmologists, Optometrists, Opticians

According to a persistent rumor, this is how schools of optometry teach their students to set prices: "Tell the customer that the price will be $75. If he doesn't flinch, add '. . . for the frames.' Then say, 'As for the lenses, they'll cost $95' and, if he doesn't flinch, add '. . . each.'"

Whether the rumor is true or not, the fact is that many customers, especially those in small towns where competition is not keen, overpay for contact lenses and spectacles, and this can hold true even in metropolitan areas, where optometrists compete with one another by offering "One-hour service!" or "Buy one pair, get one free!" or "Budget Eyewear . . . $39."

The question of how to treat one's vision problems is not a simple one, because the answer may be:

1. Have an examination by an ophthalmologist (an M.D. with additional training and accreditation as an eye specialist), and have his prescription filled by an optician (a technician who does nothing but manufacture lenses and fit them into frames);
2. have a refraction (for visual acuity) done by an optometrist (a practitioner licensed to perform vision tests and to prescribe and provide corrective lenses and frames); or
3. pick up a pair of ready-made reading spectacles avail-

able in various standard lens prescriptions for less than
$10 in local variety stores.

The argument in favor of ophthalmologists stresses that, unlike optometrists, they can, by examining the eyes, find symptoms
of other problems, such as diabetes, that optometrists may not be
trained to detect. In addition, because their income does not depend on the sale of lenses and frames, they are unlikely to recommend lenses (or a change in a current prescription) unless they are
clearly called for.

Optometrists, like ophthalmologists, are trained at schools of
optometry and are licensed by the state. But the curriculum at
these schools is far more limited than that of a medical school,
and the criteria for state licensing of the graduates vary widely
from one state to another, as do the specifications of which procedures must be performed by an optometrist and which may be
delegated to noncertified assistants. In extreme cases, one optometrist can set up a chain of offices staffed entirely by nonlicensed
technicians. And although some optometrists invariably refer to
an ophthalmologist people with conditions that they cannot treat,
others may not.

Optometrists also suffer a conflict of interest. Because they
earn relatively little from doing a refraction, their main source of
income derives from the sale of lenses and frames. As a consequence, they may prescribe lenses when the need for them is marginal, or they may prescribe contact lenses in cases where
a financially disinterested ophthalmologist would advise against
them because of the conformation of the patient's eyeball.

Some vision problems can be alleviated simply by finding a
suitable pair of ready-made spectacles from a rack in the local
variety store. Although some states prohibit the sale of these spectacles, the consensus of qualified experts is that the prohibition
exists to protect the incomes of ophthalmologists and optometrists rather than the health of the public. On the other hand, the
people most likely to buy these ready-mades—elderly consumers,
many of whom suffer from farsightedness, which normally increases with age—run the risk of overlooking glaucoma, cata-

racts, and other treatable conditions that also become more likely with increasing age.

Complaints against optometrists usually center on overcharges, uncomfortable frames, or unsatisfactory lenses. Overcharging can be avoided by comparison shopping on the basis of a highly detailed estimate, not only for lenses but for the specific model of frame and any other special charges for plastic lenses, protective coatings, tinting, and other extras.

Frame discomfort is usually correctable, even though two or three visits may be necessary to solve the problem. (Most optometrists will adjust frames as a professional courtesy, whether or not the customer is their own.)

Complaints about unsatisfactory lenses—usually involving contact lenses or bifocals—present a more difficult problem. The first-time user of either contacts, bifocals, or trifocals must undergo an initial period of adjustment, and it is often difficult to know whether the optometrist's urging the customer to be patient is or is not an attempt to evade responsibility for a genuinely faulty prescription. There should be a clear understanding in advance that the optometrist will replace the lenses at no additional cost if the discomfort persists after a specified adjustment period—usually 30 days. Lacking such an agreement, the dissatisfied customer might consult an ophthalmologist about the appropriateness of the optometrist's prescription and the accuracy with which it has been followed in the manufacture of the lenses.

Complaints against the professional performance of ophthalmologists and optometrists can be filed with the respective professional associations and with the state department of professional licensing. Complaints about overcharges or deceptive advertising by optometrists and opticians can be filed with the Better Business Bureau and the state attorney general.

Hearing Aids

Because some degree of hearing loss is an almost inevitable part of the aging process, the elderly constitute a particularly vulnerable market for overpriced or ineffective hearing aids—especially those sold through television and newspaper advertising.

Anyone with a hearing loss should disregard the free offers of hearing tests made by the manufacturers of hearing aids and should, instead, be tested by an otolaryngologist or a certified audiometrist, preferably one associated with a hospital or a nonprofit institution devoted to hearing problems. A disinterested professional will recommend the appropriate type (and perhaps make) of hearing aid or conclude that a hearing aid will not alleviate the problem. Under no circumstances should you agree to buy a hearing aid without a competent professional examination.

Although many hearing-aid companies offer a "money back guarantee," many buyers complain that the time limit is too short or that the seller insists on retaining a "restocking charge" of 15 percent or more. For this reason, the contract should be read carefully and thoroughly.

Nursing Homes

The majority of complaints against nursing homes, usually filed by the resident's children, involve mistreatment or neglect. And these tend to surge immediately after the periodic media exposés about horrific conditions in a specific establishment.

Many of the media horror stories describe nursing homes that have a high proportion of indigent patients, a tight budget, and, consequently, a high turnover of their low-paid and poorly trained staffs. But complaints are also filed against expensive homes on the grounds that the residents "are not getting what we're paying for."

Mediation of these complaints is difficult for the families of residents because the residents' testimony may well be inaccurate. Because mild paranoia and mental confusion are not uncommon among the elderly, complaints about theft of personal property or physical abuse can't always be taken at face value. Nevertheless, mistreatment—overmedication, physical restraint, and interactions that rob the elderly of their dignity—does occur and, if it is confirmed by other residents, should be reported and investigated promptly.

Complaints should be addressed to the nursing home's administrator first. The social services departments of some states and counties have well-trained ombudsmen who visit each nursing home periodically and listen to residents' complaints confidentially and impartially. If these ombudsmen discover chronic complaints from several residents, they attempt to mediate them with the home's administration first. If mediation is unsuccessful, they report ongoing problems to the state department of social and health services or to the state licensing authorities. In the absence of an ombudsman system, complaints should be filed directly with these state offices.

LAWYERS

In his orientation lecture to newly recruited young lawyers, the senior partner of a large and respected law firm would say, "If your client doesn't complain about your bill, you simply haven't charged him enough." In addition to complaints about lawyers' excessive fees, there are two other areas of widespread client dissatisfaction: inadequate professional performance (usually procrastination or failure to respond to telephone calls or letters) and theft or improper use of the client's assets.

Delays

Many clients complain that their lawyers have not acted promptly and aggressively on their behalf, that they have failed to introduce or emphasize relevant evidence, that the case has been dragging on for months or, more significantly, that they have failed to win a favorable verdict or outcome.

Although some lawyers are less conscientious than others, and although some of them take on a greater work load than they can handle properly, the slow pace of many, if not most, lawsuits is due not to the lawyer's apathy or neglect but to "the law's delay"—that is, overcrowded court calendars and the opposing attorney's skill in winning delays and postponements in the hope that witnesses will disappear and the case will "go away."

As for failure to win a favorable verdict, most clients, because they are biased and without legal experience, tend to be more sanguine than their lawyers about what is admissible as evidence, what the law "ought to be," and the probable outcome of the case. Indignant clients are usually certain that "if they just see it my way," justice will prevail and the court system will reward their cause. Their lawyers, more familiar with the vagaries of judges and juries and the neutrality of the legal system, are, or should be, far less certain about what kind of "justice" will be wrought.

Misconduct

Gross professional misconduct by lawyers takes several forms, and its reported incidence has risen in recent years. The increase has been attributed to various causes, among them a rise in reported alcohol and drug abuse among lawyers, the television portrayals of lawyers with a life-style far more affluent than most lawyers enjoy, and the oversupply of lawyers, which makes earning an adequate living difficult for many of them.

The most serious professional misconduct involves stealing from the client. The theft can take various forms: borrowing or stealing from a client's estate or trust fund, siphoning off the proceeds of a personal-injury claim, billing for services not rendered or needed, tampering with the probate process in order to steal from the deceased's estate, and engaging in a conflict of interest by representing two parties whose positions are opposed.

With the exception of Kansas, Maine, New Mexico, and North Dakota, all states have established funds to reimburse victims of malfeasance by their lawyers. The sponsorship of these funds differs from one state to another, but most of them have been established by the legal profession and are supported by fees paid by its members. Few of these funds are able to reimburse the victims in full, however, and many of them are on the verge of depletion because they are paying out more than they receive. Nevertheless, they may provide some restitution for the victims of unscrupulous lawyers. Unfortunately, the most likely victims— widows and wards in guardianship and people who are what have been called "legally illiterate"—are unaware of their victimization or of the existence of these funds or other avenues of redress.

Most lawyers carry malpractice insurance, the premiums for which have been rising steadily, reflecting an increasing number of client claims and a corresponding increase in demands for defense and adverse judgments and settlements against attorneys. Malpractice insurance covers *negligence* in practice, not intentional acts or theft. While risk-management by attorneys in efforts to lower their premiums may improve the service they render to clients, it can also lead to overcautious practice, which can raise the client's final bill.

Overcharges

You may be able to avoid surprisingly high fees by asking in advance about your lawyer's hourly rates and bearing in mind that this rate applies not only to face-to-face meetings and courtroom appearances but also to the many hours of research and preparation that your case may require. Although your lawyer may be able to provide a ballpark estimate of your total fees and costs, there is no predicting the course that the lawsuit will take. In the end, you must trust the lawyer to behave professionally.

Complaints

Complaints about lawyers' ethics, including overcharges, should be filed with the state bar association or the state supreme court, whichever regulates the profession in your state. But your expectations of redress, except in a truly egregious case, should be tempered by the fact that, nationwide, approximately 95 percent of complaints are quietly dropped and, although some members of the American Bar Association are responsive to public complaints that "the fox is guarding the chicken coop," secrecy about complaints is still the rule. The disciplinary staffs of many state bar associations are overworked, and complaint investigation does not have high priority.

In Oregon, complaints filed against lawyers are open to the public as soon as they are filed, and in other states, reforms are under way. In most states, however, files are not available unless and until the bar association's investigation has found preliminary evidence of wrongdoing or has taken official disciplinary action against the offending lawyer.

In some situations it may be more effective to seek the help of another lawyer—one who is presumably more responsive. A discreet telephone call from him or her to your first lawyer about marginal behavior may be enough to restore matters to a professional level. And the possibility of the second lawyer's involvement in your complaint to the bar association can enhance your credibility and may correct the situation more promptly.

SCHOOLS AND COLLEGES
Public Schools

Parents' complaints against public schools generally center on the child's rejection from or placement in a particular class or a particular school, the general quality of the educational program, or the interaction between a specific teacher and their child.

Some complaints about rejection or placement have a firm basis in law. Federal law requires that the state provide education for every child, regardless of physical or mental conditions that challenge learning. If your child is barred from schooling on the grounds that he or she is incapable of participation in schoolwork, and you receive no satisfaction from the principal, you should confront the board of education—perhaps even threaten a lawsuit. Such lawsuits have been successful in forcing communities to provide special transportation, visiting teachers who specialize in learning disabilities, television links to the classroom, or whatever else is needed to ensure that the exceptional child's basic educational needs are met.

Complaints about the child's placement in a class for slow learners or a vocational-education track (or rejection from an advanced class for gifted children) must be filed first with the school principal and then, if necessary, with the superintendent of the school system. To be effective, the complaint should be based on objective testing and evaluation by an independent specialist—an educational psychologist, otologist, or ophthalmologist, for example—rather than a parent's opinion of the child's abilities.

All too often a child is placed in a special education or vocational class because of physical or behavioral problems rather than learning problems, and such an assignment is unlikely to be of any benefit. On the other hand, some parents whose child has not been placed in a class for gifted children may have a somewhat exaggerated notion of their child's academic abilities or performance.

Complaints about assignment to a specific school generally stem from a community-wide assignment plan that is intended to reduce racial segregation. Although appeals are possible in most school systems, they need to have a sounder basis than proximity to the child's home. Once the appeal process has been exhausted, a lawsuit is the only alternative, but it is unlikely to be successful since it can be based only on procedural issues and not on your subjective view of what is best for your child. A more practical alternative may be to explore "magnet" schools, which, in many communities, enroll students on the basis of their interests rather than their place of residence.

The professional competence of a child's teacher is a source of distress to many parents, but few of them are willing to file a complaint for fear of retribution against the child by the teacher. And there have been instances in which the identity of a parent who was promised confidentiality by the principal was disclosed to the child's teacher.

Even when filed, complaints against teachers are unlikely to be successful—in part because their validity is very difficult to prove, in part because teachers and principals are prone to jealously protect their "professional judgment" against criticism from laypeople, and in part because the tenure system or a teacher shortage may make removal or transfer of a teacher difficult if not impossible.

Complaints filed by an individual parent are easily dismissed as coming from a "crazy." Complaints filed jointly by a group of parents of classmates are less easily dismissed, especially if they take the form of a statement providing specific examples of the teacher's behavior and signed by all members of the group. Here, again, the complaint should go first to the principal, then to the superintendent of education and, if necessary, to all members of the school board.

From time to time capricious and arbitrary actions of a teacher, a principal, or a board of education infringe on the civil rights of a student. Some parents, having exhausted the appeal process, have begun litigation on the child's behalf. Although the American Civil Liberties Union eventually came to the aid of some of these parents, others used their own funds to begin litigation. You may feel, as they did, that the cost of litigation is a small price to pay to demonstrate support of your child and to memorialize it by having his or her name attached to a Supreme Court decision.

Complaints Against Private Schools

Because many parents' very high expectations of private preparatory schools are based on the excellent and widespread reputations of such schools as Exeter or Andover, they are likely to be disappointed with the performance of the very expensive yet inadequate imitations of these models.

Private schools below the first tier face many problems. Low teacher salaries attract inadequately prepared teachers and cause high teacher turnover. This occasionally causes the sudden cancellation of courses that were advertised in the catalogue and may have constituted a major motivation for the child's enrollment. And despite a higher teacher/pupil ratio than is found in their public counterparts, they cannot offer the wide variety of courses and the elaborate library and laboratory facilities that the best public high schools can provide. Moreover, because they are largely independent, some of them can establish arbitrary (and sometimes bizarre) rules and regulations that would not be tolerated by an educational bureaucracy responsible to the general public.

But private schools are not entirely independent; they are regulated at least to some extent by one of the regional accreditation organizations that set standards for independent schools and monitor their compliance. Before registering their child, therefore, parents should check on the school's accreditation and, if possible, visit classes. And if their complaints against the school cannot be settled internally, a complaint to the accrediting board is in order. As in the case of complaints against public schools, complaints by a group of parents (though more difficult to organize because parents may not share a geographic community) are far more effective than individual complaints.

Complaints Against Vocational and Trade Schools

Private, for-profit vocational schools tend to appeal to an easily exploitable clientele—high school dropouts, high school graduates with substandard academic records, and others who find themselves adrift in a labor market that increasingly demands well-developed skills. As a result they have been the subject of a rapidly growing number of complaints. These complaints include unqualified instructors, equipment that lags behind the latest technological developments in almost every field, promises of job placement that are not fulfilled, negotiating government loans for obviously unqualified students who remain responsible for the loans even if they drop out, and filing for bankruptcy, leaving the student with a loan balance to pay off.

The student considering vocational education should recognize that it is basically expensive. If a community college, the public counterpart of the private vocational school, charges its students only about 30 percent of the actual costs, how, then, can a profit-making vocational school promise good training at reasonable rates? Before enrolling in a private vocational school, therefore, the student should carefully research the community colleges and vocational-technical high schools in the vicinity to discover whether more competent training is available at substantially lower cost.

The student still interested in a for-profit vocational school rather than a community college should demand precise figures from the school on the percentage of students who drop out before completing a certain course and the percentage who are actually placed in related jobs through the school's efforts. Job placement statistics should be scrutinized carefully and in detail. One vocational school that offered training in the "travel and hotel industry," for example, counted as "placements" some graduates whom the school placed as valet-parking attendants at a local hotel. Another possible source of information is students who have completed (or failed to complete) the course—not necessarily the students offered as "references" by the school.

When a student loan is involved, the enrollment contract should include provisions for pro rata refunds if the student drops out before completion and for protecting the student from loan payments if the school goes bankrupt. Because this has proven to be a widespread and serious problem area, the student should in no circumstances undertake a large federal loan that must be repaid whether or not the full course of study is completed.

Complaints against private vocational schools should be filed with the state's vocational education commission or the board regulating higher education.

Complaints Against Colleges

Unlike complaints against secondary schools, complaints against colleges are generally filed by students rather than parents. These complaints range across a large spectrum: failure to be admitted to a desired course, failure to obtain a refund of tuition, unfairness

of a grade, inadequacy of instruction, and sexual harassment. (In a few isolated cases dissatisfied students have filed lawsuits alleging that the course descriptions in the college catalogue constituted deceptive advertising, but the courts have not upheld them.)

Complaints about failure to be admitted to a desired course are likely to increase as shrinking budgets produce overcrowded classrooms, but an appeal to the instructor to "make just one more place" may be effective if the student's motivation for enrollment is a sound one; the need of the course to fulfill a graduation requirement or a prerequisite is more likely to gain approval than the fact that an afternoon course is more compatible with the student's sleeping habits than one that meets at 8 A.M.

Complaints about unfairness of a grade should be taken up with the instructor. The grade is unlikely to be changed, but the instructor's justification of it may do much to help the student earn a better grade on subsequent assignments.

Some complaints against "bad" teaching—the instructor's foreign accent, speaking style, or unapproachability—may be justified but unresolvable. Not every college instructor is a Mr. Chips, and many teaching fellows or teaching assistants are hired not for their teaching abilities but for their research skills. Hence, students may have to lower their expectations. On the other hand, a complaint addressed to the department chairperson and signed by a substantial proportion of students in the course may produce some corrective action.

Complaints that cannot be resolved by the individual instructor or the department chairperson may be carried to a higher level. Many colleges have an ombudsman—an individual whose specific function is to mediate impartially between students and faculty. In the absence of an ombudsman, complaints can be filed with the dean of the college.

Complaints about racial or sexual discrimination or sexual harassment can be filed with the administrator appointed to deal with such matters. The precise title of this official will vary from one campus to another, but his or her identity can be found rather easily by inquiring of any administrator. In such situations, however, a lawyer should be consulted, because complaints of this nature are very difficult for the layperson to prosecute single-handedly.

Serious complaints that cannot be resolved at the campus level can be addressed to the state commission that regulates higher education. Here, too, a complaint signed by a group and offering objective information is likely to get closer scrutiny than one signed by an individual and consisting largely or wholly of undocumented opinions. Because institutions are concerned both with their legal liability and their reputations, a well-constructed letter from an attorney is likely to produce a substantive response. Legislators who control the budget of a public institution may also help with a complaint that cannot be resolved by the administration.

PUBLIC UTILITIES

The rates and services of public utilities that supply consumers with gas, electricity, and water are regulated by the state utilities commission. Some of these commissions are consumer oriented and monitor closely the rates charged to customers, the return on investment permitted, the treatment of customer security deposits, and the methods of accounting used. Other commissions are, to use the euphemism of a stockbroker, "investment favorable," meaning that they permit the regulated utilities to reap liberal profits for their shareholders.

Similarly, some public utilities are customer-friendly, offering free repair of electric appliances, free or discounted devices that conserve electricity or water, and other courtesies. Others retain a nineteenth-century "the public be damned" attitude.

Complaints about rates, therefore, are futile unless they are organized in the form of a widespread political protest against the actions of the utilities commission. The utilities commission will, however, accept complaints about the misclassification of an account—as residential rather than industrial—or about billing errors and late payments if these cannot be resolved by the utility. The utilities commission is located in the state capital.

TELEPHONE SERVICE

Long-Distance Carriers

With the breakup of AT&T and the advent of alternative long-distance carriers such as MCI and Sprint, the Federal Communications Commission and other consumer protection agencies have been flooded with complaints about unauthorized switching of their long-distance service from one company to another—a practice known as "slamming."

Some of these complaints are not valid because subscribers didn't read the fine print that authorized such a switch when they entered what they thought was a promotional prize contest. But others have proved to be entirely justified.

Federal Communications Commission rules require that, before signing up a new customer, a long-distance carrier must obtain from the consumer one of the following: (1) written authorization, (2) electronic authorization via an 800 number, (3) oral authorization witnessed by an independent third party, or (4) by sending, at the customer's request, an information package that includes an authorization in the form of a business-reply postcard and waiting 14 days after receipt of the postcard (to give the customer time for a change of mind) before notifying the customer's local telephone company of the change.

Subscribers whose long-distance service has been switched without their consent can pay their normal telephone bills without including the long-distance charges. Eventually these charges must be paid, but at a rate no higher than that charged by their former company.

Complaints are also generated by what is called "alternative operator services." These companies, which solicit as subscribers hotels, motels, airports, hospitals, and other locations patronized by transient users, charge substantially higher rates than the regular carriers (AT&T, MCI, Sprint) and share their profits with their subscribers. As a consequence, many travelers are shocked by the exorbitant long-distance charges that appear on their hotel bills.

Federal Communication Commission rules require that the companies offering alternative operator services affix a sticker on or near their telephones that displays the company's name and states that rates will be quoted on request. In addition, when calls are placed, these services must identify themselves to the callers and give them an opportunity to hang up or offer to connect them with the long-distance carrier of their choice.

Repair Service

The advent of privately owned telephones has created problems that did not exist when telephone companies supplied the instruments and assumed maintenance responsibility for the entire system—for the telephones as well as all connecting wiring linking the instrument to the exchange. Today the telephone companies limit their responsibility to the wiring outside the residence, leaving the subscriber responsible for all internal wiring as well as the telephones.

Subscribers faced with a phone that's "out of order" can't be certain whether the fault lies with the instrument or its in-house wiring or with the company's system. If they call the telephone company's repair service and the fault turns out to involve internal wiring or a telephone, they will be faced with a substantial bill for the repair.

To alleviate this problem, many telephone companies offer, for a monthly payment, a kind of insurance policy covering the telephones and the internal wiring, but most consumer advocates advise against it. They point out that system malfunctions rarely affect individual subscribers and that inquiring of a neighbor can determine whether the problem is areawide. If it is not, disconnecting each telephone, one at a time, is likely to identify the faulty instrument. And if the problem turns out to be in-house, the consumer can choose between discarding the defective instrument or calling a private telephone service company, which is likely to correct the problem less expensively than the telephone company itself.

(900) Numbers

Encouraged by the profitability of toll-free (800) long-distance calls, so called because the recipient rather than the caller pays the toll, long-distance telephone companies devised the (900) number, for which the company bills the caller a per-minute charge. The long-distance carrier subtracts a service charge and turns the money over to the client who has subscribed to the (900) service. Although the charge for the call is uniform for all parts of the country, the cost can be extremely high, even if the call is a brief one. The system has led to widespread abuse and fraud and, consequently, to a volume of consumer complaints sufficient to generate a hue and cry for state and federal regulation.

Typically consumers call a (900) number in order to gain information or a service they regard as valuable. In some localities, for example, city records can be obtained and parking tickets can be paid by calling a (900) number. But although some (900) numbers do provide the caller with legitimate information (for example, stock quotations, weather forecasts for distant cities, or sports scores), most, if not all, of this information is available from other sources, usually at little or no cost. Sports and weather information, for example, is readily found in any major newspaper, and stock quotations are available from a cable channel or the caller's broker. (900) numbers are also used in some television-originated opinion surveys, although no professional pollster regards as valid a survey whose respondents consist only of individuals willing to pay for a (900) call.

Many (900) numbers connect the caller with a dating service, sexually explicit conversations, and other salacious materials. The content of such calls is protected as free speech by the First Amendment, and despite the fact that they may offend some citizens, they are not illegal if the callers are adults and are aware of the nature of what they are buying and the cost of the call.

On the other hand, many of the (900) numbers are advertised by individuals and companies whose intent is clearly fraudulent (see Chapter 9). One entrepreneur, for example, used a (900) number to market reservations for flights to the moon. Some fraudulent companies who have become aware of the growing public suspicion about (900) numbers have taken to using (976) numbers. Calls to these numbers are also charged to the caller at exorbitant rates. In addition, some callers to (800) numbers have found themselves billed for the call, although these charges appear on a separate bill rather than on their regular telephone bills. The Federal Trade Commission advises callers to disregard such bills.

Radio and television stations also promote contests and sweepstakes by asking viewers to call a (900) number to enter. Some states view these as lotteries and therefore illegal, and the Federal Trade Commission is issuing guidelines for the use of (900) numbers in sweepstakes, including a requirement that organizers must state the odds of winning.

The abuses of (900) numbers have reached such proportions that the long-distance carriers, in compliance with FCC rules, require businesses using (900) numbers to include a statement, both in their advertising and at the outset of the phone call, that informs callers of the cost of the call and tells them that they may hang up within a few seconds without being charged. Statements in programs aimed at children must tell callers to hang up unless they have parental permission. Customers can ask that a (900) number be blocked from their phone line and can ask for a one-time forgiveness of charges incurred inadvertently. They can refuse payment of (900) charges without being cut off from local or long-distance phone service.

Perhaps the largest problem, however, stems from the unauthorized use of (900) numbers by children in a household. Some parents report that their telephone bills are running to hundreds of dollars because their unsupervised children regard calling (900) numbers as a form of after-school recreation.

Although the long-distance carriers are not permitted to reject (900) accounts, they can exert control by refusing to bill the (900) account's callers on their telephone bills. In effect, this forces the (900) account to bill customers directly—a process so uneconomical and ineffective as to reduce their incentive to use (900) numbers.

Complaints to the local telephone company about excessive or unauthorized charges meet with various responses. The local companies point out, correctly, that the responsibility for (900) numbers lies not with them but with any one of a number of long-distance carriers, and not necessarily the company that handles your regular long-distance calls. Nevertheless, you will be charged for calls to them on your regular telephone bill. Although the carrier can be readily identified by the first three digits of the (900) number, some local companies refuse to disclose the information to complaining callers. Consumers can get this information, however, from a free kit published by the National Association of Information Suppliers at (800) 737-NAIS. Most long-distance carriers offer a one-time forgiveness of these bills, but this policy varies with each carrier.

Complaints concerning billings for (900) numbers should be filed (for intrastate calls) with the local telephone company and, if unresolved, with the state public utilities commission, the Better Business Bureau, or the attorney general's office.

The major interstate carriers have established the following toll-free numbers for lodging complaints on (900) billings:

AT&T: (800) 222-0300

MCI: (800) 444-3333

Telesphere: (800) 346-6329

U.S. Sprint: (800) 366-0707

Complaints can also be lodged with the Informal Complaints and Public Inquiries Branch, Enforcement Division, Federal Communications Commission, Suite 6202, Washington, DC 20554. Complaints about fraud should be addressed to the attorney general's office and the nearest office of the Federal Trade Commission.

In October 1992, Congress passed a bill requiring strict regulation of 900 numbers and empowering the Federal Trade Commission to issue rules and prohibit deceptive practices. In addition, the FTC is to work out dispute-resolution mechanisms for billing errors and to require the blocking of (900) dialing from households that request it. These measures should do much toward cleaning up the (900) and telemarketing industry.

CABLE TELEVISION

When cable television service began to burgeon, many communities were so eager to enjoy its benefits that they impulsively awarded franchises that embodied no regulatory constraints. Some communities, in fact, offered cash subsidies to induce cable companies to serve their residents. As a result, cable television service is an unregulated monopoly that has thus far successfully evaded rate regulation at the federal, state, and local level, and cable companies have been able to raise their rates at will. To date, public protest has proved weaker than the cable companies' lobbying efforts in the battle over rate regulation.

Although a bill regulating the cable industry was passed by Congress late in 1992, and although telephone companies have now been permitted to compete with cable companies, these developments are likely to lock the barn after the horse has been stolen.

Complaints about installation fees, billing errors, and the often erroneous imposition of exorbitant late fees should be filed with the Mass Media Bureau, Federal Communications Commission, 2025 M St., NW, Washington, DC 20554. Complaints can also be filed with the local franchising authority, usually the cable communications office of the city or county licensing department. Although the terms of most franchises preclude any rate relief and may prevent immediate complaint resolution, an accumulation of complaints may significantly influence renewal of the franchise.

HOUSEHOLD MOVING

A household move—especially interstate—is almost inevitably stressful, often involving a change of job, regrets over leaving the old community, concerns about unknown aspects of the new one, and a general feeling of disorientation. (It is during a household move that children are most likely to have accidents.) The physical household move itself is, of course, a major source of this stress, but careful planning can reduce, though probably not eliminate, worries about "the movers."

Although your first impulse in planning a move may be to reduce total weight, this is best done after you get a mover's estimate of the total weight of your household goods. Movers' rates are based on a sliding scale: the greater the weight, the lower the rate per hundredweight. Hence, before deciding to abandon some heavy items, such as refrigerators, find out whether their inclusion crosses the "break point" and gives you a lower rate per hundredweight for the entire load, in which case taking them along may be worthwhile.

Once you get this general estimate, you can determine what to take along and what to dispose of through a classified ad, a "moving sale," or gifts to friends, neighbors, or charitable organizations. Major appliances, for example, are relatively heavy, and the decision to take them along should be based on their age and current replacement or market value. This sorting-out process should leave you with a very firm understanding of what goes and what does not.

In some cases, you may be able to reduce moving costs by sending some heavy goods that weigh several hundredweight—such as books—by motor freight rather than with the mover. Motor freight requires sturdy packaging and imposes a minimum charge, but it may save you money if the weight of these items does not reduce the remaining load to a point at which it carries a higher rate per hundredweight.

Estimates

Once you have determined exactly what you plan to move, try to get some word-of-mouth recommendations of movers from friends or neighbors who have moved recently. (If your move is employment-related, your new employer may have some recommendations along with some relocation assistance.) But such recommendations should be used only as a starting point. A check with the Better Business Bureau for any complaints against the moving company or its local agent may modify your list of possibilities. In addition, a mover who is not licensed to do business in the state of your destination should probably be rejected because your load will have to be transferred somewhere along the line to a company that can take it to your final destination. Obviously, this additional loading and reloading increases your risk of loss or damage.

Each moving company that you invite for an estimate is required to give you two pieces of printed information. The first, *When You Move: Your Rights and Responsibilities,* a pamphlet published by the Interstate Commerce Commission (see Chapter 16), is useful but not cheering. Like too many government "consumer" publications, it has been so heavily influenced by the industry that it is heavy on the consumer's responsibilities and light on the rights. The second piece of printed information (which the mover may not offer voluntarily but is required to give you if you ask for it) is far more relevant. It is an official record, which the mover must submit to the ICC, of the company's performance over the past year in terms of damage and loss claims, delays, and billing errors. Although a deplorable record may cause you to reject a company, a good record won't guarantee a good move.

Even the most exemplary moving companies may hire freelance drivers who, in turn, may hire one set of casual laborers at the point of origin and another at the destination. And the quality of your move will depend more on them than on the reputation of the company although, of course, the better companies tend to hire the more reliable drivers. Perhaps more important is the reputation of the local agent for the parent company.

Once you have selected two or three moving companies, ask for estimates of four types:

1. *A per-hundredweight estimate.* This estimate is based strictly on the actual weight of your shipment, which is determined by weighing the truck on approved scales before and after your goods have been loaded. You have the right to be present at the weighing, but

this right is likely to be inconvenient to exercise. In any event, the driver will notify you after the weighing about the amount of your actual bill. Although experienced estimators are fairly accurate, your actual load may weigh more than the estimate, but under ICC regulations, your final bill may not exceed the estimate by more than 10 percent and you have 30 days in which to pay any amount over the estimate.

2. *A binding fixed-price rate.* Because this rate is guaranteed by the mover, you know exactly what you'll pay at the destination, but if you obtain the estimate a month or more before the move, it is important to specify just how long the rate is "locked in," since it may be subject to change over time.

3. *An estimate for packing and unpacking by the mover* (in conjunction with either the per-hundredweight or the fixed rate). This arrangement not only saves enormous labor at a time of stress and provides professional protection for fragile valuables (such as a grandfather's clock) but also strengthens your claim in the event of damage.

4. *A schedule estimate* that guarantees that both the pickup and the delivery will occur between narrowly specified dates (usually two or three days).

Although interstate moving rates are set by the Interstate Commerce Commission, movers are not required to comply with them strictly. Consequently, the actual estimates you receive may vary considerably. Some companies include various ICC-authorized extra charges—for the presence of an elevator at either location, for example, or for county excise taxes at the destination—that more competitive movers are willing to overlook or absorb. Some movers will quote a lower rate because your load will fill a truck that is scheduled for a move to a nearby destination on or near the same date. Others will offer a discount from ICC rates simply because they want your business. Given the fact that moving charges are not regulated, you can bargain with each estimator. Because they are usually paid on a commission basis, they are likely to offer you the lowest possible rate rather than lose your move.

Insurance

Influenced by the industry, the Interstate Commerce Commission has set the mover's basic liability for loss or damage at an extremely low rate: currently 60 cents per pound. This means that you'll collect about $18 if your $3000 computer is destroyed and perhaps 75 cents for a treasured ceramic bowl. You can buy several types of additional coverage. The least expensive pays for your damaged items on a depreciated basis, a figure on which you and the mover may not agree. A more expensive coverage reimburses you on the basis of "replacement cost." Both coverages are available with a sliding scale of deductibles.

You can insist on higher coverages for specific items, but the mover has the right to refuse coverage of more than $100 per pound, which may not cover expensive computers, works of art, or antiques. However, the company that issues your homeowner's policy may offer an "in transit" policy that covers your household goods, and this may be more liberal and less expensive than the coverage offered by movers.

Most moves involve minor scratches, dents, and breakage, but it is difficult to prove that these occurred at the hands of the movers. Hence, if your belongings are not especially valuable, you may decide to forgo additional coverage. Of course, should the truck catch fire en route and burn to the ground, you will get nothing but the basic coverage; but this occurs so rarely that you may as well take your chances. On the other hand, if your belongings include antiques, valuable clocks or chandeliers, or other fragile items, you'll probably want the additional coverage.

Loading and Unloading

As each of your belongings is loaded, its nature and condition are entered on an inventory sheet. Because you are required to sign the inventory sheet (and thus acknowledge its completeness and accuracy), you should pay careful attention to each of the entries and dispute, if necessary, any notation of "scratched" or "damaged" that strikes you as inaccurate or exaggerated. This is, of course, more easily said than done, what with a crew loading at a rapid pace and the other distractions that are inevitable on moving day, but you should record all differences of opinion on the inventory.

The same procedure occurs at the destination, where each item unloaded is checked off the inventory. Here, again, careful supervision is necessary if your claim for loss or damage is to have high validity.

Payment

Although the ICC regulations allow movers to demand full payment in cash or by certified check before unloading your goods, it may be possible to negotiate other terms with a specific mover, especially if your credit is good and the mover wants your business. On the other hand, if the mover insists on full payment, it's a good idea to have some extra cash on hand for any "extras" that are legitimate—if, for example, you did not have a fixed-price agreement and your load weighed more than the mover estimated, or if you were not on the spot when the moving truck arrived.

Complaints

Complaints against movers generally involve delays, loss or damage, and overcharges. Filing a complaint with the ICC may add a black mark to the mover's record but the ICC will do nothing to resolve it. If the mover violated the agreement to deliver by a specified date, you should request from the moving company an "inconvenience form," on which you should list the costs you incurred as a result of the delay.

Loss or damage and charges that exceeded the estimate should also be reported, first, to the mover. If the mover does not resolve your complaint, your next step is the nearest regional office of the Interstate Commerce Commission. A complaint can also be filed with the state attorney general if the moving company has an official agent in the state. But these government agencies are less likely to resolve your complaint than a lawsuit—in small-claims court if your loss does not exceed its limitations (see Chapter 12).

Moves Within Your State

Intrastate moves are governed by a state commission, whose aggressiveness in consumer protection is likely to vary from state to state. At their best, these commissions establish a rate schedule to which movers must adhere. Although they are interested in consumer complaints for record purposes, they are unlikely to adjudicate them. Here, again, a lawsuit is likely to be the most effective route to restitution.

HEALTH AND FITNESS CLUBS

The physical fitness fad of the 1980s, which continues to flourish in the 1990s, led to a proliferation of firms that provide (or promise to provide) a wide array of equipment and facilities alleged to enhance their members' muscular vigor, general health, and social lives. Many of these firms are so inadequately capitalized that they go into bankruptcy shortly after opening, but their members often lose more money than their operators.

Health clubs rank among the top five categories of complaints received by some state attorneys general, but the cases are extremely difficult to resolve—largely because of bankruptcies. Hence, your best defense is extreme caution when reading the membership contract and making arrangements to pay for membership.

Many health clubs, shortly before they are scheduled to open, advertise introductory memberships at seemingly attractive rates. Some of these clubs, apparently relying on these introductory fees for capitalization, fail to open. Others do open but without the equipment or facilities promised in their initial advertising. Still others merge with another health club at a location extremely inconvenient for some members. And still others go bankrupt shortly after opening, leaving their members with no way of getting back their membership fees. The basic problem is that health club membership requires a long-term financial commitment with little assurance that the promised long-term benefits will materialize.

Because of widespread consumer complaints, some states have passed laws governing the operation of health clubs, and in these states the abused consumer should file a complaint immediately with the attorney general's office. But whether or not your state has regulatory legislation, you should, when offered a membership contract, pay particular attention to the following:

Is there an initiation fee? Because such fees are rarely refundable when the membership contract is terminated, their size is extremely significant.

Does the contract include an "escape clause" to cover termination of membership before contract expiration (1) if the member is dissatisfied, becomes ill, or loses interest, (2) if the member moves, or (3) if the club moves its location or merges with (or is taken over by) another club?

Another crucial consideration is the method of financing the membership fees. Many health clubs persuade prospective members to get a bank loan for the initial membership fee. Under this arrangement many members who become dissatisfied simply stop making payments to the bank and then find themselves in the hands of a collection agency. Whether or not a bank loan is involved, stopping the payment of membership dues because of dissatisfaction does not solve the problem. As long as the contract is in force, you may well find yourself in the hands of a collection agency.

If you decide to join a health club, resist the temptation to sign up for a long-term membership. Despite the club's sales pitch, insist on a month-to-month membership so that you can decide whether you are getting your money's worth.

CLEANERS

Carpet Cleaners

Because the carpet-cleaning business consists of a large number of intensely competitive small firms, it's not surprising that deceptive advertising is rampant and that consumer complaints abound. For the most part, these involve overcharging, unsatisfactory results, and failure to replace furniture in its original position and to clean up the premises after the job has been completed.

Some obvious danger signals are lowball pricing ("Your whole home for $99!"), discount coupons, and other special offers. Because fine-print disclosures and unspecified extras almost invariably raise the bill for the job significantly above the promotional price, it is essential to get a firm, on-premises written estimate before hiring a carpet cleaner. It is also important to get a written guarantee that certain spots will be removed (or a stipulation that they are simply not removable).

The best gauge of the reliability of a carpet cleaning company is word-of-mouth recommendations from friends or neighbors or from the dealer who sold the carpeting. Lacking these, references from the company or a call to the local Better Business Bureau can at least help weed out the chronic offenders or those who ignore consumer complaints.

Complaints about overcharges, shoddy workmanship, or deceptive advertising should be filed with the Better Business Bureau (which may be able to mediate the issue) and the state attorney general's office. On the other hand, if another company is called in to do what the original company promised but failed to do, a suit in small-claims court may recover the original company's charges, especially if the second firm substantiates the poor work of the original cleaner.

Dry Cleaners

Complaints against dry cleaners generally involve loss or damage of garments. Loss of a garment is unlikely to be denied if you have retained a receipt, but the value of the lost garment is often disputed, especially if you can't produce any evidence of its original cost or are unwilling to allow for depreciation. If this kind of dispute cannot be mediated by the local Better Business Bureau, your alternatives are filing a complaint to the attorney general's office or a suit in small-claims court.

Damage to a garment presents a more complex problem. Although the Federal Trade Commission requires that manufacturers sew a permanent and easily found care label into each garment, it does not monitor these labels for accuracy. Hence, although a "Dry-Clean Only" label correctly warns the wearer not to wash the garment, it does not guarantee that the garment will survive dry cleaning intact. Often, for example, trim on the garment, such as beads, appliqués, buckles, or buttons made of some kinds of plastic, simply dissolve when dry-cleaned.

Reputable dry cleaners who maintain a list of vulnerable products and of manufacturers whose care labels have proven unreliable are likely to reject such items or brands for cleaning or to accept them with the clear stipulation that cleaning will be done at your own risk. But many smaller firms are less cautious and, in any case, the person serving at the counter may be inexperienced or too rushed to notify you about the risk.

Although by accepting a garment for cleaning, the dry cleaner implies that it can be cleaned safely and effectively, you can avoid problems by removing vulnerable buttons or buckles and by identifying the nature of specific spots. Suede garments are especially vulnerable to unskilled cleaning and should be sent to a specialist despite the high cost.

Legally, the manufacturer whose care label specifies dry cleaning is responsible for replacing garments that fail to survive the process, but except in the case of garments that are wear-dated, the manufacturer may be difficult to identify, although the retailer may be willing to make the adjustment on the manufacturer's behalf. If complaints to the manufacturer or the retailer are ineffective, and if the claim against the cleaner cannot be mediated by the local Better Business Bureau, a lawsuit in small-claims court may be the most effective means of redress, but if the cleaner specified that the garment would be cleaned at your risk, you have no recourse other than the hope of a good-will adjustment.

U.S. POSTAL SERVICE

If the Postal Service were a private corporation, it might well draw the attention of the Federal Trade Commission for deceptive advertising in connection with its widespread television commercials that promote Priority Mail service. Although the commercials promise two-day delivery, this reflects only wishful thinking on the part of the post office and is not guaranteed. Some Priority Mail packages have lingered in the hands of the Postal Service for as long as nine days. And, although Express Mail service guarantees next-day delivery, a substantial number of post offices are exempted from this deadline. Furthermore, if a piece of Express Mail does not get delivered as promised, the Postal Service will refund the fee but will take no responsibility for the (often very serious) consequences. Similarly, the Postal Service assumes no responsibility for the consequences of misdelivery of certified mail.

Complaints about the U.S. Postal Service generally center on late delivery (or nondelivery) of mail and are easy enough to file. Each post office provides a multipart prepaid postcard on which patrons can detail their complaints. One part of the card goes to the local postmaster, the other to Washington, D.C. But although the complaint process is easy, satisfactory resolution is rare. Complaints about delivery usually get a computer-generated letter of apology. And insurance claims or the tracing of a misdelivered piece of certified mail or the receipt for a money order can take weeks to process. Complaints about mail orders and other transactions involving the mail are dealt with by the U.S. Postal Inspection Service (see Chapter 16).

Despite the rapidly increasing volume of first-class mail, continuously rising postage rates indicate that the Postal Service has failed to benefit from economy of scale, and its charges for insured package delivery are usually higher than those of such private carriers as United Parcel Service.

Although a volume of complaint postcards that focus on a specific local post office may produce some improvement, the consumer with an item that requires expeditious and safe delivery may be wise to compare the Postal Service with one of the private carriers in terms of cost, convenience, and reliability.

6

Money Matters

ALTHOUGH MOST CONSUMER complaints involve money already spent, a substantial number involve money that has been borrowed or saved. In fact, many consumers who are ultra-cautious about their buying habits seem to be rather casual about their saving and borrowing practices. This carelessness can, of course, cost them far more in the long run than an occasional bad buy.

BANKS AND CHECKING

Some years ago, in an attempt to warm up its cold, bureaucratic image, the nation's second largest bank saturated the print media with the slogan, "You have a friend at ———." Months later, when the message had become embedded in the public consciousness, a competitor, the nation's fourth largest bank, bought the same amount of media space and struck back with the slogan: "You have a banker at ———."

Since that time, mergers and acquisitions have made banking even more impersonal and bureaucratic. Local bank managers, no matter how friendly, are simply agents of policies formulated thousands of miles away, and customers' accounts are processed almost entirely by computer and automatic teller machines. What this means is that a personal relationship with a branch manager is no guarantee that your check won't bounce or that overdraft charges will not be applied to your account.

Choosing a Bank

Although these days banks no longer offer free toasters for new accounts, and mergers have left consumers with fewer banks among which to choose, banks still compete for customers by advertising various extras, such as monthly interest, free traveler's checks, a free safe deposit box, free notary service, and other benefits. But these ads rarely mention costs that the customer may incur: for account maintenance, returned checks, stop-payment orders, overdrafts, certified checks, the electronic transfer of funds, and other services that the customer may need. This is why, before deciding to open an account, you should scrutinize an itemized description of *all* bank charges, including interest rates for savings accounts and loans.

Bank Errors

Discrepancies between the bank statement and your checkbook can generally be straightened out at the branch level if you can produce documentary evidence in the form of canceled checks or withdrawal or deposit slips. Before making a complaint, however, you should review this documentation carefully because in most cases the bank's figures turn out to be correct. The usual culprit is a spouse who has misplaced a withdrawal ticket or forgotten the amount of a hastily written check.

Many of these discrepancies arise from the use of "electronic transfers" into or out of an account or the use of a bank card in automatic teller machines or "point of sale" terminals. Federal

rules regulating these transactions are usually provided by the
bank that issues the bank card, and a careful reading when the
card is issued is likely to prevent most problems.

More serious errors involve the bank's clearing a postdated
check or one on which the customer has stopped payment. Because bank errors in this area constitute serious violations of the
Uniform Commercial Code, the bank is likely to correct them
promptly, provided you have kept a careful record.

Bounced Checks

Most checks returned "NSF" (not sufficient funds) were written
not intentionally by petty criminals but unintentionally by spouses
who neglect to coordinate their check-writing or by people who
are careless about their current account balance or who assume
that checks they have deposited in their account have cleared. But
the consequences can be severe, regardless of intent.

In all circumstances, the payee has the right to charge the
writer of the check a fee, which is usually specified by state law. In
some cases, the payee will notify the payer and ask for a good
check, but he is not required to do this. He can, if he wishes, turn
the check over to a collection agency, with possibly dire results for
the payer's credit rating. And, if the amount of the check is high
enough, he can file a criminal complaint against the payer. The
prosecutor, however, will look at the check-writer's intent and
prior history as well as the damage done before deciding to go
forward with a criminal charge.

If the check was returned through the bank's error, the bank is
obligated to write to the payee an explanatory letter, clear the customer's record, and give reimbursement for any returned-check
charges. But the bank is not responsible for checks it has returned
because checks that you deposited to your account have not yet
cleared.

Federal law requires that local checks be credited to your account within three business days and out-of-state checks within

seven business days, but some banks, as a courtesy, credit all checks on the following day.

Stopping Payment

Many consumers, when they have bought a product or a service with which they are immediately dissatisfied, attempt to resolve the problem by stopping payment on the check they wrote to pay for the transaction.

In the overwhelming majority of cases, this tactic is not only ineffective but downright dangerous, both financially and legally. It is dangerous because the payee has the right to treat the stopped check as a "bounced" check, placing the payer in the situation described above. And, if the stopped check represented payment for an automobile or other large purchase, the seller can charge the buyer with theft. It is, moreover, ineffective because the check is likely to have been cleared before the stop-payment order goes into effect and, even if payment is successfully stopped, it immediately antagonizes the payee and gives him or her additional powers, thus making any reasonable adjustment unlikely.

In the following very limited situations, you can legitimately instruct your bank to stop payment on checks and transfer requests:

- if your checkbook has been lost or stolen;
- if you have, by mistake, issued two checks for the same transaction (payment should be stopped on the second check);
- if the payee claims that your check has been lost in the mail and requests a replacement, and you find that the check has indeed not cleared;
- if you have disclosed your bank account number in the course of a mail or telephone transaction;
- if the transaction permits a cooling-off period *and you*

notify the payee within the time limit for cancellation in person or by certified mail.

Postdated Checks

The postdating of a check in the anticipation that funds will be in your account by the date on the check is not illegal, but it can cause you considerable difficulty. First, the payee may, inadvertently or not, present the check for payment before its date, and second, the bank may clear the check. Although both these actions are illegal, punishing the offender(s) is extremely difficult and, in any event, does not extricate you from the problems that may ensue.

No business or collection agency has the right to demand a postdated check but if writing such a check is for some reason absolutely essential, you should write on the face of the check in bold crayon or marker directly above the date: "NOT PAYABLE BEFORE————." You may be able to get further protection by negotiating a signed agreement that the payee will not present the check before its date.

Late Payments

The date that payments are due on loans, credit cards, and mortgage payments, and other installment debts must be clearly specified on the monthly statement or payment coupon. But this date specifies the time by which the payment must be in the hands of the lender (regardless of the vagaries of the U.S. Postal Service), not the date on which the mailed payment must be postmarked. Many consumers, accustomed to the postmark deadline imposed by the Internal Revenue Service and state tax authorities, assume that banks and other lenders operate by the same rule. Although they may be surprised at incurring late charges as a result of this misconception, these charges are perfectly legitimate.

In these days of computerized billing, playing due-date

"chicken" can result in lightning-quick overdue notices and possible compromise of your credit rating.

Filing Complaints

According to the Office of the Comptroller of the Currency, loans constitute the major category of their complaints, and more than half of these involve credit cards. In the second largest category—deposits—more than half involve checking accounts. But the OCC determined that the bank was correct in 47 percent of the loan complaints and in 37 percent of the deposit complaints. Hence, although a discrepancy between the bank's figures and your own may generate a good deal of anxiety and anger, it's important to check your statement and the bank rules before assuming that the bank is at fault.

If your dispute with a bank or a credit union cannot be settled at the branch level, you should appeal to higher authority within the institution. If this yields no results, the next step is to complain to the nearest office of one of the following regulatory authorities that has jurisdiction over the bank or credit union. Branch addresses and telephone numbers can be obtained by calling the federal information number: (800) 726-4995.

- *National banks:* Director of Consumer Activities, Comptroller of the Currency, Dept. of the Treasury, 49 L'Enfant Plaza, SW, Washington, DC 20219, (202) 287-4265.
- *Banks insured by the FDIC:* Federal Deposit Insurance Corporation (see p. 296).
- *Banks that are members of the Federal Reserve System:* Consumer Affairs Division, Board of Governors, Federal Reserve System, Washington, DC 20551.
- *Federal savings banks:* Office of Thrift Supervision, Consumer Affairs, 1700 G St., NW, Washington, DC 20552, (800) 842-6929.
- *State-chartered banks:* the state banking commission.

- *Savings and loan institutions:* Office of Thrift Supervision, Consumer Affairs, 1700 G St., NW, Washington, DC 20552, (800) 842-6929.
- *Federally chartered credit unions:* National Credit Union Administration, 1776 G St., NW, Washington, DC 20456, (202) 682-2950.
- *State-chartered credit unions:* state agency that regulates credit unions or the Federal Trade Commission.

CREDIT

When we apply for a loan, a mortgage, or a credit card, we usually take for granted that the lender will thoroughly investigate our general creditworthiness, and we provide whatever references and documentation required to prove it. What we often fail to do, however, is to check out the lender. We may feel that since we owe the money, we have control of the situation and need not be concerned about the quality of the institution we owe.

This can be a mistake for several reasons that have nothing to do with the fine print of the loan agreement. For one thing, some lenders frequently make clerical errors on creditors' accounts, resulting in late fees and unjustified charges for which the borrower is in no way responsible. For another, some lenders are far more rigid than others about their treatment of late payments and the imposition of penalties, and therefore are more prone than others to put delinquent accounts into the hands of a collection agency. Moreover, some lenders prove to be virtually inaccessible. Because their telephones are constantly busy and because they disregard written complaints, billing errors and other disputes remain unresolved for months.

Checking on a creditor is not easy because state attorneys general and bank regulators are loath to release complaint records, though the Better Business Bureau and word-of-mouth recommendations may be of some help. In general, you are likely to fare better with a bank with which you have done business or at least with a local institution than with an unknown lender in a distant city. Classified advertisements for "credit repair" and unsolicited offers of loans, especially if your credit rating is unsatisfactory, should be disregarded, because they are almost invariably fraudulent.

Credit Cards

In today's marketplace, credit cards have become virtually essential. Without one, it is nearly impossible to rent a car, guarantee a hotel reservation, buy mail-order items by telephone, or, in some situations, cash a check. And, properly managed, they are useful in handling a household's monthly cash flow. Moreover, as we shall note, a credit card receipt can provide you with important protection for your credit card transactions.

Credit cards can, of course, encourage you to buy more impulsively than you might if you had to open a wallet or reach for a checkbook, and they are clearly inflationary, since the merchant who accepts them pays about 3 percent for the privilege and passes this cost on to all of us. (Some canny consumers wangle a discount by offering the merchant cash or a check instead of a credit card.)

Although it is illegal for institutions to send consumers unsolicited credit cards, advertising for applications—by direct mail and in the media—is vigorously competitive and often misleading. Hence, the right choice of a credit card often calls for a very careful reading of a lot of fine print.

Choosing a Card. Your choice of credit card should be based primarily on whether you pay off the account in full each month or use it as a continuous source of revolving credit and cash advances. If you are among the 25 to 35 percent of cardholders who pay off the entire balance each month, the rate of interest charged—although it is conspicuously advertised—is of no significance, and you will be best served by the card that charges the lowest (or no) annual fee or one that offers a cash rebate on your charges. If, on the other hand, you regularly make only a part payment each month and use the card as a form of revolving credit, the interest rate becomes important.

Whatever your style of credit card use, it is crucial that you read the fine print on the credit card application. This spells out not only the general conditions governing its use but, more important, the interest-free grace period, the penalties that apply to late payments or to charges that exceed your established line of credit, and the method used in calculating interest on purchases made while a balance is still outstanding.

Consumer complaints about credit cards generally center on these issues, and they are difficult to resolve because the cardholders agreed to the terms of the contract, whether or not they read them carefully. Some issuers of credit cards, for example, disclose in fine print that there is no grace period—that is, that the cardholder is charged interest from the day on which a transaction is posted.

It is always possible that the original issuer of your card (perhaps your bank) will sell its credit card business to another institution in another state. Although the buyers of these accounts are obliged to honor all the terms of your original contract, they have been known to breach them. In addition, mailed payments to the new owner may take several days longer and may not be posted promptly. Hence, when this kind of transfer occurs, you may decide to cancel your card and apply for a different one.

Billing Errors. Complaints involving billing errors are not difficult to resolve if you are careful to retain all sales slips until they can be reconciled with the statement. If the credit card issuer claims a charge item that you deny or dispute, it is required to send you a copy of the disputed charge slip with your authentic signature or other evidence that you authorized the transaction. If the dispute involves the amount of the charge, you should be able to produce a copy of the charge slip showing the amount charged at the time of the transaction.

Although no signature is required for goods or services ordered from catalogues by telephone or mail, the invoice that accompanies such orders will show the credit card number as well as the amount charged and hence can be used to reconcile discrepancies on the statement. But extreme care should be used in disclosing a credit card number to unknown vendors, especially those who use a post office box as an address and who solicit business through television commercials or classified advertisements.

When you notice an error or discrepancy, you should send an explanation within 60 days (or two billing cycles) to the issuer, who must acknowledge this explanation within 30 days. Meanwhile, you are not required to pay the disputed amount and will not be charged interest on it unless, within 90 days, the issuer determines that there was no error. In that case, you must pay the charge, together with accrued interest. If you continue to refuse payment, the issuer can report you to a credit bureau as in default but must (1) give you the name of the credit bureau and (2) inform the credit bureau that the default is the result of a dispute.

Loss of a Card. If you lose a credit card, you are required to notify the issuer immediately in order to prevent the possibility of incurring charges through unauthorized use of the card. But even if you fail to notify the issuer, you cannot be held responsible for more than $50, and many issuers waive this charge. This is why "insurance" policies that promise to protect you against unauthorized use are probably not worth their premiums. (Similarly, insurance policies that promise to pay your balance should you become disabled are highly overpriced relative to the risk involved.)

Transaction Problems. Although some credit cards offer such fringe benefits as collision protection on rented cars and extended warranties on certain purchases, their main advantage is the protection they offer you in unsatisfactory transactions.

If, for example, you charge airline or cruise tickets and the airline or cruise company goes out of business before you use the tickets, the credit card company will simply cancel your indebtedness and, if possible, charge it against the vendor. And if you have a dispute with a vendor who has failed to deliver promptly or who has delivered defective or unsatisfactory merchandise, you have the right to withhold the credit card payment for the transaction (at no interest) until the dispute is settled. If it is settled in your favor, the credit card issuer will cancel the charge and refuse to pay it to the vendor. But this protection is limited by the following conditions:

- The amount involved must exceed $50.
- You must show evidence of having attempted to resolve the dispute with the vendor and allow 60 days for a response.
- The purchase must have been made either in your home state or within 100 miles of your mailing address *but in most states a mail order is assumed to have taken place at the residence of the buyer, no matter where the seller is located.*

Under this arrangement, credit card issuers have returned to consumers many thousands of dollars that were charged for unsatisfactory purchases and for tickets bought from airlines and travel agencies that went bankrupt before the tickets could be used.

Debit Cards

Apparently feeling that they have saturated the market for credit cards, many banks have turned to marketing "debit cards." As the name implies, the merchant who accepts such a card debits the cardholder's checking account immediately (sometimes electronically) and the cardholder must be certain to maintain a sufficient balance to withstand the debit.

The advantages claimed for debit cards are that (like credit cards) they eliminate your need to carry substantial amounts of cash and (unlike credit cards) they prevent heedless splurging. The disadvantages are that you lose the benefit of the credit card's twenty-five-day grace period and that you are likely to be unprotected in the case of a transaction dispute.

Your liability for unauthorized use of your debit card is $50 if you notify the issuer within two business days, but it escalates to $500 if you do not. There is no limit for unauthorized use if you fail to notify the issuer within 60 days.

Some banks offer debit card users a 1 percent rebate on all charges. This is not especially generous, because the users must maintain (at very low interest if any) a balance large enough to cover all their planned and unplanned purchases.

Credit Repair

Obtaining a credit card is obviously difficult for people who have declared bankruptcy or who are the targets of a collection agency. But there are circumstances in which financially responsible people also encounter problems. People who have been living or working overseas for a long period of time, for example, or who have immigrated from a foreign country, are unlikely to have a credit history recent enough to satisfy the issuer of a credit card. And consumers who are first-time applicants for a credit card or a mortgage may be denied credit because credit bureaus do not record payments for rent, utilities, or other recurring bills that the applicants pay regularly.

In such circumstances, many consumers are tempted to respond to advertisements in newspapers and magazines that promise, for a fee payable in advance, a credit card "no matter what your credit history." These offers, which are almost invariably deceptive, are discussed in Chapter 9.

Although it may take a considerable period of time, a simple and low-cost way to establish credit is to apply at a bank for a "secured" credit card. Under this arrangement, the applicant deposits in a savings account a sum of $500 or more. He or she is then issued a credit card with a line of credit equal to the savings deposit balance and guaranteed by that deposit in case of default on the payments. If the payments are made regularly for a specified period of time, the applicant will be issued a regular unsecured credit card, the possession of which will indicate a satisfactory level of creditworthiness.

Mail-Order Loans

Consumers who lack a credit rating or have an unfavorable one are unlikely to be able to negotiate a loan with a bank or other reputable lender. Although they may resort to a "personal finance" company, which offers loans at very high interest to risky borrowers, many of them fall victim to firms that, like those advertising credit cards to people with poor credit, promise loans by mail. As in the case of mail-order credit cards, these offers are invariably deceptive and usually fraudulent (see Chapter 9).

Debt Consolidation

Consumers who find themselves overwhelmed by debts, whether through improvidence, illness, or loss of a job, may be tempted by various offers to consolidate their debts by taking out a loan—the kind of loan often offered by the fraudulent mail-order firms described above.

A legitimate way to work one's way out of this kind of situation is offered in many communities by the Consumer Credit Counseling Service—a nonprofit organization sponsored by lenders to help hard-pressed debtors and—not incidentally—to help the lenders recover what is owed to them. This organization may persuade the creditors to accept a lower level of monthly payments or to offer the debtor a moratorium that will permit financial recovery. It will not deal, however, with debtors who have no current source of income.

The debt consolidators who advertise, on the other hand, often conceal not only the fees they charge for the consolidation but also the percentage of the debtor's payment that actually goes to satisfy the creditors. Almost invariably, they make the situation worse than it was before the debtor engaged their services.

Credit Ratings

Three out of every four Americans, whether they are aware of it or not, have dossiers in the files of one or more of the many credit-rating bureaus that provide merchants and lenders with an assessment of their creditworthiness.

Although pressures and threats of regulatory legislation by the Federal Trade Commission and by a coalition of state attorneys general have diminished some of the more flagrant abuses, credit bureaus, through inaccuracies and inefficiencies, still cause problems for many solvent consumers. In fact, consumers who pay their bills promptly may be unpleasantly surprised when their application for a credit card or charge account is rejected on the grounds of a poor credit rating.

The unsatisfactory credit rating for consumers who pay their bills promptly may be the result of

- confusion with someone else who has a similar or identical name;
- a clerical error on the part of the credit bureau;
- a trivial unpaid charge dating many years back, which the consumer either overlooked or disputed;
- a current debt that the consumer is disputing.

If you are denied credit on the grounds of an unsatisfactory rating, you are entitled by law (1) to obtain from the lender the identity of the credit-rating bureau that issued the unsatisfactory rating, (2) to obtain from that bureau, free of charge, a copy of your credit report, and (3) to write a brief statement rebutting the unfavorable rating, which the credit bureau is required to append to your report.

By law, the credit bureau must investigate your rebuttal and, if it is found to be true, must delete any inaccurate information. If, however, the information is accurate, the bureau can maintain it on the report for seven years. Bankruptcies remain on a credit report for ten years.

If you have not been denied credit, you can currently obtain a copy of your credit report for a fee ranging from $2 to as much as $20, depending on state law, but one of the largest credit bureaus, TRW, in settlement of a lawsuit brought against it by the Federal Trade Commission and a coalition of state attorneys general, offers consumers who have not been denied credit a copy of their credit report once a year without charge and additional copies for $7.50. TRW has agreed, also, to make the report more understandable by the consumer. Although TRW is one of the largest credit bureaus, it is too early to judge whether the practice has reduced abuses and complaints. The other two largest credit bureaus—Equifax and Trans Union—have also agreed to modify their practices under consent orders by the coalition of state attorneys general.

This course of action has come none too soon, because not only is the typical credit report coded in ways that make it incomprehensible to the consumer but credit bureaus have been notoriously lax about adding the consumer's rebuttal statement to his or her report. And, although credit bureaus are supposed to exchange information among themselves, consumers have no way of knowing how many, or which, credit bureaus maintain a file on them or which lenders use which credit bureaus.

Legislation strengthening the regulation of credit bureaus and requiring them to provide toll-free telephone numbers failed in the Congress in 1992 but may be reintroduced in the near future. Meanwhile, you can obtain a copy of your credit report by writing to the following addresses:

Equifax Information Service Center
P.O. Box 740241
Atlanta, GA 30374

Trans Union Corp.
1561 E. Orangethorpe
Fullerton, CA 92631

TRW National Consumer Relations Center
P.O. Box 749019
Dallas, TX 75374

A recently established service (Credco, Inc., 2141 Palomar Airport Rd., Suite 200, Carlsbad, CA 92009, 800-443-9342) offers, for a charge of $24, information on the payment status of all your accounts and the names of any companies that have asked for your credit history. This service is also marketed through some local banks.

If, after filing a valid rebuttal statement, you continue to get an unfavorable credit rating, you should file a complaint with both the Federal Trade Commission and your state's attorney general. But the best course of action is to avoid a negative credit rating by attending promptly to any disputed billings as soon as they are received. Because a creditor is entitled to report you to a credit bureau the moment your account becomes delinquent, you may discover, if you wait until the last possible moment to pay a bill or settle a dispute, that you have waited too long.

Mortgages

Because a mortgage is a long-term debt and the total interest charges can cost you more than any other expenditure made during your lifetime, comparison shopping is crucial, and the terms of the mortgage should be scrutinized with the greatest care. Regardless of the state of the economy, competition among potential lenders is keen, and the creditworthy consumer is likely to have a wide choice.

When the mortgage market becomes active because of a drop in interest rates, a great many unscrupulous lenders and mortgage brokers appear on the scene. These mortgage brokers have been able to victimize thousands of consumers eager to buy or refinance a home. The typical scam involves advertising a seductively low rate, collecting appraisal and other fees from the applicant, and, after an unconscionable delay, failing to deliver a mortgage or offering one at much less attractive terms than those originally advertised.

The only protection you have is to demand full disclosure of all terms in writing and a deadline on the application. If a satisfactory mortgage is not delivered, and you have paid for an appraisal fee and a credit check, you are entitled to get copies of both, although other costs may be impossible to recover.

In any mortgage, two clauses are of paramount importance. First, you should demand a clause permitting prepayment without penalty. This clause will allow you to satisfy the debt with a single payment of the balance at any time should you benefit from an inheritance or other windfall or should you have an opportunity to refinance your property at a lower interest rate. It also allows you to make larger-than-normal payments to reduce the term of the mortgage and, thus, the total amount of interest paid.

The second clause provides for automatic transferability—that is, the right to transfer the mortgage on the same terms to any buyer of your property. This right can be highly attractive to many potential buyers.

Another feature worth bargaining over is the "escrow"—that is, an amount added to the monthly payment that does not reduce the principal but is held for the payment of taxes and insurance on the mortgaged property. In most states, thanks to the lobbying efforts of banks and other lenders, escrow accounts yield no interest, and thus you may find yourself paying monthly advance installments on tax and insurance bills that may be paid from the escrow account only annually or semiannually. Escrow accounts give lenders an additional measure of security, but they rob the borrower of interest on a substantial amount of money.

Although mortgages are a major part of the economic life of many consumers, they are virtually unregulated by either state or federal governments. The numerous consumer complaints focus on two issues: the cost of applying for a mortgage, especially one that is not granted, and unannounced increases in the amount of the monthly escrow payment.

In shopping for a mortgage, consumers are, of course, primarily concerned with the interest rate and the number of "points" charged by the lender, but they should also compare the application costs among lenders. These costs always include an appraisal of the property and a check on the employment history and creditworthiness of the potential borrower, but they vary considerably from one lender to another. The crucial consideration is the amount that the potential borrower will be out of pocket should the loan be denied. If, for example, after paying for an appraisal, the borrower is denied a mortgage, is that same appraisal usable in applying for a mortgage from another lender? And what other application costs will be refunded if the mortgage fails to be approved within a specified time limit?

Consumers who are faced with an increase in their escrow payments should understand that an increase of as much as 50 percent in anticipation of increases in tax assessments or insurance premiums is legal, whether or not these costs have actually risen. Increases beyond that statutory maximum provide grounds for complaint.

A common practice among mortgage lenders is to charge "junk" fees, which may be labeled as a "document handling fee" or "loan administration fee." The lenders' employees usually receive incentives for charging these fees, which can amount to hundreds of dollars. When such charges appear on your mortgage application, you should demand either a justification for them or their removal.

Complaints against mortgage lenders are difficult to file because banks who issue mortgages almost invariably sell them to other financial institutions—many of which are located in distant states. The buyer may then sell the mortgage to a third party and may or may not retain the servicing of the mortgage—that is, the handling of payments and other paperwork. This makes it very difficult for the homeowner to know who, in fact, his payments ultimately go to.

Complaints against mortgage brokers who promise mortgages and accept a fee but fail to deliver them can be filed with the state attorney general and the Federal Trade Commission, but restitution is unlikely because these fraudulent brokers usually launch a vigorous advertising campaign, collect large numbers of advance payments, and go out of business before action can be taken against them.

INSURANCE

Before buying any insurance policy, you should consider the reliability of the insurance company, the promptness and fairness with which it settles claims, the coverages you want or need and, finally, the premium charged for the coverage you need. You can check the financial condition of an insurer by asking for its latest financial statement or checking its rating in *Best's Insurance Reports,* but this may not be important if the insurance companies in your state have agreed to pay on the policies of any failing company licensed to do business in the state.

More important is the matter of claim settlement. If your state's insurance commissioner does not compile and disclose complaints against specific companies, your only recourse is the Better Business Bureau or the reputation a company has among your friends and neighbors, particularly those who have had experience in filing a claim.

A number of companies have translated their policies, formerly written in dense legalese, into plain English. But, as in all contractual agreements, the policy should be read with the greatest of care, regardless of its prose style, since nothing that an agent tells you is valid and enforceable unless the print in the policy confirms it.

Life Insurance

The two most common problems consumers face in connection with life insurance are (1) buying an unnecessarily expensive policy and (2) collecting the benefits after the insured's death.

Choosing a Policy. As in all purchases, consumers who do their own research and know what they want before buying inevitably fare better than those who passively take the advice of a salesperson. This holds especially true for life insurance because the insurance agent, who stands to earn a commission not only for selling the policy but for its entire life, understandably urges the buyer to commit for the highest possible premium and the longest possible term.

In order to get the highest coverage for the lowest premium, you need to recognize that what you want is protection for your survivors in the event of your death—and not a savings or investment plan. This is why most experts agree that the best life insurance policy for most people is the *term* policy. The premiums for term policies are far lower than those of policies that promise a growing cash value over the years. Their argument is that if you invest the money saved by paying the lower premiums, you will accrue far more "cash value" than what the insurance companies will earn for you on a non-term policy. Insurance agents, in their attempt to sell cash value policies, use hypothetical projections to illustrate the growth of cash values, whereas insurance companies have generally been extremely conservative in the dividends that they pay on such policies.

Experts also point out that since an insurance agent provides little service once a life policy has been bought but continues to earn commission on it, policies can be bought more economically without the services of an agent—through banks and credit unions, for example.

Term policies are available in a wide variety of options, but one that deserves your consideration—because insurance agents are not enthusiastic about prompting it—is the "decreasing term" policy. This policy, which carries an unchanging premium for a term of twenty years or more, provides for relatively high coverage in your early years—when your mortgage balance and child-rearing costs are likely to be high—and a gradually decreasing coverage in the later years, when the mortgage and college tuition are likely to have been paid off and you will have acquired other assets to leave to your survivors.

In short, in order to develop a rational estimate of the coverage you need in the event of your sudden death, you should consider as carefully as possible your family structure, your current and future obligations, and your other assets and sources of income, both current and future. Then you should shop for the lowest premium that provides the coverage you need, keeping your savings and investment plans strictly separate from your insurance premiums.

Collecting the Benefits. Unless a life insurance policy designates your estate as the beneficiary, the proceeds pass directly to your beneficiaries without going through the probate process. And because they often represent the beneficiaries' most important asset, they should be claimed promptly.

In most cases, the insurance companies pay out the proceeds once they have received a properly executed claim form and a certified copy of the death certificate. But problems arise occasionally, some of them the fault of the insured, some due to the reluctance of the company to make payment.

If a policy has been lost, the company will provide beneficiaries with an affidavit form for specifying the loss. If the beneficiaries are not sure whether the deceased had life insurance coverage, a search through his or her bank records may turn up evidence of premium payments or dividends. Otherwise a request to Policy Search, American Council of Life Insurance, 1850 K St., NW, Washington, DC 20006, will generate, at no cost, a search through the records of more than two hundred life insurance companies.

If the company requires the beneficiaries to surrender the original policy, they should retain a photocopy of the face sheet and send the original by certified mail.

Some companies require that a claim be submitted within a specified time period—usually 90 to 180 days—after the death. Although it is doubtful that courts would uphold this restriction, beneficiaries can avoid problems by submitting the claim promptly.

Occasionally, insurance companies refuse to make payment on grounds that the original application was fraudulent—that is, that the insured did not mention on the application a hospitalization, a chronic illness, or a physical condition. It is important for beneficiaries to understand that the burden of proof in such a situation lies with the insurance company, which must prove (1) that the omissions or misstatements were deliberate rather than due to memory lapses, (2) that the facts omitted or misstated were related to the death, and (3) that the company had a right to rely on the insured's statements in deciding to issue the policy. Generally, companies are unlikely to charge fraud on policies that are more than two years old.

Most policies cover death by suicide after they have been in force for two years. On newer policies some companies may argue that an accidental death was in fact a suicide. Here, again, the burden of proof lies with the company.

Occasionally an insurer will refuse payment on grounds that the policy had lapsed because premiums were not paid. This refusal should not be accepted until the policy itself has been scrutinized. Some policies specify that a certain amount of insurance remains in force even if premium payment is terminated; in others the cash value of the policy may be used for premium payment.

In the event of irreconcilable conflict with a life insurance company, the beneficiaries should file a complaint with the state insurance commissioner (see Chapter 15). If this fails to produce results, an attorney should be consulted. Tempting though it may be, the attorney should not be engaged on a contingency basis (see Chapter 14), because a single letter from the attorney (which obviously should not earn him or her one-third of the proceeds—the typical fee under a contingency arrangement) is likely to produce results. Insurance companies are notoriously reluctant to have juries decide between then and an innocent, bereft, and impoverished survivor.

Homeowner's Insurance

Homeowner's insurance covers not only damage to your residence and its contents but also certain claims that may be made against you by others—for example, your breaking of an expensive vase while visiting a friend's house or a claim against you by a delivery man who slipped and fell on your front porch. For most homeowners and for many apartment dwellers, this kind of insurance is essential, but the amount of coverage needed requires careful thought.

Insurance companies are willing to insure virtually anything against almost any contingency, but if you recognize that the basis of insurance is a bet that something bad will happen, and that the odds in this bet favor the "house"—in this case the insurer—you may not want to insure against risks that you can afford to cover yourself. Thus, you may or may not want to insure the contents of your home for "full replacement value," which will escalate your premiums periodically. On the other hand, if fine jewelry, expensive computers, and other high-value items are not covered by your policy, you may want to buy additional coverage for them. In any event, recognizing that "Fred," your friendly insurance agent, gets his commission not from you but from the company and that his earnings increase with every additional coverage he sells you, it's important to develop some immunity against Fred's friendly sales pitch.

Homeowner's policies come in several forms, each with its own series of exclusions, some of them tricky. A policy may, for example, protect you against damage to your home caused by a tree falling on it during a windstorm but may not cover the cost of replacing the tree. Or a policy may exclude flood damage unless the damage was caused by "water driven by wind." Your primary protection against a disallowed claim is to read every clause in the policy very carefully and demand understandable answers to your questions before deciding to buy it.

Because homeowner's policies do not cover earthquake damage, some homeowners buy separate earthquake coverage. Although consumer advocates are somewhat divided on its value, most point out that earthquake damage very rarely exceeds the deductible 10 to 20 percent of the face value of the policy.

Automobile Insurance

As is the case with life insurance, drivers who know precisely which coverages they need and who shop around for them will fare far better than those who drop in on the most convenient insurance office or buy a policy from the first salesperson who comes calling.

Companies differ from one another not only in the premiums they charge for identical coverage but also in the promptness and fairness with which they settle claims. And it is not true that the companies with the lowest premiums have the most recalcitrant claims adjusters. Some indication of a company's settlement record may be obtainable from the state insurance commissioner (some commissioners publish comparative ratings and premium charges). And *Consumer Reports* periodically surveys its members on their experiences with automobile insurance.

On the other hand, some consumers are undeterred by a company's poor record in settling claims because, they argue, unless the claim involves collision or comprehensive coverage on their own vehicle, the problems will be confronted by the other driver involved in the accident.

Many drivers, relying on their past records, decide to buy the minimum liability coverage required by state law and to forgo collision coverage on the grounds that they are most unlikely to get involved in a culpable collision. They overlook the fact, however, that anyone borrowing their car may not be as careful a driver as they are and that if the borrower is not adequately insured, the owner of the vehicle may have liability for all injury and property damage caused by the borrower.

On the other hand, if the value of your car is relatively low—say, $2,500—collision insurance is a poor buy, since in the occurrence of any serious damage the insurer will declare the car "totaled" and offer only its minimal current market value instead of paying more to have it repaired.

When your vehicle is damaged in a crash, the insurance company has the right to ask for multiple repair estimates. It cannot, however, require you to use the cheapest one unless it suspects that other estimates are not bona fide or unless it has a contract with a specific body shop. Some insurers will stand behind the work of repair shops, especially if they directed you to one of them.

Complaints

When an insurer fails to pay a claim in full, a complaint should be filed with the insurance commissioner of your own state and, if necessary, in the insurer's corporate home state. Most commissioners, however, will not pursue individual complaints and, since such claims lie outside the province of the state attorneys general, your only recourse is a lawsuit in small-claims court or through a private attorney.

INVESTMENTS

The major reason why some consumers fare badly with investments is their failure to recognize two facts: (1) that there is no such thing as a totally risk-free investment and (2) that there is a direct relationship between yield and risk—that is, the higher the yield, the higher the risk, and the lower the risk, the lower the yield.

Money hidden in a mattress will be safe (unless the house burns down), but its value will inevitably be eroded by inflation. On the other hand, the overwhelming majority of lottery participants, or racing fans who bet on 50-to-1 long shots, do not retire on their winnings. Prudent investors make a thoughtful decision about how much yield they would like as opposed to how much risk they can tolerate and then choose their investments on the basis of their own careful study or rely on the advice of a full-service brokerage firm or an investment adviser. Since neither alternative guarantees the anticipated results, problems often arise.

We shall deal first with problems of investors who rely wholly or partially on the advice of professionals and later with the problems encountered by do-it-yourselfers.

Full-service Brokerage Firms

Full-service brokers charge higher commissions than "discount" brokers, but they justify the difference on the grounds that, unlike the discounters, they provide their customers with investment advice based on extensive research.

Problems may arise because such brokers face a conflict of interest in two ways: first, they earn a commission each time the client buys or sells stock in accordance with their advice, whether the client gains or loses in the transaction; second, they may be motivated to recommend new issues for which their firm earns an underwriting fee. For both these reasons, their advice may not be entirely objective or in line with the customer's particular needs or interests.

Most complaints against full-service brokers center on what is called "churning" of the complainant's account—that is, frequent buying and selling that earns the broker a commission but does not necessarily produce gains for the customer. A rising number of complaints have involved churning of mutual funds, because such activities can yield the broker a commission as high as 7 percent compared with perhaps 1 to 3 percent earned on the average stock transaction.

Complaints are also lodged by customers who set up a "discretionary" account, authorizing their broker to buy or sell stocks on their behalf without their specific authorization of each transaction. (In this situation, customers have few legal grounds for complaint if the broker's actions are consistent with their having given him unqualified authorization to act on their behalf.)

In a rising market, many customers report very happy results from their brokers' recommendations, often not realizing that a rising market tends to raise all stocks. Moreover, they are not aware that a "buy" recommendation by a large brokerage firm can create sufficient demand among its own customers to raise the market price of a company's stock, at least temporarily, even though the fundamentals of the company do not change. On the other hand, customers tend to blame their brokers when the market as a whole is dropping precipitously.

The only way you can assess the long-term soundness of a broker's recommendations is to check periodically—perhaps quarterly but certainly semiannually—the percentage change in the value of your portfolio against the percentage change in the broadly based Standard & Poor's 500 Index. It is unlikely that changes in an individual portfolio will exactly and persistently match changes in the S&P (in part because brokerage commissions will reduce its value), but if the values lag consistently and significantly behind it, the broker is benefiting from the account more than you are.

Complaints About Full-service Brokers. Complaints about churning or about ill-fated recommendations are not easy to resolve—especially if the brokerage agreement signed when the account was opened mandated arbitration of disputes rather than legal action. In 1987, the U.S. Supreme Court upheld the right of brokers to enforce mandatory arbitration with no appeal to the courts, but a recent study by the Government Accounting Office has questioned the impartiality of this arbitration process and the independence and competence of the arbitrators. The study found that investors win about 60 percent of the time but that they recover, on average, only 45 percent of their claimed losses. Investors who retained lawyers fared significantly better than those who did not, as did investors who claimed less than $20,000.

Thanks to recent action by the North American Securities Administrators Association, however, records of brokers' past behaviors are now available to complaining investors and may be usable in supporting a complaint. The complaint must be filed within a year of the investor's discovery of a potential fraud and within three years of when it was committed.

The broker's defense—that is, that the client was free to reject the recommendations—is a fairly strong one. But egregious abuses should be reported in writing to the compliance officer of the brokerage firm and, if the complaint is not resolved, to the stock exchange on which the transactions were executed, to the National Association of Securities Dealers (800-289-9999), and to the Office of Consumer Affairs and Information Services of the Securities and Exchange Commission (Washington, DC 20549), as well as to the state's regulatory agency. Whether or not an individual grievance gets resolved, these agencies will act if it appears to constitute part of a consistent pattern.

Problems with Investment Advisers

Financial advisers are so poorly and inconsistently regulated that in some states virtually anyone can hang out a shingle and charge people for investment advice. At the more professional level, some advisers offer to analyze a client's portfolio on a fee-per-session basis, whereas others take full charge of the client's portfolio for an annual fee based on its value.

If an adviser is affiliated with an investment institution, a product, or a service—a family of mutual funds, for example—or if he or she earns sales commissions from the investments bought for the client, the conflict of interest is the same as that facing the full-service stockbroker. But even the "independent" adviser who claims to have only the interests of the client at heart is far from infallible. It is crucial to recognize that nobody can accurately predict the direction of the investment market as a whole or the future value of any particular security and that the recommendations of even the most incompetent or dishonest adviser have about a 50 percent chance of being right.

Problems of the Do-It-Yourselfer

Because *over the long run* common stocks have proved to be a more profitable investment than bonds or savings accounts, individuals who have devoted a good deal of time and effort to studying financial information and business reports and who monitor their portfolios regularly and carefully have increased the value of their holdings substantially over the years. But these individuals have avoided pitfalls that have entrapped a great many "small investors."

Great Ideas and Hot Tips. Successful independent investors, recognizing that they do not have as much financial information as the professionals, tend to take a long-range view and to be modest in their hopes for income and capital appreciation. Consequently they restrict their choices to stocks that appear relatively safe and that do not promise spectacular yields.

Unsuccessful investors, by contrast, hope to "make a quick killing." They may, after a visit to an overcrowded fast-food restaurant, buy its stock, not bothering to look at the company's financial statement, which may show a high level of debt or a consistent annual decline in sales. Or they may invest in a current but transitory fad—such as tanning salons.

The unsuccessful investor is also vulnerable to invitations to participate in various unorthodox schemes. Companies whose shares are traded on the major exchanges must satisfy certain requirements established by the Securities and Exchange Commission and by the markets themselves. Although this does not protect the investor against possible loss, it does certify that the company is a going concern that is actively doing business.

A significant number of serious complaints—most of them unresolvable—are made by individuals who have been invited to invest in enterprises that are not listed on any exchange, such as mortgage companies, new inventions, and local ventures of various kinds. Many people, for example, are solicited to invest money in a company established to provide mortgages to home buyers. Although there is nothing illegal about such enterprises, some of these companies promise a rate of return that indicates either that the company will invest in extremely risky mortgages or that the investors will never see their money again.

The same holds true of invitations to finance a new invention or franchise. Because banks and venture-capital fund managers are constantly looking for promising loan applicants and for investments in promising legitimate enterprises, independent investors should ask themselves why they have been approached as potential investors. State and federal laws generally require investment schemes to file a prospectus disclosing detailed information that can be independently verified. Perhaps the principals involved in fraudulent schemes select victims who are unaware of this requirement.

Unfortunately, the regulatory agencies, state or federal, are usually unable to resolve complaints about these schemes—generally because the firm has gone out of business or has simply left town, leaving its promoters and the investors' funds completely untraceable.

Discount Brokers. The do-it-yourself investor, having no need for the research and advice offered by full-service brokerage firms, saves as much as 70 percent of the brokerage commissions by using discount brokers. These firms offer no advice or recommendations but merely execute the customer's orders as directed.

Complaints against these firms tend to center on their failure to execute the customer's order to buy or sell a security at a fixed price. But not all such complaints are well grounded. If, for example, a customer instructs the broker to buy 100 shares of XYZ Corporation at 37, his order may not be executed even when the market price is 37 because other buy orders that preceded his may have absorbed all the shares offered at 37. But if the stock drops to 36½, the order should be filled and the broker is responsible for making good on it. Failure to do so is grounds for complaint. (This general rule may not apply to over-the-counter stocks, the market for which is not as strictly regulated.)

To guard against misunderstandings, customers should, whenever they place an order with a broker, ask for a confirmation number or the name of the person taking the order. Many brokerage firms record telephone calls, but this is for their protection rather than the customer's.

Complaints against discount brokers should be made through the same channels as complaints against full-service firms: first the compliance officer, then the agencies listed on pages 158–59.

Concern about the solvency of a broker—full-service or discount—is not warranted provided that the broker is a member of SIPC, an institution that, like the FDIC, protects customers' holdings up to a specified maximum against a broker's bankruptcy or other problems.

Mutual Funds

Many investors who cannot afford the time involved in monitoring their investments or the fees charged by financial advisers or the substantial amount of cash required for diversification obtain a measure of all these benefits by investing in mutual funds.

Because these funds invest in a wide variety of securities, they provide diversification, and because they require a relatively small initial investment and permit very modest additional investments, they enable the investor to make periodic contributions that tend to even out market fluctuations. And because part of a fund's expense fee pays for financial advice, the investor benefits from professional advice at a negligible cost.

Of course, not all mutual funds are equally attractive. Some charge an initial sales fee (load); others impose a fee when a member withdraws (reverse load); still others impose no load; but there is no evidence that the "load" funds perform better than their "no load" counterparts. Some are admittedly "aggressive" (the euphemism for high risk), others conservative. Some emphasize dividend payout, others the appreciation of capital.

Complaints against mutual funds usually involve spectacularly poor performance in comparison to other similar funds. And, although mutual funds are regulated by the Investment Company Act of 1940, the shareholder's most effective recourse may be a class action lawsuit, in conjunction with other fund shareholders, against the fund's directors. This sophisticated process should be undertaken only after consultation with a law firm that specializes in such cases (see Chapter 14).

OTHER PITFALLS

Although participation in the legitimate financial markets by no means guarantees success, there are other potential investments that virtually guarantee a loss. Many of these, although marginally legal or clearly illegal, have enticed substantial numbers of consumers into parting with their money.

Pyramid Schemes

A pyramid scheme initially solicits the consumer to earn commissions by signing up as a sales agent for a company in order to sell distribution rights to new recruits, who, in turn, sell distribution rights to others. Hence the term, *pyramid scheme*. Commissions earned on sales of the product are secondary to commissions earned on the sales of distribution rights or the recruitment of new "agents"; the product itself may be worthless or, in some cases, nonexistent.

Anecdotes about the big money made by those at the top fuel the recruitment process but, as the number of recruits increases in geometric progression, those at the top of the pyramid get rich and those at the base are doomed to disappointment. State regulators have been reluctant to take action against pyramids because the victims are motivated by greed, and some of the early investors are themselves perpetrators of the enterprise. Even in states where pyramid schemes have been outlawed as fraudulent, enforcement has been difficult because courts have differed as to what constitutes a pyramid scheme.

When the plan involves the actual selling of a bona fide product or service, it is not an illegal pyramid scheme, but its major appeal is the promise to reward the sales agents with special commissions on additional sales made by sales agents whom they recruit. And these recruited sales agents are offered the same promise.

Such plans have become the source of large numbers of complaints, which charge that sales pitches misrepresented the product, that products ordered were either delivered late or were unsalable and unreturnable, or that the parent company went bankrupt immediately after unloading a large supply of the product on its "agents."

The fact that a multilevel marketing scheme may have been declared illegal in some states should be sufficient to make the potential investor cautious. A call to the state's business license center can verify whether the enterprise is licensed to do business in the state. But the mere fact that a license has been issued is no guarantee of moral or financial integrity or profitability at the level at which you enter.

Business Seminars

Many people who have been dismissed as a result of corporate mergers or who are seeking a career change are attracted by advertisements for "seminars" on setting up one's own business, becoming a consultant, and other enterprises. Typically, these seminars, usually held in hotels on weekends, require either a very substantial admission fee, the purchase of text materials, or both. In some cases, the total investment runs to several thousand dollars.

Dissatisfaction with these seminars has become so widespread that the Federal Trade Commission has ruled that participants may cancel their purchase or commitments and demand a refund within three business days of the seminar (see p. 211). But many participants report that their cancellation notices have been disregarded and that their total investment has been lost. State consumer protection agencies have been largely ineffective because many of the organizers are transients or go out of business shortly after collecting substantial amounts of money from their victims.

LIVING REVOCABLE TRUSTS

Many consumers—especially the elderly—receive mail or telephone solicitations from firms offering them the preparation of a living revocable trust. Some of these advertisers sell books containing do-it-yourself trust forms. Others offer personal preparation. Although the promotion and sale of these products and services are not illegal, many people who buy a living trust discover that they have been sold, often at an excessive price, something from which they will derive no benefits whatever.

For some individuals—especially those who have substantial and varied assets or a complex family structure—a living trust can provide very significant benefits, but before responding to such solicitations, you should answer three basic questions:

1. Given my financial and personal circumstances, will a trust offer me enough benefits to justify its initial cost and the continuing costs and inconvenience of record-keeping, monitoring, and periodic updating?
2. Given the wide variations in state laws and the complexity of some of them, will a one-size-fits-all, do-it-yourself trust document comply with the laws of my state, or may it contain phrasing that renders it invalid?
3. If a trust seems useful, would it be preferable to have it drafted by an attorney who will consider my personal situation and best interests in setting up a comprehensive estate plan?

What a Trust Can and Can't Do

The advantage most often stressed by the sellers of living trusts is that assets placed in a trust avoid the costs and delays involved in the probate of your will. But this can be a valuable feature only if the probate process in your state is lengthy and expensive. In some states, for example, probate costs are based on the value of the estate, but in other states they are not. And the complexity of the probate process varies from one state to another; in many states the cost of probate is lower than the cost of preparing and supervising a living trust. Hence, before buying a living trust, it's wise to consult an attorney about the cost of the probate procedure in your state and, if necessary, other ways of avoiding it.

A revocable living trust is often advertised as providing greater flexibility than a will. Again, this is true in some circumstances, but even when a trust is established, a will is still essential to designate a guardian for minor children and to dispose of property not held by the trust. And, contrary to some claims, a living trust does not in most cases eliminate or reduce all tax payments or the obligation to file a return.

Instead of responding to a mass-mailed solicitation about a living trust, you might consult a lawyer, who is presumably concerned with your best interests over the long term rather than the immediate profit earned from the sale of a trust document and will give you a detailed explanation of why a trust is—or is not—advisable in your case. If it is recommended, the lawyer can prepare a trust document expressly tailored to your personal and financial situation. The cost of this is likely to be no higher (and may, in fact, be considerably lower) than what you would pay for the several pages of boiler plate from the "trust mill" firms that solicit you.

CHARITIES

Charitable donations are often made on the basis of habit ("Let's do what we did last year") or as a result of social pressure from a soliciting next-door neighbor, a church, or an employer's charity drive. This method of giving, though not necessarily effective, is relatively safe. But millions of dollars go annually to charities that prey on the public's generosity and are outright frauds.

Most of us are confronted year-round, but especially at Thanksgiving and Christmas, with appeals from unknown individuals and organizations for various causes that appear to be worthy: food and shelter for the homeless, support for Vietnam veterans or war orphans, Christmas toys for poor children.

Fraudulent solicitations for charitable causes constitute one of the most vicious, pervasive, and persistent consumer scams that operate nationwide. They are vicious because they victimize generous people and have a chilling effect on legitimate contributions. They are pervasive because they require little or no capital investment and can work effectively in any part of the country. And they are persistent because very few victims file complaints and because punitive action is virtually impossible since these fraudulent solicitations tend to be short-lived and disappear before any corrective action can be taken.

Fraudulent appeals may arrive through the mail, by telephone, or by a personal solicitation at the potential donor's door. Some of them use names very similar to those of established charities in the hope of confusing potential donors. Others claim to be sponsored by local associations of firemen, police officers, or sheriffs. Often the appeal involves the selling of tickets or merchandise, the proceeds from which will allegedly go to some worthy cause. In all of these schemes, the appeal is immediate, and potential donors are offered no opportunity to verify precisely where their contributions will go or how they will be used.

The safest policy is never to respond to such appeals without (1) obtaining printed information about the organization and (2) checking on its status with the state office that requires the registration of all charities—usually the office of the secretary of state or the attorney general. This office will be able to verify whether the organization is registered (and therefore minimally qualified) as a charity, whether it has filed an annual report, whether it has specified the proportion of its receipts used for administrative costs, and whether this figure is an estimate or the result of an audited financial statement.

Complaints against fraudulent charities should be filed with the state attorney general's office, but, for the reasons we have cited, the likelihood of reimbursement for a fraudulently obtained contribution is small.

COLLECTION AGENCIES

Most of us, having had no dealings with collection agencies, assume that the people they pursue are deadbeats who are trying to evade legitimate debts. But this is far from the truth. Many honest, solidly middle-class consumers find themselves hounded by a collection agency through little or no fault of their own, and they should be prepared to deal with it.

Innocent people can suddenly find themselves dunned by a collection agency through a variety of errors and mishaps:

- Often two similar names are confused, and consumers find themselves dunned for a debt incurred by someone whose name differs from theirs only by a middle initial. The same kind of clerical error can credit consumers' regular and punctual payments to the wrong account, leaving theirs delinquent.

- Physicians, dentists, hospitals, banks, and other institutions occasionally misaddress their bills, and when these are returned "not at this address" (perhaps only because the apartment number was omitted), they automatically turn the bill over for collection instead of trying to track down the debtor's address or verify its accuracy.

- In many cases, consumers have applied for bank loans to pay dues to health clubs or camping clubs that shortly go out of business, leaving them with payments for services no longer available. In such situations, consumers who stop their loan or installment payments may well find their loans turned over for collection; they should, instead, review their contracts and promptly exercise their cancellation rights in compliance with the contract and with state law.

- Some consumers who are dissatisfied with an item or a service but are unable to obtain a refund or an adjustment try to solve the problem by terminating their regular installment payments. This tactic almost inevitably leads to dunning by a collection agency and may put the consumer's credit at risk.

- If a customer's check bounces, some payees automatically turn the account over for collection instead of notifying the customer and asking for a good check. And, as we have noted, a customer who stops payment on a check (see p. 135) is almost certain to hear from a collection agency.

- In some cases, firms that are contemplating bankruptcy automatically turn over all their accounts receivable to a collection agency in the hope of realizing some quick cash.
- The statute of limitations on debt, after which a debt is not legally collectible, may run 4 to 6 years, depending on state law. (The clock stops if the debtor leaves the state, fails to provide a forwarding address, or is otherwise unaccessible to creditors, but it may start running again if the debtor acknowledges the debt in writing.) Many collection agencies, however, ignore this limit, assuming the debtor is unaware of it. Hence the debtor may be confronted for payment of long-forgotten debts incurred in the distant past.

Solvent consumers generally fall into the hands of a collection agency as a result of disputing a bill, and they can avoid the problem by settling any disputes promptly, in writing, with copies retained for possible complaints to a consumer protection agency or an attorney. And a complaint should be filed promptly if the creditor will not resolve the dispute. Otherwise, the creditor can not only turn the matter over to a collection agency but can also report the "delinquency" to the consumer's credit bureau. Although the consumer has a legal right to notify the credit bureau that the debt is the result of a dispute, credit bureaus have been notoriously lax about promptly adding such a statement to the credit report.

On receiving a collection agency notice, you may be prompted to get in touch with the creditor—the dentist, the hospital, the department store—who alleges that you incurred the debt. This is unlikely to be effective because your original creditor, having sold the account to the collection agency at a discount, no longer has an interest in it or in you. The collection agency, on the other hand, having bought the account, is interested in wringing as much money out of it as it can—including interest, attorney's fees, and late charges if possible.

For upright, law-abiding, bill-paying citizens, the first experience with a collection agency may well be frightening. It almost

invariably includes a list of threats, ranging from ruining the debt-
or's credit rating to wage-garnishment and even arrest—a legal
impossibility in the absence of criminal behavior. The initial written notice may look like a court summons or other government
document, even though federal law prohibits this practice. And
the collection agency's follow-up telephone calls are likely to be
shocking.

Illegal though such behavior is, the callers may well be insult-
ing, abusive, threatening, and even obscene. They may misrepre-
sent their position or the firm for which they work, their right to
collect the debt, or the consequences of delaying full and immediate payment.

Psychologists offer an interesting explanation for this behavior. They point out that collection agents, like everyone else, see
themselves as decent human beings, but since they find themselves
daily badgering debtors who have become delinquent through bad
luck or poor judgment, their positive view of themselves is threatened. Hence, they can maintain their self-image only by trans-
forming the debtor into a thief, a cheat, or a deadbeat, terms they
use frequently in their telephone calls.

If the debt is *not* legitimate, your first step is to refute the collection agency's claim by submitting documentary proof of your
payments or of an error in identification. If this rebuttal is persuasive, the collection agency is likely to abandon the pursuit, and if
the debt has been reported to a credit bureau, the credit bureau
must add to the report the fact that the debt is disputed.

If, despite the rebuttal, the collection agency persists in its efforts, your course of action becomes more difficult. If you ignore
the collection agency's claim, you run the risk not only of damaging your credit rating but of adding interest charges and lawyers'
fees to the debt and having a judgment made against you that can
result in liens against your property and garnishment of your pay.
But the alternative—paying the debt and then trying to recover it
through small-claims court—runs the risk of failure to win your
case.

If the debt is legitimate, the following summary of both your rights and the rights of the collection agency should help you chart a course of action.

The Debtor's Rights

The collection agency is required by law to send the debtor, along with the initial notice, an itemized statement of the indebtedness, including any interest, late charges, or collection fees. These extra charges must not exceed those specified in the original credit or purchase agreement or those authorized by local law. And the interest rates and other conditions specified in the original agreement may not be changed without the debtor's approval. State usury laws may limit the interest rate, and federal law prohibits "unfair, abhorrent, onerous, or unconscionable" loan contract terms or collection agency practices.

In some states, collection agencies are prohibited by law from calling a debtor more than three times a week, and these calls may not be made between 9 P.M. and 8 A.M. Only one of these calls may be to the debtor's workplace—but not if the employer prohibits such calls. A direct call to an employer is permitted only to determine the debtor's whereabouts. If the debtor requests in writing that the collection agency not contact him or her again, the agency may not continue to call or write except to notify the debtor of legal action, which it does have the authority to take.

Collection agencies are not permitted to harass, embarrass, intimidate, or threaten debtors in any way. They may not threaten violence or criminal prosecution or use abusive or offensive language. They may not publish lists of debtors or claim to represent a government agency. Whether or not your debt is legitimate, you need to understand that no matter what the collection agency threatens, it cannot seize property or garnish wages until it has the approval of a court, who must notify you to appear and present your version of the facts. In any event, the court will not permit the collection agency to seize everything you own and drive you naked into the street. Although the court may authorize the collection agency to garnish your wages or other payments, it is not permitted to touch social security income or any form of government payment other than wages or salary. And in no circumstances can anyone be jailed for nonpayment of a debt.

All of these prohibitions and restrictions would seem to offer you significant protection, but violations are widespread, and enforcement is usually too slow and sporadic to be of help in individual cases. If violations persist, however, you should advise the collection agency that you plan to file complaints with the state attorney general and with the Federal Trade Commission. This threat may alter the behavior of the collection agency, but whether it does or not, you ought to follow it up promptly. Neither of these regulatory agencies is likely to be of direct help to you, but if a significant pattern of violations builds up against a specific collection agency, action is likely to be forthcoming, especially at the state level.

The Collection Agency's Rights

The collection agency is entitled to demand the entire amount of the debt and to reject any offer of installment payments, especially if the original agreement authorized payment in full in case of default on an installment. It can ask (but cannot legally demand) payment by a series of postdated checks. Under federal law, the collection agency may not deposit such checks before their payment date, and banks are prohibited from clearing them, but because these rules are widely violated, you should be cautious about writing postdated checks (see p. 136). If a postdated check bounces, the collection agency can take a separate legal action, and in such circumstances the law will almost certainly rule against the debtor.

The collection agency has the right to apply for a court judgment authorizing it to seize your property or garnish your wages. The suit must be filed in the court closest to your place of residence or the place where you incurred the debt. You must be served papers in connection with this judgment so that you can appear in court to dispute the debt-collection action or, in some cases, arrange for a schedule of payment.

Your Best Course of Action

If the debt is a legitimate one—that is, if it is not due to the kinds of error noted above—your best course is to pay the debt, even if it requires getting a loan, since interest charges on a conventional loan are likely to be significantly lower than the collection agency's escalating interest charges, attorneys' fees, and possible court costs. But if you can't get a loan because your credit rating has been damaged by the collection agency's actions, you may have to rely on the kindness of family or friends. Alternatively, a consultation with the local office of the Consumer Credit Counseling Service (see p. 270) may result in a mutually satisfactory payment schedule. But such counseling is available only if you have a regular source of income and can agree to the proposed schedule of payments.

BANKRUPTCY

Many consumers faced with overwhelming debt that they see no prospect of paying off consider bankruptcy as a way of reorganizing or canceling their obligations. Nationwide, the number of personal bankruptcies currently approaches one million a year, and it will continue to rise as credit card binges, health problems, or sudden loss of jobs leave people with no way of paying their short-term and long-term debts.

The Problems

There are, however, two problems connected with bankruptcy that do not make it the panacea it appears to many harassed debtors. To begin with, the bankruptcy procedure often costs more than the potential bankrupt can afford. Filing for bankruptcy requires a statutory court fee of $120. And lawyers' fees can raise the total cost to as much as $1,000. Hence, the debtors who can afford the bankruptcy procedure can usually afford to pay off at least some of their debts and to negotiate with other creditors, whereas those who are penniless can't afford to file at all. Although it is possible for potential bankrupts to represent themselves in court, most people find the procedure far too complex and intimidating.

The second problem has to do with credit rating. Bankruptcies are automatically reported to credit bureaus, and a record of bankruptcy remains on the bankrupt's credit report for ten years, no matter how exemplary the credit record after the bankruptcy. Although occasionally a bankrupt has been able to get a loan or credit from lenders who trust that there is no longer any outstanding debt, in most cases the person is likely to experience serious difficulty not only in financing a home or a car but also in getting a job from an employer who checks credit ratings as part of the hiring process or a landlord checking on suitability as a tenant. And, although the social stigma of bankruptcy has diminished in recent years, it has by no means disappeared.

In general, then, bankruptcy should be avoided if at all possible. One way is to talk candidly with creditors in the hope of arranging for a suspension or reduction of payment. Since the creditors are aware that if the debtor goes bankrupt they may get nothing at all, they may be willing to compromise. A second possibility is a conference with the Consumer Credit Counseling Service (see p. 270).

Forms of Bankruptcy

If bankruptcy seems inevitable, the debtor can choose between two forms. Under Chapter 7 of the bankruptcy code, by far the most common form, the debtor sells or releases all assets (beyond a minimum "homestead" exemption established by state law) to satisfy the creditors to the extent possible. The remaining balance of the debts is canceled, and the bankrupt is then free from debt.

Under Chapter 13, the debtor is permitted to keep some assets and agrees to pay off the creditors in full but with lower payments over a longer period of time. Under this arrangement the debtor is permitted to keep a percentage of the equity he or she has in the home, cars below a certain value if they have been paid for, and a limited amount of personal property, such as wedding rings and household effects.

Exploring the Alternatives

The consumer who is heavily indebted or is being hounded by a collection agency should avoid the widespread scams that offer "credit repair." If negotiation with creditors or consultation with the Consumer Credit Counseling Service cannot solve the problem, the debtor should consult a lawyer who specializes in bankruptcy proceedings and can give advice on which form of bankruptcy, if any, is appropriate.

7

Travel

CONSUMER PROBLEMS WITH travel rarely involve large sums of money, but they rank high in terms of disappointment and frustration. Although the purchase of a defective item is annoying, the situation can generally be resolved. But there is no immediate remedy for being bumped off the last flight that can get you to a friend's wedding on time or arriving at a hotel after a tiring drive only to learn that there is no record of your reservation.

With the exception of airlines, the travel industry is virtually unregulated, but even strict regulation can lead only to monetary compensation and cannot make up for a missed wedding or a spoiled vacation. For this reason, it is crucial to plan carefully and to deal only with reliable suppliers.

TRAVEL AGENCIES

Once you recognize that travel agencies earn their commissions from airlines, hotels, cruise operators, or auto rental agencies, it's easy to understand why they may not always quote you the lowest fare or rate. In addition, because some airlines offer travel agencies special incentives, you may find yourself with a less than ideal itinerary or fare on the airline of the agency's choice rather than yours. Lastly, airfares are in a state of constant flux that can confuse even the most conscientious agent.

Frequent travelers are often able to establish a long-term relationship with a reliable travel agent who will make an effort to save them money, but most travel agents regard the sale of a one-time airline ticket between, for example, New York and Washington, D.C., as a nuisance. Hence, the infrequent traveler with a simple itinerary may do better by making reservations directly with the airline by telephone. Even if you use a travel agency, you would do well to check with two or three airlines to ensure that the agency has quoted you the lowest possible fare. Similarly, hotel and auto rental reservations can be handled easily through toll-free numbers on a do-it-yourself basis.

Because a number of travel agencies have collected large amounts of money from customers and gone out of business before issuing the tickets ordered, it is extremely important (1) to use a travel agency that is well established, (2) to use a credit card for all transactions since the credit card company can cancel charges made for undelivered services, and (3) to scrutinize all tickets for coding that may signify restrictions or nonrefundability.

Many consumers who file complaints against travel agencies claim that they bought vouchers for overseas hotel accommodations and that, on arrival, the hotel denied ever receiving payment. In such circumstances the traveler has no alternative but to pay the hotel bill on the spot and then file a claim against the travel agency. Other complaints involve prepayment for cruises that never materialized. This is no problem if the vouchers were bought or the prepayments made on a credit card (see p. 141). But if the vouchers were paid for in cash and the travel agency has gone out of business, the customer is likely to have no recourse whatever. Travel offers made through mailings or newspaper advertisements need to be carefully investigated. Hidden costs, "blackout periods," or unsuitable dates may make them no bargain.

Complaints against travel agencies can be filed with the local Better Business Bureau, the state attorney general's office, and the American Society of Travel Agents (P.O. Box 23992, Washington, DC 20026). Complaints about tours can be directed to the U.S.

Tour Operators Association, 211 E. 51st St., Suite 12B, New York, NY 10022.

AIR TRAVEL

The major complaints about airlines center on misleading (if not downright deceptive) advertising, overbooking (resulting in what passengers call "bumping" and the airlines call "denied boarding"), missed connections due to flight delays or cancellations, and lost or damaged baggage.

Overbooking is an abuse for which the consumer has clear-cut remedies. Remedies for canceled or delayed flights, on the other hand, are entirely at the discretion of the individual airline. Coverage for lost or damaged baggage is spelled out on the airline ticket, which few if any travelers read.

Airline Advertising

Although several states, as well as the National Association of Attorneys General, have attempted to regulate airfare advertising in order to eliminate flagrant deception, the federal government claims exclusive jurisdiction, and the abuses remain largely uncorrected. The advertising of prices has come under criticism on several grounds. Many ads prominently feature a "bargain" one-way fare that turns out to be available only with a round-trip purchase. Moreover, such ads often omit taxes and departure fees. Perhaps more important, the bargain fares are available for only a limited number of seats, and frequently these seats are sold out before the ad appears.

The footnoted phrase "some restrictions may apply" covers a multitude of serious limitations. These may include advance purchase, nonrefundability, restrictions on itinerary change and days of travel, holiday "blackouts," and a compulsory Saturday overnight stay at the destination. Although federal law requires that important restrictions be spelled out in the offer, many consumers overlook them and are disappointed when they attempt to book the advertised flight.

These bargain offers are part of the airlines' technique of "yield management"—that is, their effort to manipulate their fares in an attempt to fill every seat on every flight. Thus, the bargain fares are more likely to be available on unpopular flights, such as "red-eyes" and flights to low-traffic destinations on low-traffic days of the week.

For some travelers, the bargains may be genuine. But for those who can't tailor their plans to comply with the restrictions, the "bargain" ends up costing hundreds of dollars more than the advertised price. Travelers can to some extent avoid disappointment by doing some comparison shopping among airlines, booking well in advance, and asking the reservation agent questions about refundability, changes of itinerary, and other limitations.

"Denied Boarding"

In line with their efforts to fill every seat on every flight, airlines regularly overbook some flights on the assumption that a calculated percentage of passengers with reservations will fail to show up for the flight. When this percentage is miscalculated, a certain number of passengers with reservations will be "bumped"—occasionally after they have already boarded the flight. There are, however, fixed federal penalties for overbooking. The airlines are required to display these prominently at ticket counters, but often the display is less than conspicuous.

When a flight has been overbooked, the airline's first step is to ask for volunteers who are willing to take a later flight in return for an incentive, which may consist of a free ticket or a cash bonus in addition to a confirmed reservation on a later flight. Because the incentive is not fixed but may be subject to the supply of volunteers, prospective voluntary bumpees can sometimes raise the ante to a point at which a later flight is acceptable.

If the number of volunteers is insufficient to eliminate the overbooking problem, the surplus passengers will be denied boarding *involuntarily,* their sequence being determined in accordance with the airline's rules on boarding priority. The federal rules for the compensation of involuntary bumpees are as follows:

No compensation will be paid (1) if the passenger did not comply with the airline's rules on check-in time or flight confirmation or is found not acceptable for transportation under the airline's usual rules, (2) if the flight is canceled, (3) if overbooking was due to substitution of a smaller aircraft for safety reasons, (4) if the passenger is offered accommodation in a different class at no additional cost (or is given a refund of fare difference if he is seated in a less expensive class), or (5) if the airline can book the passenger on a flight scheduled to arrive at his final destination within one hour of the scheduled arrival of the overbooked flight.

Passengers who are entitled to compensation will receive a payment equal to the value of their flight coupons (based on the regular one-way fare including tax but less any discount) or $200, whichever is less, provided that the overbooking airline can provide alternative transportation. This is construed to mean transportation that arrives at the passenger's next stopover (of 4 hours or more) or his final destination no later than 2 hours (for flights in the U.S. and its possessions) or 4 hours (for international flights) after the scheduled arrival of the overbooked flight.

If the airline is unable to provide alternative transportation, the penalty is doubled to twice the cost of the flight coupons or $400, whichever is less.

The airline may offer the passenger free tickets in lieu of cash payment, but the passenger has the right to reject the offer. If the passenger elects a cash payment, the payment must be made in cash or by check at the time and place where the overbooking occurred, but if alternative transportation provided by the airline prevents payment, it must be sent to the passenger within 24 hours.

Passengers need not accept any airline payment and

may seek compensation through court action or in some other way.

Delays and Cancellations

In general, airlines have no legal responsibility for the passenger's meals, lodging, or missed connections when flights are canceled or delayed, no matter what the reason. Nor is the airline responsible for damages resulting from a missed connection or a late arrival. The traveler who misses a cruise departure, a lecture commitment, or a crucial business meeting should presumably have booked an earlier flight. And, contrary to widespread belief, the airlines are not required to provide long-distance telephone calls, meal vouchers, alternative transportation, or lodging for passengers stranded by delays or cancellations.

In reality, however, airlines often do attempt to alleviate passengers' problems—sometimes as company policy, sometimes at the discretion of the station manager. For this reason, the stranded passenger has everything to gain and nothing to lose by asking for help.

Complaining in these circumstances requires tact and courtesy. The traveler, seriously inconvenienced, may be tempted to vent frustration on the airline's agent, who not only is not responsible for the problem but has probably already withstood a barrage of angry complaints from a full planeload of passengers. As in all complaint situations, a civil tone and an objective explanation of the problems caused by the delay may be far more effective than a mere ventilation of one's grievance.

Lost or Damaged Baggage

The computerization of baggage transfer has significantly reduced the amount of checked luggage that airlines misdirect, but, although permanent loss of luggage is rare, delays due to misdirection remain.

The reimbursement policy for lost baggage is set by agreement among all the airlines and is uniform. Unless you declare and pay for additional coverage, which few travelers think of doing, the domestic airlines' liability for checked baggage is limited to the depreciated value of the contents, with a maximum of $1,250, but you must be able to document the value of the lost items, and a claim will be considered only if you file it before leaving the airport. (On international flights airline liability is limited to $9.07 per pound, regardless of content.)

Most airlines will replace or repair a piece of luggage that was obviously damaged en route. But anything packed in cartons or other nonluggage containers is checkable only if you waive the right to any coverage.

Pending recovery of the lost baggage (which is highly probable, though it may take several days), the airline is not obliged to provide money for emergency toilet kits, medications, or clothing or to deliver the baggage to your final destination, which may be miles from the airport. But some airlines will provide the bereft traveler with basic necessities—a toilet kit, for example—and some have been known to deliver the recovered luggage to the traveler's destination, even though in one case it was 60 miles from the airport.

Even though baggage loss has become less common, you should never pack in your checked luggage anything that you will need shortly after arrival—medications, for example, or a set of notes and slides for an imminent presentation, or a formal gown needed for a closely scheduled occasion.

Complaints

Complaints about airline problems should be addressed to the Office of Consumer Affairs, U.S. Department of Transportation, 400 7th St., S.W., Room 10405, Washington, DC 20590, (202) 366-2220. Unless they involve clear violations of federal regulations (with respect to overbooking, for example), such complaints are unlikely to be resolved on an individual basis. But, taken with others, they may lead to some legislative action. After all, the government did not institute regulations on overbooking until it had been flooded with many thousands of complaints from victims.

HOTELS, MOTELS

Short of threatening to get undressed and go to sleep on a sofa in the lobby, there is little you can do when a hotel/motel, for one reason or another, fails to honor your reservation.

Most hotel/motels will hold a telephoned reservation until 6 P.M. on the day of arrival, but if your plans are definite, you can give the hotel/motel your credit card number and get a confirmed reservation that is presumably guaranteed no matter what time you arrive. Guaranteed reservations can usually be canceled by telephone before 4 P.M. on the day of arrival. But if you change your plans and fail to cancel, your credit card account will be charged for the room. To avoid problems, you should, when making a reservation, ask for a confirmation number or the name of the clerk taking your reservation and insist on the same information when canceling a guaranteed reservation.

These general reservation rules do not apply to some accommodations in resort areas during the "high" season. These places may insist on advance notice of three days or more for cancellations, even though the reservation may have been made only 48 hours in advance. Hence, if you use a credit card, you should confirm the reservation policy before making a commitment.

If you arrive with a confirmed reservation only to find the hotel/motel fully booked, you have, unfortunately, little recourse. Reputable hotel/motels will usually try to find you alternative accommodations, but these may not always be comparable in price or quality. If the hotel/motel is part of a chain, you should file a complaint with corporate headquarters, but you are unlikely to be mollified with anything more than a computer-generated form letter prefabricated for such situations. If the overbooking seriously

disrupted vacation plans, a letter to the travel agent who booked
your reservation and to the travel editor of both a local and a
national newspaper may at least make you feel better and perhaps
help others avoid the same problem.

Disputes over billing can result from clerical error (in the
charging of bar, restaurant, and room-service bills to your room)
or from your failure to get precise information about the room
rate and other charges before registering. Some hotel/motels offer
free local telephone calls; others impose hefty surcharges (even on
local and toll-free calls). Some hotel/motels use, for long distance
calls, carriers that charge far more for a call than the familiar ones.
It is best to inquire in advance about these extras.

If you cannot resolve a billing dispute locally by taking a firm
stance, a threat of a complaint to corporate headquarters may be
helpful. Cases of serious overcharge can, of course, be dealt with
by the state attorney general's office. Small-claims court is likely to
be ineffective because the suit must be filed in the community
where the hotel/motel is located, which is, presumably, at some
distance from your home.

CRUISES

There are two reasons why travel agents would rather sell cruise
tickets than anything else in their inventory. The travel agent who
arranges an individual trip for you may earn commissions on airline tickets and possibly auto rentals and hotel reservations but
earns nothing on your meals, admission tickets, taxi fares, and
similar expenses. But by selling you a cruise ticket, the agent gets
a commission on your total outlay by making a single, brief telephone call instead of having to make half a dozen calls to airlines,
hotels, and car-rental companies and wait for their several commissions to arrive.

A second reason is even more important. In return for a high
volume of ticket sales, some cruise lines classify some travel agents
as "preferred suppliers" and reward them with generous supplements to the standard 10 percent commission. Obviously these

travel agents are likely to steer you to the more generous cruise lines.

This situation can be either an advantage or a disadvantage. The possible advantages are, first, that the high-commission cruise line is likely to be large and reliable and, second, that you may be able to wangle a rebate of part of the high commission if the agent is eager to make the sale. If not, you are quite likely to find the same cruise offered by a more flexible agent.

The disadvantage, of course, is that the agent may steer you to a different cruise line—and even a totally different itinerary—from what you had in mind or might enjoy most. If you have researched the plentiful cruise brochures and have decided on a definite itinerary, you should probably ignore the agent's sales pitch. On the other hand, the agent's recommendations may lead to a satisfactory vacation, and bargaining on the price—especially very shortly before the cruise is scheduled—can save you a substantial amount of money. Before you decide that you are getting a bargain, however, it's wise to comparison-shop the same cruise among discount agencies that specialize in last-minute bookings.

If you decide to stick with your own choice, it is imperative that you read all the fine print on the sales contract to determine where your money will be between the time you pay for the tickets and the time you go aboard. Some states require cruise operators to post a bond or to maintain a trust fund to reimburse ticket holders in case of cancellation. And some operators maintain an escrow account. If the money is kept in escrow, you will get it back should the cruise fail to materialize. Otherwise it may well be at risk.

The fine print on the contract will not reassure you about your rights to sue the company for negligence, breach of contract, or personal injury. Cruise lines have the right to insist on the specific venue of the lawsuit, preventing you from filing suit where the company does business or where you bought the ticket. In addition, they attempt to set a time limit on the filing of a suit. Typically you must notify the company of your injury within six months and file suit within a year.

As these limitations indicate, your only resource for complaint settlement is likely to be the American Society of Travel Agents (P.O. Box 23992, Washington, DC 20026) or a private attorney.

AUTOMOBILE RENTALS

Instead of automatically signing up with one of the national rental companies or arranging the rental through a travel agency, you may be able, if you plan ahead, to make substantial savings by comparison-shopping the rates of local rental companies at your destination. And many renters report satisfaction with the small, local companies that rent older cars and trucks.

Rental Agency Advertising

Before making a decision based on a magazine or newspaper advertisement, you should scrutinize the fine print for conditions that may make the advertised "bargain" or "special" rate almost meaningless; sometimes these restrictions may not appear in the advertisement at all. The same precautions apply when reserving a car rental through a travel agency, because the display on the agency's computer screen usually provides rates only and omits the "fine print" extras.

There is probably no large-scale business or industry in which misleading advertising and deceptive practices are more widespread. As a consequence, many renters discover that it is impossible to rent a car at the advertised price and find themselves, instead, paying double or triple the rate that attracted them. To protect yourself, therefore, you should clarify with the rental agency the following issues, some of which may not be disclosed in the advertisement or voluntarily by the agent at the rental counter.

Availability. Is the offer limited to specified dates or locations? Some advertisements specifically exclude certain locations, but others simply indicate that the offer is "valid only at participating locations," leaving the prospective renter guessing.

Reservations. Is advance reservation required (and guaranteed) or will the specified type of car be available at any time? Most rental companies offer a "free upgrade" if your original choice is not available, but this upgrade may be a gas-guzzling full-size sedan instead of the subcompact model you reserved.

The number of "free" miles included in the basic charge and the cost of mileage in excess of this allowance. Per mile charges as high as 30 cents or more are not uncommon.

The refueling charge. Although the customer is expected to pay for the gas he uses, some companies impose a substantial fixed refueling charge no matter what the fuel level when the car is returned.

Penalties for early return. Many bargain "per week" rates become inapplicable if the renter returns the car after only three or four days.

Geographic restrictions. Does the contract permit the renter to drive the car into Canada, Mexico, or even another state?

Airport charges. Many companies add a surcharge of as much as 10 percent if the car or you are picked up or dropped off at an airport.

Drop-off charges that apply if you return the car to a different branch of the company. Renters have been charged as much as $150 for dropping off their rental at a branch only 60 miles from the site of their original rental.

Whether the rate is based on a calendar day or a 24-hour day. With the former, you will be charged for an entire day if you return the car at 10 A.M. With the latter, you will not be charged if the rental started at 11 A.M.

Whether there is an extra charge for an additional driver.

The cost of the collision damage waiver (CDW) and your
liability for damage, loss, and other costs if you accept or
reject it.

If you have not been attracted by an advertisement but simply
walk up to the counter of a rental agency, you should scrutinize the contract with the foregoing issues in mind, even though
you are likely to be in a hurry to get into the rental car and on
your way.

Collision Damage Waiver

The most serious consumer exploitation—in terms of both the
number of complaints and the amount of money involved—is the
collision damage waiver (CDW) that rental companies offer as an
option. At least two states have prohibited it as exploitative because (1) it is many times more expensive than normal collision
insurance, (2) it offers substantially less coverage, and (3) although
it is represented as a form of insurance, it does not fall under the
jurisdiction of the state insurance commissioner. (In these states
the renter's liability for all loss or damage is $100, but the rental
firms have responded by raising their rates, reducing the number
of cars available, or, in some cases, refusing to rent cars to drivers
who do not arrive by air.)

In the many states where CDW is still available, counter clerks,
because they are either offered a commission for selling the enor-
mously profitable CDW or are required to meet a weekly quota of
sales, are likely to exaggerate either the risks that the renter assumes by rejecting it or the protection that CDW provides.

The rental firm should (but generally does not) tell you that
you may not need the CDW if you have personal collision coverage on your own car or coverage through certain credit cards. You
should also be informed that some CDWs do not offer you complete protection. Some do not cover you if the damage or loss was
caused by your own negligence, and some exclude damage if you
have drunk *any* alcoholic beverage, taken *any* drug—even

aspirin—or driven in a manner that might be construed as even 1 percent negligent.

Other CDWs do not cover damage or loss of the vehicle by theft or vandalism, all of which are covered by the conventional automobile policy. And although liability for personal injury is included in the basic rental charge rather than in the CDW, the amount covered may be minimal, leaving you, if you are involved in a serious accident, liable for whatever damages exceed this minimum coverage.

Before assuming that your personal automobile policy covers your use of a rental car, it makes sense to check with your insurer. Even if rental cars are covered, your maximum collision coverage may be limited to the replacement value of your own subcompact and may not be enough to cover damage or loss of a new full-size rental car.

Certain charges resulting from an accident in a rental car may not be covered either by your personal policy or by the CDW. In the event of an accident, for example, the rental company may charge you not merely for repairs (which are generally calculated at the retail price) but also for towing the disabled car to the point of origin for repair (even though a company repair facility may be located closer to the scene of the accident). You may also be charged for the company's loss of use of the car (a totally arbitrary figure) or for the company's loss of the car's "sweetheart" trade-in allowance on its next fleet purchase from the manufacturer. And credit card coverage is no panacea. To begin with, credit card coverage is *supplementary*—that is, it will cover only loss not covered by your own insurance policy. Moreover, approximately 25 percent of claims against credit card insurance are rejected—presumably on the same grounds that cause CDW rejections.

The safest policy to follow is to base your decision about CDW on (1) an inquiry to your insurance agent or company as to precisely which of the several liabilities your own collision policy covers and (2) an assessment of the actual risk you run by self-insuring for whatever liabilities your own policy does not cover. If you are a safe driver (in terms of your recent accident experience) and if your itinerary involves an area that is neither geographically nor socially hazardous, you may decide to assume the risks your-self. Insurance companies base their rates on exaggerations of the actual statistical risks. Is a CDW at more than ten times normal insurance rates worth the money? On the other hand, you need to estimate the increased risk you run in driving an unfamiliar car through unfamiliar territory.

Complaints should be filed with the Federal Trade Commission or the attorney general's office in the state in which you rented the car as well as in your own state. A suit in small-claims court is likely to be impractical since the suit must be filed in the state in which the car was rented, which is usually not your state of residence.

CAMPING CLUBS

Complaints against camping clubs—organizations that promise their members camping facilities, either in one location or in a nationwide chain—generally center on high-pressure sales tactics or bankruptcy of the camping organization. Since neither type is easily resolved, extreme caution—or outright avoidance of such enterprises—is your best protection.

The sales pitch of camping clubs is highly seductive. It usually begins with a mailing that offers the recipient a no-obligation gift—commonly an outdoor grill or a set of luggage—simply for coming to visit the club grounds. Although the fine print may set age, marital status, and income limits for the recipients, or require them to listen to a sometimes lengthy sales pitch, the gift offer is genuine, although the quality of the gift is often questionable.

Because the prospective customer usually makes the trip in fine weather, the club will appear at its best, and the sales staff is invariably adept at stimulating the customer's fantasies about endless summers spent basking in nature's bosom at very low cost. In addition, the salesperson's assurance that the membership may be bequeathed to the customer's children has especial appeal to elderly people who do not stop to ask whether the camping club will be in business for the next couple of decades. A closing statement about a "special price good only today," all too often results in the euphoric signing of a check and a contract before customers have thought realistically not only about their probable use of the facilities but also about the terms of the contract and the total cost.

Because bankruptcies are not uncommon among camping clubs (in which case members are likely to get nothing at all for their substantial membership fee) the prospective member should, before signing any contract, get satisfactory answers to the following questions:

How long has the club been in business, and what experience has the management had in operating it?

Is the club subject to periodic financial audits, and are recent past reports available?

Will the club disclose data on the resale of memberships?

What rights do members have? Does membership include title to any property?

What is the policy regarding reservations?

What facilities are currently offered, and what are planned? If new property or facilities are planned, have the necessary land-use permits been obtained?

Is the club open to nonmembers and, if so, how much do they pay?

Does the club own, lease, or simply have the right to use the facilities? What is the length of the lease or the mortgage, and are there any restrictions to members' rights to use the property?

What are the club's bylaws or rules on the use of the facilities, and how may they be changed?

In addition to the initial fees, are there further fees or assessments, and what are the provisions for raising the payments?

Do members have the right to sell or bequeath their membership?

Under the laws of many states, you may cancel a camping club contract within three business days by mailing a certified letter to the club, but it is quite possible that your euphoria will not subside within this time period. In that case, your financial obligation may continue to haunt you long after your interest in the club activities has waned. Worse yet, the club may go out of business and sell your long-term contract to a collection agency.

Complaints against camping clubs can be filed with the attorney general, but if the club is in bankruptcy a claim should be filed with the appropriate bankruptcy court.

8

Housing

WHETHER WE OWN or rent our living quarters, their cost represents a major budget item, and our satisfaction with them significantly influences the general quality of our lives. Although the housing market is governed largely by national and local economic conditions, the choices (and the mistakes) we make are what finally determine our day-to-day level of contentment.

REAL ESTATE

Because all major changes in one's life generate stress, it is not surprising that the transfer of a home from seller to buyer is generally fraught with tension and anxiety for both parties. But the problems each faces are clearly different.

Buying a Home

Difficulties and disappointments in buying a home arise from two sources: (1) impulsive, "love at first sight" buying—often at an excessive price—and (2) the assumption that the realtor, whom the buyer selected, is an agent of the buyer rather than the seller, who pays the realtor's commission.

Love at First Sight. It is not uncommon for buyers, exhausted by a long and fruitless search, to come upon the house of their dreams and, on the spot, hand the realtor or the seller an "earnest money" check and sign a binder agreement committing them to go through with the purchase.

This is a serious mistake for two reasons. To begin with, a buyer unfamiliar with the neighborhood may overlook some disadvantages that can't be discovered by a cursory walk-through. One buyer, for example, bought a condominium without realizing that the railroad track behind it, which appeared unused, carried hundred-car freights at night that whistled when approaching a nearby crossing. Another, charmed by a house in a retirement community, failed to discover that the community mailboxes were almost a mile distant. A third bought a home bordered by a creek that deposited five feet of water into its basement—but only about once every two years, when a high tide coincided with a northeast gale. Yet another discovered that, because of a local geologic formation, water rates in that neighborhood were eight times higher than those in adjacent communities.

Equally important is the fact that most home buyers understand as little about house construction as they do about their automobile engines. Hence, they buy a house that may have seriously defective wiring or plumbing or misrepresented insulation or a leaky roof or a chronically wet basement.

Price and Condition. You can avoid paying too high a price or buying a home with serious defects by spending time on research and money on outside consultants. A careful reading of real estate advertisements, for example, can reveal the asking prices of similar houses in the same neighborhood. Tax records, available at the local assessor's office, can provide a comparison among the houses' current assessed values and may disclose the price the current owner paid for the home you've chosen to buy. And an independent appraisal can contribute reliable information to your data bank.

Of course, there are always intangibles for every individual buyer: the quality of the school district, for example, or the attractiveness of the grounds, or the view from an upper floor. But these intangibles, however they are valued, should be added to a firmly established "going price" for very similar homes.

Paying a fair price is not the only consideration because running expenses can, over the long term, be even more important. Once you are seriously interested in a house, you should demand and examine tax bills, utility bills, insurance policies, and all bills for any recent renovations or repairs that the seller claims to have made.

Buying a home with serious structural defects can be avoided by making the purchase "subject to a satisfactory inspection" and hiring a qualified *independent* appraiser or inspector to evaluate the house in every structural detail. Some of these inspectors provide a warranty that will pay for the correction of any defects they may have overlooked. If a trustworthy independent inspector is not available, it is usually possible to find a contractor who is expert in a specific area—roofing, plumbing, wiring, drainage—that is of concern to you.

Although neither the seller nor the agent is required to tell you anything about the condition of the house, an increasing number of states require the seller to execute a detailed disclosure form that describes many more features than merely the condition of the roof, furnace, plumbing, and wiring. Some forms include questions about neighborhood noise, the presence of termites or carpenter ants, the presence of asbestos or lead-based paint, and the adequacy of the water supply.

The use of these forms was instigated by realtors to protect themselves against lawsuits on grounds of misrepresentation, and some realtors will not list a property until the seller has filed such a form. But the protection they offer the buyer is limited. Because the form requires the disclosure of *known* defects, the seller may plead ignorance about some conditions; in any event, proving misrepresentation and collecting compensation may be difficult if not impossible. Buyers in states that do not require the disclosure form can nevertheless insist on one as a condition of the sale, but the form should not take the place of a thorough inspection.

The Realtor's Role. More than two-thirds of all lawsuits against realtors are brought by buyers who charge misrepresentation. And surveys show that most buyers believe that the realtor represents them rather than the seller, even though the agent's actual relationship may be revealed (in some states) somewhere in the fine print of the earnest money form. A few realtors do act specifically as buying agents—that is, they act only for the buyer and serve only the buyer's interest. But this arrangement is opposed by many large real estate brokers and is not widespread.

Meanwhile, it is essential to recognize that a realtor, even though selected by you, has a fiduciary relationship with the seller, who pays the commission, and hence is invariably concerned with the seller's best interests. This is why you should not reveal any information—personal financial data, job status, closing date on the property you now own, mandatory job move, or anything else—that may enhance the seller's bargaining power. Because getting the highest possible sale price is to the advantage of both the seller and the realtor, you should not expect the realtor to bargain very hard unless the alternative is no sale at all.

One common tactic among realtors involves tiring prospective buyers by showing them a series of clearly unsuitable or marginal properties and saving for the end of the tour one that is "exactly what you're looking for" but is highly overpriced. Another is to exaggerate the desirability of the property and to create a sense of urgency by implying that other prospective buyers are about to make an offer.

Complaints against individual realtors are difficult to resolve because the occupation is loosely regulated. Many realtors are independent contractors with little or no supervision by the agency for which they work. Most state licensing authorities tend to be biased in favor of the realtors and are unlikely to remove their certification in the absence of obvious fraud or deception. Nevertheless, complaints should be filed—first with the owner of the agency and, if necessary, with the state licensing authority.

Offers, Earnest Money, and Binders. Because a house represents the highest single expenditure you are likely to make, and because its financing can obligate you for decades, every part of the transaction should be put into writing and scrutinized with the greatest care.

Your initial offer, in addition to specifying the price you are willing to pay, should include a time limit for the seller's acceptance (often 72 hours) and a suggested date for completing the transaction. It can embody several conditions: a satisfactory professional inspection of the premises, your ability to obtain financing at a specified interest rate and for a specified term, or the sale of your existing home—all within a specified time period.

If your offer is accepted, or your offering price negotiated, you will be expected to sign a contract and pay a sum of money known as earnest money or a binder, often as much as 10 percent of the agreed-upon price. It is the terms of the contract and the payment of the binder that give rise to the vast majority of disputes and lawsuits.

Even though you have signed the earnest money agreement, it is not valid until the seller has signed it. Until then, he or she can legally sell the house to a higher bidder or simply remove it from the market. Once the seller has signed it, however, he or she is expected to remove the house from the market and hold it for you. Hence, the purpose of the binder is to compensate the seller in the event that, for whatever reason, you fail to complete the purchase. This is why, *unless the contract clearly specifies it,* the binder is not refundable. In addition, most contracts that are "subject to obtaining financing" give the seller the right to sell the house to any other buyer who comes along with a full cash payment, providing that you are given the opportunity to buy it (usually within 48 hours) for cash. If you are unable to obtain a conventional mortgage, however, it is possible that the seller will offer you a contract at terms competitive with those of the commercial lenders.

If the contract includes a "subject to inspection" clause and the inspection reveals defects, you have the right to a full refund, but in most circumstances the seller will agree to remedy the defects or to discount the selling price by the amount you will pay to remedy them. Occasionally the seller, for one reason or another, is unable to complete the sale by the date specified in the contract. In this situation you are, of course, entitled to the return of your binder—either from the seller or the realtor, depending on who has possession of your money.

Because of the complexity of the contract and the substantial amount of money involved, it's advisable to have a lawyer review the contract before you sign it. Realtors occasionally suggest that you can save legal fees if you and the seller use the same lawyer for the transaction. But this invariably creates a conflict of interest and should be avoided, no matter how amicable the relationship between you and the seller.

Selling a Home

Pressure to Sell. A major difficulty the seller faces stems from being forced to sell the home as quickly as possible. The couple that has retired and plans to move usually can, if they choose, fix a selling price for their home and wait indefinitely for an offer that meets or approaches it. Not so the owner who must move by a certain date because of a change in job or family circumstances. As the deadline approaches, panic mounts and the asking price drops.

But, unless the seller desperately needs cash, a precipitate drop in the asking price is not inevitable. Opinion varies among realtors as to whether an empty house is more marketable than a furnished one, but many feel that the empty house is easier to sell because it gives more scope to the potential buyers' imaginations and does not put them off with furnishings or a decor that may not be to their taste. Given a trustworthy realtor, the seller can usually move to the new location, no matter how distant, confident that a sale— and even the closing—can be handled by telephone and fax or overnight mail. The outcome depends, of course, on the integrity of the realtor. In such situations, the services of an on-the-scene attorney provided with clear instructions and authority may be a good investment.

The Realtor. Sellers tend to complain mostly about the commissions realtors make and the quality of their performance. They are particularly incensed when a realtor earns several thousand dollars in commission by selling the house less than a day after signing the agreement to represent them. Such sellers tend to be unaware that the realtor may have spent many futile days showing the buyers other properties.

On the other hand, some sellers become perturbed as their home remains on the market for months and "the realtor isn't doing a damned thing." These sellers fail to realize that realtors can do nothing when the housing market is depressed because of high mortgage rates or economic recession.

Because it is prepared by the realtor, the printed agreement that commits you to use a realtor's services is certain to benefit the realtor over you in every possible way. But almost any condition specified in this printed agreement is subject to negotiation.

For example, the agreement will specify a commission that is standard within the geographic area, but there is no reason why a commission with a specific realtor cannot be negotiated. (In fact, in areas where realtor competition is severe, some realtors offer a reduction in commission of their own accord.) And, although the standard agreement calls for payment of the full commission even if you find a buyer through your own efforts, there is no reason why the agreement cannot be negotiated to reduce the commission in such an eventuality.

The agreement also specifies an expiration date—usually 60 to 90 days after signing. But negotiating for a 30-day expiration date can put the realtor under pressure to find a buyer in a hurry. In any event, agreements running for more than 90 days should be avoided.

The agreement should also specify precisely the realtor's responsibilities. Will the home be photographed? Where and how prominently will it be advertised? Will the realtor arrange and be present for "open house" showings? Will the realtor arrange all but the legal details of the closing? Will the realtor sell the home on an exclusive basis or will it be added to the community's multiple listing, thus greatly increasing its exposure? Does the realtor have access to a nationwide multiple listing?

In general, comparison shopping among realty firms and interviewing a number of their agents is likely to be effective.

The Transaction. The fact that a realtor turns up a buyer puts the seller under no obligation to accept an offer. Although competent realtors will not present buyers who are financially unqualified, the ultimate responsibility for selecting a buyer is the seller's alone. On the other hand, the seller who rejects a clearly qualified buyer on the basis of race, sexual orientation, or other irrelevant characteristics may run into trouble not only with the realtor but with government antidiscrimination or fair-housing agencies.

All the advice offered to the buyer earlier in this chapter applies equally to the seller. Because the sale of a house is a large and very important transaction, reading all the documents carefully and enlisting the help of a competent lawyer constitute inexpensive and essential insurance.

CONDOMINIUMS

A condominium can be bought from one of two sellers: the developer who is in the process of selling units to new purchasers or the owner of a unit in an established, owner-controlled condominium. The former type of purchase is somewhat hazardous because the developer may make promises that will not be kept or describe facilities that may turn out to be wishful fantasies. Some states require developers to disclose certain information to prospective purchasers; others do not.

Because a condominium is governed entirely by its membership, you should scrutinize not only its financial records and the bylaws but also the minutes of the past year's meetings. The financial records will disclose periodic increases in taxes, utilities and maintenance costs—all of which require increases in membership dues. They can also tell you something about the condition of the buildings and grounds, the size of the reserve fund, and the care and foresight with which expenditures are made.

The minutes of the membership meetings may reveal not only current issues facing the membership but also areas of disagreement and contention and—more important—the values of the members with respect to the cash reserve, expenditures on cosmetic structural improvements, the hiring of maintenance staff, insurance coverages, and other matters that affect the monthly dues. The voting record at membership meetings may also disclose a strong consensus or the existence of sharply disagreeing cliques.

The bylaws should be reviewed for restrictions not only on such matters as pets, the parking of recreational vehicles, and the number of occupants per unit but also on the owners' right to rent their units. When a significant percentage of the units are currently rented, it is safe to assume that the owners regard their units as an investment rather than a residence, and this may affect their attitudes and decisions.

Although, in rare instances, bylaws must be changed to comply with changes in state or federal law, they are usually changed by a majority vote of the board. For this reason, it is important to determine (from the bylaws) the definition of a quorum and (from the minutes) the "democracy" of the membership meetings—that is, whether decisions are reached through broad consensus of the membership or by a small clique.

It is also useful to pay a social visit to as many of the current owners as possible. This is not to imply that condominium owners should be bosom friends, but a brief visit can reveal such details as whether the current owners get their ideas of decor from K-mart, Madison Avenue decorators, or somewhere in between—and their tastes may influence decisions about the decor of the common areas.

Disputes in connection with condominium membership may center on a change in the bylaws, the interpretation of a current bylaw, or a board decision about expenditures. In any case, they

are difficult to resolve, especially if only one member is the disputant. The member who feels abused may be able, through active
"politicking," to enlist enough support from other members to
effect a change, but otherwise the only recourse is through alternative dispute resolution (see Chapter 13) or a lawsuit (see Chapter 14).

LANDLORD-TENANT PROBLEMS

Over the past two decades, the supply of rental housing has decreased sharply as rental units have been converted into condo-
miniums or cooperatives. This situation has led, in many parts of
the country, to a chronic shortage of apartments and, consequently, a seller's market.

The printed leases presented to you invariably favor the landlord. Once signed, they commit you to pay the stipulated rent on
time for the duration of the lease, and they cannot be terminated
except by mutual consent. But despite their legalese, they may be
negotiable in terms of their duration, the amount of rent, or other
concessions, especially if the landlord has a high level of vacancies
or regards you as a particularly desirable tenant.

Even though a lease favors the landlord, it does offer you protection not only against rent increases during its term but also
against eviction because of sale of the property or for any other
reason except conduct that is deliberately destructive or unsafe.
Despite a landlord's threats, no contested eviction can take place
without authorization by a local court.

Tenants who rent on a month-to-month basis have very little
protection against termination of the arrangement and, aside from
giving timely notice, the landlord has virtually no obligation to
continue it.

Because landlord-tenant relationships are governed by state
law, which is often modified by local law, it is manifestly impossible to provide here any hard-and-fast information that will be
applicable to all situations. Nevertheless, some federal laws regarding discrimination are universally applicable.

It is illegal for a landlord to reject a qualified tenant on grounds of race, religion, or physical disability. A landlord may, however, prohibit the presence of pets, though no such prohibition can be imposed during the term of a current lease. A landlord may prohibit the presence of children in the absence of local regulations to the contrary.

If parking is one of the amenities provided, it should be clearly specified in the lease, and any restrictions on parking (of boats, for example, or recreational vehicles) should also be spelled out.

Tenants frequently complain about a landlord's failure to maintain the rented premises or to make needed repairs promptly. Most state laws require that problems that threaten a tenant's health—an infestation of roaches, for example, faulty plumbing, or an inoperative refrigerator—must be corrected promptly, usually within 48 hours. Other maintenance or repair problems should be brought to the landlord's attention in writing. But suspending rent payments until the problem is corrected is not legal. It is permissible, after the landlord has been given adequate notice under the provisions of the lease and state law, to have the repairs done by an outside contractor and to deduct the cost from subsequent rent payments.

Many landlord-tenant disputes center on the landlord's refusal to return a cleaning or damage deposit on the grounds that the departing tenants left the premises in worse condition than when they arrived. You can protect yourself against this situation before signing a lease by insisting on a "walk-through" in the company of the landlord and noting on a checklist any preexisting conditions—especially uncleanliness and damage—that may eventually give rise to a dispute. Once the landlord has signed this checklist, you can use it, on your departure, to assess the condition of the premises objectively.

In the absence of a dispute, state law requires the landlord to return the deposit within a reasonable time. If there is no government housing agency that can mediate a landlord-tenant dispute, and if the landlord is unwilling to participate in alternative dispute resolution, the best remedy for the tenant is a suit in small-claims court.

Complaints involving safety or health hazards should be addressed, if the landlord refuses to correct them promptly, to the city or county housing or construction department.

MOBILE HOMES

Although mobile homes constitute an efficient and economical source of housing for many segments of the population with limited incomes—semiskilled workers and young marrieds, as well as retirees—the strong social prejudice against them results in zoning restrictions that in many areas prohibit their placement on individual lots and confine them to mobile home "parks."

This creates a situation in which the owner's home, which often represents a substantial investment, must be situated on a rented lot, the rent for which is controlled by the park's owner. Because mobile homes, despite the name, are expensive to move, and because alternative space may be scarce or unavailable, any rent increase not only affects the owner's budget immediately but also reduces the selling price of the mobile home, since a new owner will be faced with the higher rent.

In addition, once a park is fully rented and demand exceeds supply, many park owners neglect the park's facilities, not merely with respect to general appearance but sometimes to the point of endangering the health of the tenant families.

Although homeowners can find some protection in negotiating a lease that contains specific provisions for rental increases, changes in park rules, and sale or bankruptcy of the park, their ultimate security may well depend on state law. Some states strongly protect the interests and welfare of mobile home owners; others do not. In fact, an owner's decision about where to situate a mobile home should depend, in part, on a careful scrutiny of the state laws and the negotiation of as protective a lease as circumstances permit.

Complaints against park owners should be filed with the attorney general's office, the state office responsible for mobile home administration, and, if appropriate, the county or state department of health or department of zoning and land usage.

Many buyers of new mobile homes complain about manufacturing defects, since mobile homes are not covered by state Lemon Laws. When purchasing a new home, buyers should not only read the warranty carefully but should choose a dealer who seems likely to remain in business long enough to honor it. Complaints about defects in mobile homes that are not corrected by the manufacturer should be filed with the Manufactured Housing and Construction Division of the Department of Housing and Urban Development, Room 9158, Washington, DC 20410, (202) 708-2210.

Relocating a mobile home is not only expensive but, to judge by consumer complaints against the movers, often hazardous. Any move should be covered by a very specific contract detailing liability for leveling, connection of utilities, and other tasks that movers, in the absence of a written contract, often refuse to perform.

Complaints about the moving of a mobile home should be filed with the Interstate Commerce Commission for interstate moves and with the state transportation commission and the attorney general's office for intrastate moves.

TIME-SHARING

Time-sharing has become increasingly popular as an economical way to enjoy a recreational facility—a boat, a seaside cottage, or a condominium—without investing in its total cost and upkeep. In its simplest form, two or more people buy a boat in partnership, share its purchase price and other costs, and agree that each partner has the right to use the property at certain times—on alternate weekends, for example, or during each partner's annual vacation. The success of informal time-sharing depends essentially on the congeniality of the partners and the stability of their relationship.

Commercial time-sharing, on the other hand, can be more hazardous because it is more complex, and many participants report disappointment if not downright victimization. Hence, before entering into a time-sharing agreement, you need to think carefully about your own plans and purposes and the kind of commitment the contract requires.

There are three forms of time-sharing, and they differ significantly. In the "right to use" form, you have no equity in the property. Your payment covers, essentially, your right to use the facility for a certain number of days each year, the dates of which may or may not be specified.

Another type—the "time-share club"—is similar to the informal partnership arrangement described above. The facility is owned by the club and controlled by its members, each of whom has the right to use it for a specified period.

The most expensive type is "fee ownership." Under this plan each participant owns a share of the property and the right to use it for a specified period. This plan is frequently used by real estate developers who build facilities—usually in popular recreation areas—with the express intent of selling them to fee owners. One inducement that the developers offer to potential buyers is the privilege of "trading" their annual time-share for a time-share in some other part of the country.

As in the case of camping clubs, many buyers, enticed by the offer of a free gift or overnight stay, visit the property under ideal conditions and, under the influence of the salespeople and their own euphoria, sign a contract without thinking carefully about their personal needs and plans or reading the fine print. High-pressure tactics—including "a special price if you sign up today"—are as common here as in the used-car business.

Among the personal issues to consider is whether you would want to spend an indefinite number of summers in the time-share facility and—if so—whether your children would feel the same way. A time-share "trade" may not be easy to accomplish unless the facility is located in a highly desirable area.

Despite pressure to "sign up today because most of the shares have been taken," it's advisable to show the contract to a lawyer, who can read it with the following questions in mind:

- What service or maintenance fees will you be charged?
- Can you sell or bequeath your rights?
- What restrictions are there with respect to use and occupancy?
- How sound is the financial condition of the seller?
- Is a list of the other time-sharers available so that joint action may be taken against the management if necessary?
- Who owns the property, and what equity or liens exist?

The laws of some states require the seller to provide the buyer with a set of disclosures, including a description of the property, the fees to be charged, and the identity of the owner of the time-share property. In addition, the buyer often has the right to cancel the contract within seven days of having received the disclosure. Whether or not your state has such laws, you should, before committing yourself, get full disclosure on each of these issues.

Complaints about time-share sales tactics and related problems should be filed with the state attorney general and the Federal Trade Commission.

9

Telemarketing, Prize Awards, and Other Scams

P OPULATION SHIFTS AND technological changes during the past several decades have brought about major changes in our buying habits—where and how we buy our goods and services. Not only has the neighborhood family-owned store given way to the distant mall and the impersonal supermarket but increasingly we are willing to buy—by mail, telephone, and fax—from strangers whose businesses may be a thousand miles away.

This development has brought us such benefits as a wider selection, the opportunity to shop in a national market, and often lower prices. But the trust we've developed through dealing with reputable mail-order firms is widely exploited by firms that offer poor value or that simply operate as new-age "confidence men." The general term for this kind of transaction is *telemarketing*.

TELEMARKETING

Telemarketing is a broad term applied to a wide variety of selling schemes that are based at a distance from the consumer's home and that routinely solicit customers by telephone, mail, television commercials, or classified advertisements. It does not apply to conventional mail-order firms or to "cold calls" by stockbrokers or by local firms soliciting orders for specials on carpet cleaning, photographic portraits, or other goods and services. In some states, a firm is defined as a telemarketer if it generates at least 60 percent of its revenues through telephone solicitation or through mailings or classified advertisements that invite a telephone or mail response.

Telemarketers use a variety of methods to reach their customers. Some use computerized equipment that dials numbers (including unlisted numbers) at random and then uses a computer-driven recording for the sales pitch. By tying up the customers' telephone lines (including emergency lines in hospitals) and answering machines, this technique has become such a widespread nuisance that some states have banned its use and the Federal Communications Commission has taken some action, but enforcement remains difficult.

The Telephone Consumer Protection Act, passed by Congress in 1991, requires the Federal Trade Commission to establish a system for listing people who do not want unsolicited sales calls, especially from automatic dialing machines. How soon this will be done and how effective it will be remain to be seen.

Other telemarketers use mass mailings of postcards to names on a list that may be taken from a city directory or some other large, undifferentiated list. And still others set up "boiler rooms" from which telephone solicitors target specific groups of customers—the elderly, small businesses, the unemployed, people with poor credit ratings—to whom they offer overpriced goods and services that may or (more often) may not be delivered.

The most vicious telemarketing schemes employ (900) numbers, enticing the caller to pay extortionate toll charges for information or services—such as home mortgages, employment opportunities, or credit repair—that either do not materialize or turn out to be valueless.

Some fraudulent companies, aware of the growing public suspicion about (900) numbers, have taken to using (976) numbers. Calls to these numbers are also charged to the caller at rates far higher than those for normal toll calls. In addition, some callers to toll-free (800) numbers have found themselves billed for the call, although these charges are billed separately to the caller by the party called and not by the telephone company. The Federal Trade Commission advises callers to disregard such bills.

Telemarketing schemes have several characteristics in common:

1. The victim has never heard of the company and has no way of checking on its reputation.
2. The victim has no way of inspecting the goods or evaluating the services offered.
3. The victim sees the product as a bargain or as meeting a need that can't be satisfied locally.
4. The victim must commit a payment (usually by credit card, check, or billing through a [900] number) with no provision for a refund. The worst of such schemes send a UPS or Federal Express truck to pick up the victim's check and deliver the merchandise, thus avoiding jurisdiction by the U.S. Postal Inspection Service.

The fundamental problem with all telemarketing is that control of the transaction belongs to the seller rather than the customer. When you place an order with a reliable mail-order house, you have not been solicited (except through a catalogue), you have decided by yourself that you want to make a purchase, and you know in advance the specifications of what you are ordering, the price and shipping charges, and the normal delivery time. The customer who falls for a telemarketer has no clear idea of any of these factors. In the worst cases, consumers have been asked to reveal their bank account numbers "just to check on your financial stability" and then discovered that their accounts have been wiped out by an electronic transfer of funds.

Abuses by telemarketers and (900) businesses will be impacted by the FTC under the recently passed Consumer Protection Telemarketing Act. Meanwhile, suspicious consumers can call the National Fraud Information Center (800-876-7060) to inquire about telephone or postcard solicitation.

THE THREE-DAY "COOLING-OFF" PERIOD

In response to an inundation of complaints about high-pressure sales, misrepresentation, and sharp dealing, the Federal Trade Commission has established the "three-day cooling-off rule," which permits buyers of anything costing more than $25 to back out of the following transactions within three days of initiation:

1. a door-to-door sale,
2. a sale where the buyer's agreement to purchase is consummated away from the seller's normal place of business—for example, at a "business seminar" or trade show conducted at a hotel, and
3. any loan (such as a mortgage) that encumbers the family home

On these transactions, the seller is required to inform the buyer about the three-day cancellation rule, and the three-day period does not begin until the buyer receives such notification. In the case of home mortgages, the lender's failure to comply with the rule may extend the cancellation period to three years.

The rule exempts purchases at arts and crafts fairs and of automobiles bought at a special location away from the dealer's regular establishment. Although the federal rule exempts telemarketing transactions, a number of states have extended the rule to include them.

Under this rule, the buyer who changes his mind must notify the seller of his intention by midnight of the third business day (Saturdays included) following the transaction, either in person or by certified mail (preferably with "return receipt requested") postmarked within the three-day limit.

But this rule has some severe limitations. To begin with, unless payment was made by credit card (in which case the card issuer may deduct the charge as "disputed"), getting the money back can be difficult, even though the rule requires a refund within 10 days. And although stopping payment on a check may be legitimate when the buyer has provided valid cancellation notice, telemarketers are remarkably prompt about getting the victim's check cleared. Many of them are recalcitrant about making refunds, and many magazine-subscription operators hire their door-to-door salespeople as "independent contractors," thus (perhaps illegally) attempting to transfer responsibility for repayment to the usually elusive and insolvent salesperson. Moreover, the rule does not apply to the sale of insurance, real estate, or securities.

Perhaps more important, the three-day period begins *when the transaction is initiated,* not when the goods or services are received. Thus, the purchaser of a $2,000 encyclopedia has no protection whatever if he bought the encyclopedia on the basis of a brochure and a shoddy encyclopedia arrives two weeks after the salesperson has departed with the down payment and a legally enforceable sales contract.

Perhaps the most serious limitation of the rule is that the most vulnerable victims—the elderly, the poorly educated, and the poor—are either unaware of it or unsure about how to exercise their rights since many sellers disregard the requirement to provide clear information about cancellation.

SOME WIDESPREAD SCAMS

Although some telemarketers are equal opportunity exploiters, selecting their victims at random through mailing lists or telephone directories, many focus their attention on one of the following groups.

Travelers

Too-good-to-be-true travel offers ("A round trip to Hawaii, only $379!") comprise 15 percent of all telemarketing frauds and cost consumers some $15 billion annually. The "catches" in these offers vary. In some cases, the victims are required to make a "good faith" deposit, which they may never see again. In others, the air travel is indeed free, but the victim is required to pay for third-rate hotel accommodations at exorbitant prices. In still others, the offer is available only for certain dates, which rarely fit in with the victim's vacation plans.

Although there are legitimate ticket consolidators who buy blocks of tickets from airlines and discount them to customers, travelers who use them should make certain they have in hand a genuine ticket (not a voucher) and a confirmed reservation before parting with their money.

Poor Credit Risks

People who have been bankrupt or who have poor credit ratings for other reasons are likely to be attracted by newspaper and magazine ads offering "guaranteed loans" or credit cards, "no matter how poor your credit rating." The loans, which involve a (900) number or require a nonrefundable fee of as much as $450, never materialize. And the credit cards turn out to be valid only for excessively priced merchandise from a catalogue published by the firm issuing the bogus card. One such firm avoided prosecution by advertising a "Vista" card, which many of its victims assumed to be a Visa card. There is, of course, no way that any person or firm can "repair" a poor credit rating (see Chapter 6).

Closely allied to credit-repair schemes are offers to "Consolidate Your Debts!" In return for a loan (at a high or often unspecified interest rate), these firms promise to take over and pay off all the victim's debts. Usually the creditors do not get paid or the "service charge" sharply reduces the payments to creditors. A debtor who is in difficulties because of unpaid bills can consult the Consumer Credit Counseling Service (see p. 270), a legitimate nonprofit organization supported by major lending institutions. But "loan consolidators" who advertise should be avoided.

The Elderly

Capitalizing on the heightened concerns of the elderly with respect to health and safety, many firms sell them a wide range of equipment that invariably fails to perform or ends up costing far more than the price first quoted.

Perhaps the most widespread scam is the sale of motorized beds and chairs that allegedly relieve various aches and pains on the basis of the salesperson's assurance that "Medicare will pay for it." The buyers soon discover that Medicare will pay for it only if their physician prescribes it, and the physician is then placed in the uncomfortable position of either authorizing the medically worthless purchase or causing the (often indigent) patient to be burdened with the full cost. Although such beds and chairs are advertised as "custom fitted," the sales contract disclaims any guarantee of the buyer's comfort.

Other scams involve the sale of medical alarms that enable the user to summon help by pressing a button and burglar alarms that connect directly to a security company but require a substantial monthly maintenance fee. Also active among the elderly are "estate planners" who sell living trusts to victims whose assets and family situations do not warrant them (see Chapter 6).

The Unemployed

Operating largely through classified ads in the "Help Wanted" columns, some firms promise "Jobs in Alaska!" or "Government Jobs!" By calling a (900) number—at a cost that can run to $45 or more—or buying a "directory," the victim receives a listing of companies in Alaska (which can be obtained at no cost at a public library) or a listing of currently available civil service jobs (which can be obtained at no cost from the U.S. Civil Service Commission).

Closely related schemes offer "Work at Home. Up to $35,000 possible for PC users!" When the advertised products require assembly, the victim invests a substantial amount for the "beginner's kit" only to learn that the finished work is unsatisfactory for one reason or another and therefore the opportunity for work never materializes.

One such scheme offered its victims 50 cents for compiling names and addresses to be used in mailing lists—a seemingly obvious scam since mailing lists are more cheaply available from city directories and other sources. Applicants were required to remit a $49 "application fee" and were promised "double your money back" if they were accepted. Needless to say, nobody was accepted.

One perennial and rather seductive offer invites victims to "Earn money by evaluating manuscripts for book publishers in your spare time—on the beach or in your kitchen." The victim receives, in return for a $45 fee, a list of book publishers and is invited to solicit them. Book publishers, of course, never use the services of inexperienced amateurs.

Small Businesses

Businesses too small to employ a professional purchasing agent are widely victimized by telephone callers who promise promotional calendars, listings in the *Yellow Pages,* or bargain prices for copier supplies. (The latter are known to the regulatory agencies as "toner phoners.") The calendars fail to arrive, the *Yellow Pages* turns out to be a copycat version of the genuine *Yellow Pages,* published in a few thousand copies and never distributed, and the copier supplies—if indeed they are delivered—turn out to be more expensive than what is available locally.

One business owner was offered vouchers for a "free vacation at a resort hotel" as an incentive for buying a large supply of overpriced business forms. When the transaction was completed, she was informed that the vouchers could be used only at specified times, that the hotel was fully booked at the time she preferred, and that she could make a reservation a month later. Since by that time the vouchers would have expired, she was left with a worthless "prize."

Automobile Owners

Some telemarketers scour the "Automobiles for Sale" classifieds and then telephone the anxious seller with an offer to advertise his or her car "nationwide" and sell it "for a better price than you can get" in return for a nonrefundable fee of $300 to $500 payable in advance. These firms advertise the car minimally if at all and always pocket the seller's fee, even though they hardly ever sell the car.

The Charitable

It is the rare householder who has not received—especially around Thanksgiving and Christmas—telephone solicitations for contributions to various "good causes"—for example, food for the homeless or toys for their children, or "drug education." The callers usually identify themselves as representing local police departments or groups with names that closely resemble legitimate and well-established charitable organizations.

Because these organizations do not provide printed information on how their funds are distributed (and in some cases use 90 percent or more of the contribution for administrative expenses), the only way to distinguish the legitimate from the fraudulent is to apply the general rule that legitimate charities do not solicit strangers by telephone. In general, charitable contributions should be thought out carefully (see Chapter 6) and not made on the spur of the moment in response to a telephone call.

"Unclaimed Funds"

In another widespread telemarketing scheme, individuals are notified that they have an unstated amount of "unclaimed funds" that the sender will remit to them in return for an advance payment or a share—as high as 50 percent—of the funds recovered. Although this practice is not illegal, people who think they may have money coming to them need not share it with anyone but can claim the entire amount. These funds can come from three possible sources:

FHA Mortgages. Homeowners who at one time had an FHA mortgage but have sold their homes before the mortgage was paid off may be owed a refund for an overpayment on their mortgage-insurance premiums. This possibility can be verified by writing to the U.S. Department of Housing and Urban Development, P. O. Box 23699, Washington, DC 20026.

Abandoned Bank Accounts. When a bank account (usually a passbook account) has been inactive for a certain period of time, the balance is turned over to the state. Although the state has the right to use this money, the state treasury department will refund it on application by the legitimate owners or their heirs.

Unpaid Insurance Policies. It is possible that a life insurance or endowment policy remained unpaid because it was never submitted for payment or because the insurance company was unable to locate the beneficiaries. If no such policy can be found in a search through family papers, Policy Search, American Council of Life Insurance, 1850 K St., NW, Washington, DC 20006, will, at no charge, circulate the insured's name to more than two hundred insurance companies to check against their records.

"Congratulations! You Are a Guaranteed Prizewinner!"

A widespread scam that victimizes people of all ages and most income levels begins with a bold-type postcard notification that they "are the guaranteed winners of TWO of the following prizes." The prizes range from $25,000 in cash and a luxury automobile to a watch or a $200 gift certificate. Most of these offers require a payment of some kind before the prize is shipped—the purchase of several hundred dollars' worth of vitamins, for example, or a payment to cover "shipping charges" or "federal taxes." The prize, if it ever materializes, turns out to be a $5 watch or a gift certificate that can be applied only to high-priced and generally useless merchandise offered by the promoters.

In many states, the awarding of prizes or contest awards must have no strings attached, and demand for any payment from the "winners" is illegal. But, as we shall note, enforcement is extremely difficult, and many "winners" pay hundreds of dollars for the $15 "stereo set" and an unneeded supply of vitamins or a lifetime supply of pencils.

"Business Seminars"

People who are unemployed or who feel that they are in blind-alley jobs are particularly vulnerable to these itinerant scams (see Chapter 6). The only available protection against any of these schemes is the three-day cooling-off period, but often the victim's enthusiasm does not subside until this grace period has expired.

DOOR-TO-DOOR SALES

Because door-to-door selling is extremely expensive in terms of its sales costs, potential customers can be virtually assured that it offers no bargains. In fact, this kind of sale—whether the product is a magazine subscription, an encyclopedia, driveway resurfacing, or aluminum siding—ranks among the top ten consumer complaints to most regulatory agencies. Nevertheless, door-to-door sales continue to flourish, in part, perhaps, because many of its victims are so lonely that they welcome the opportunity to chat with anyone—even someone whose purpose is to exploit them.

Magazine Subscriptions

Magazine salespeople promise enormous savings to the customer willing to buy, with monthly payments, long-term subscriptions to several magazines. In some cases, the magazine publishers never receive the victim's money; in others, the bargain turns out to be illusory or the monthly payments turn out to be far higher than the customer can afford.

Victims who have second thoughts after the three-day cooling-off period has expired and therefore stop payment on their checks may well find themselves in the hands of a collection agency.

Contractors

A different but equally pernicious scam—which persists despite its merciless and hilarious exposure in the movie *Tin Men*—involves contractors who knock at the victim's door and announce that "Since we're in your neighborhood with all our equipment, we can resurface your driveway [or install storm windows or aluminum siding] at a special rate." Chapter 5 discusses this problem.

COMPLAINTS

Complaints about all the scams enumerated here should be filed with the attorney general's offices of your own and the offender's state, the local office of the Better Business Bureau, the Federal Trade Commission (in the case of an out-of-state or multistate company), and the U.S. Postal Inspection Service (if the mails were used in any part of the transaction). But, although a volume of complaints may lead to investigation and enforcement, the prospects of restitution are slim.

Although the U.S. Postal Inspection Service has put a stop on orders to some telemarketers and has obtained some refunds for some customers, many telemarketers evade such surveillance by using the telephone for initiating the transaction and Federal Express for picking up the customer's check (or cash). In addition, many telemarketers are adept at running an intensive campaign, collecting vast amounts of money, and going out of business just before complaints to the Federal Trade Commission or the state attorneys general reach a sufficient volume to justify an investigation. The telemarketers resurface under a new name almost immediately, because the business is as mobile as it is profitable.

The recently established National Fraud Information Center (800-876-7060) seems likely to speed up the detection and prosecution of these scam artists. Operated jointly by the National Consumers League and the Alliance Against Fraud in Telemarketing, it accepts complaints and provides information on a wide variety of fraudulent operations.

Because the likelihood of restitution is low, you can best protect yourself against victimization by refusing to do business with any unfamiliar organization that solicits business actively and:

- does not use the U.S. mails for soliciting business or for sending the merchandise;
- asks for your credit card number or bank account number by mail or telephone;
- refuses to send printed information in advance of your purchase or donation;
- makes a limited-time offer that requires an immediate response or otherwise pressures you to make an immediate decision.

3

Sources of Help

10

Complaining

M ANY CONSUMERS FAIL to make complaints, especially when the money value of the abuse or deceit is small. Some of them feel that only "cheapskates" complain about trivial amounts. Others are skeptical about getting a satisfactory response from companies and cynical about the efforts of the regulatory agencies.

Despite these reservations, however, there are several sound reasons for complaining. To begin with, a rising volume of complaints, either to a company or to a regulatory agency, is likely to bring about some reform, and your letter may be the straw that breaks the camel's back. Moreover, even if your complaint gets no response, your realization that someone in the company had to read it and send it on to the responsible person or department can help vent your anger and frustration. And, taken with all the other complaints, it can help to empower the consumer in an increasingly dehumanized economy.

AT THE POINT OF SALE

If an item or a service proves defective or unsatisfactory—if, for example, a new dress fails to survive its first dry cleaning, or if the special-ordered custom-made window blinds have not shown up

223

several days after the promised delivery date, or if the speakers on your new stereo can't be balanced—the first step is to ask the retailer for exchange or refund. (Complaints about cars are an exception, which we've discussed in Chapter 3.)

Sellers' responses to customer complaints cover a broad spectrum—from full and cheerful accommodation to downright refusal to make any adjustment regardless of the validity of the complaint. But if the first person you complain to offers no satisfaction, ask to speak to a supervisor. Except in boutiques and mom-and-pop enterprises, there is a chain of command that may include not only the department manager and the store manager but also a corporate headquarters.

At this point, if you have charged your purchase to a credit card, you should notify the credit card issuer in writing that you are disputing the charge. The charge may well appear on your next statement, but you will not be required to pay it until the dispute is resolved (see Chapter 6).

If the local higher-ups provide no satisfaction, your next step is a letter to the retailer's company headquarters, although merely asking the local manager for the company's address may produce some action. Headquarters may be more concerned than the locals about customer satisfaction and, more important, may better understand the concept of implied warranty (see Chapter 4) and the seller's obligation to fulfill contractual promises to the buyer. They may also be interested in monitoring the volume of complaints against each of their outlets.

If a retailer's headquarters offers no satisfaction, a complaint to the manufacturer is in order. Usually, the manufacturer's name and address are printed on the product or its packaging but if not, you can probably find them in Standard and Poor's *Register of Corporations,* available in the reference section of most libraries, or in the *Consumer's Resource Handbook,* available free of charge from the Consumer Information Center, Pueblo, CO 81009. Standard and Poor's guide is the more useful of the two because it lists the corporate officers by name and function. (Products imported from Taiwan, China, Korea, and Singapore usually carry no manufacturer's name, and the retailer or the distributor is likely to be your last resort.)

Increasingly, the packaging of manufactured products includes a toll-free consumer information number, but these are something of a mixed bag in terms of effectiveness. Some of them (Whirlpool is a model of excellence) will connect you with a technician who can walk you through a problem to help you solve it yourself. Others provide the names of local authorized repair services. Still others seem to be aimed largely at acquiring data on complaints for the benefit of the company's marketing, research, or production departments rather than helping the consumer.

WRITE AWAY

If your problem is a simple one (the toothpaste pump isn't pumping or a brand-new computer disk has a bad sector), and the local retailer is recalcitrant, a telephone call will probably get you a replacement. But if the problem is more complex, a letter will probably get better results.

As in all complaints, anger, sarcasm, and threats are likely to be ineffective and possibly counterproductive. The better tactic is to assume that the manufacturer is as unhappy as you are about your purchase and that your problem constitutes an exception to the generally high quality that the company assumes to be standard in its products or service.

In fact, some manufacturers are concerned not only with the quality of their products but also with the behavior of their authorized dealers. For example, a woman whose new television antenna proved unsatisfactory got no satisfaction whatever from the local dealer who sold and installed it until she wrote a letter to the antenna's manufacturer. A week later the dealer showed up to install a satisfactory replacement.

In any written complaint, a certain amount of wry humor may work. One consumer's complaint about a set of unsatisfactory coffee mugs, which opened with "Don't you wish it were made like

Rubbermaid? I certainly do, especially since the coffee mugs I bought *were* made by Rubbermaid!" resulted in a prompt and apologetic replacement. Another successful complaint, about an inefficient vegetable peeler, began by asking the company's president whether he had asked his wife to try it out before putting it on the market.

Your letter should be quite specific about what you found wrong with the product and what you want done about it. Do you want a repair or a replacement, or would you prefer a substituted product? You should also spell out, if it's appropriate, what the retailer did and did not offer to do, and support your complaint with copies of documents or a log of your telephone calls.

If you are complaining about a service—a cruise or a car rental, for example—set a realistic value on what you paid for but didn't receive, what expenses you incurred because of unsatisfactory service, and your personal inconvenience and loss of time.

The letter should be addressed to the president or the chief executive officer, even though you can be sure that the secretary will intercept it and route it to the proper person. But it's often effective to identify an appropriate vice president in the Standard and Poor's listing, address your letter to this person, and send a copy to the boss. By creating a certain amount of intracompany tension, this tactic doubles your chances for an effective response. The boss may direct the subordinate to "handle it," and the subordinate may conclude, correctly, that the best way to prevent escalation of your complaint is to satisfy you promptly.

Allowing for postal and corporate sluggishness, you should wait about two weeks before taking further action. If you've had no response, and your dissatisfaction or distress has not diminished, you might enclose a copy of your initial letter in a second letter—also temperate in tone—in which you state specifically what your next moves will be by adding, after your signature,

> copies for possible submission to:
> [your state] Attorney General
> Federal Trade Commission
> [your state] Insurance Commissioner

or any other appropriate regulatory agency, industry-wide arbitration panel, or trade association (see Chapter 16).

These alternatives may produce prompter action than filing a lawsuit in small-claims court and are less expensive than hiring a lawyer to file a full-fledged lawsuit. If, on the other hand, they produce no results, your next step is to enlist the help of one of the agencies listed in Chapters 15 and 16.

11

The State Attorney General

O NE OF THE MOST inexpensive and potentially effective tools for settling a consumer dispute—and certainly the simplest—is a complaint to the consumer protection division of your state's office of the attorney general.* This resource is available in varying degrees to consumers in every state. And the complaint process costs nothing, leaving you free to pursue other avenues should it prove unsuccessful.

The attorney general, as the state's lawyer, is responsible for enforcing state laws, among them the laws regulating what are called "unfair and deceptive trade practices." Although some of these practices (such as mergers and monopolistic behavior) are so complex as to be of interest primarily to businesses and their lawyers, many others, such as deceptive advertising, bait-and-switch tactics, and telemarketing fraud, obviously affect consumers who have been or may be victimized directly.

This is why most state offices of the attorney general have set

---

*In some states a consumer protection unit, office of consumer affairs, or fraud unit is administered by the Department of Justice, the governor's office, or local city and county district attorneys. New York City has its own (very aggressive) Office of Consumer Affairs, which supplements the (equally aggressive) Consumer Protection Unit of the state attorney general's office. California funds consumer protection through county district attorneys' offices, many of which have proven highly effective. The 1992 Sears automobile repair case, which had nationwide impact, was initiated by the Special Operations Division of the Contra Costa County District Attorney's Office.

up consumer protection divisions dedicated to protecting individual consumers and legitimate businesses against abuse and seeking redress when they have been abused. By taking action against offenders, the consumer protection division can at best get restitution for abused customers or at least punish the offenders, driving them out of business when necessary. See Table 11.1, page 237, for a list of state consumer protection divisions.

The aggressiveness and efficacy of any state's consumer protection division depends on a number of local factors. On the negative side, the state's budget may severely limit the division's staffing, resources, and activities. And the budget may depend, in turn, on the political ideology of the state legislature. In addition, a wide variety of business lobbies—used-car dealers, for example, or realtors—may persuade legislators to restrict the office's mandate or activities. Lastly, the attorney general, for personal or political reasons, may tend to favor business interests rather than those of the consumer. As a result, some state attorneys general fight far less aggressively than others for the rights and welfare of the consumer.

But there is a positive side. Because the attorney general's office concentrates most of its budget and resources on abstruse legal issues that are of little direct interest to the voting public, the effectiveness of its consumer protection division—established specifically to help the abused citizen—can be a powerful influence on the attorney general's reelection. (The gratitude of a consumer who has received a $2,000 refund from an offending firm may well be expressed not only in a thank-you letter but also in the voting booth.) In addition, an aggressive consumer protection division can show that each year it recovers millions of dollars for the consumer—significantly more than its cost of operation.

Consumer protection is the one area where attorneys general are given policy authority and prosecutorial discretion by the legislature. It is therefore the most politically sensitive function they perform. Basically, the successful consumer protection unit effectively polices the marketplace, ensuring that scams are exposed, that the playing field is level, and that the consumer's dollars go to businesses that provide the best products and services for the lowest cost. Rip-offs flourish in states with weak consumer protection agencies and avoid those which aggressively defend consumer interests.

Because budget restrictions, lobbyists' efforts, and the political climate vary so widely among states, it isn't possible to provide here a win-loss scoreboard or even a definitive list of the functions and restrictions of every consumer protection division. In general, however, the following restrictions apply, and you should be aware of them before filing a complaint.

Most state consumer protection divisions cannot involve themselves in:

- providing you with legal advice or representation.

- disputes between individuals. In the case of a used-car purchase, for example, they can intervene if you bought the car from a dealer but not if you bought it from a private party, because attorneys general are limited to enforcing consumer laws only in trade and commerce and not in private transactions.

- disputes involving "licensed professionals"—lawyers, doctors, accountants, beauticians, et al. Although they may mediate a dispute about billing, they are generally prohibited from dealing with disputes regarding quality of performance and will therefore refer them either to the professional association (such as the state or county bar association) or to the state's board of professional licensure.

- grievances involving performance that inconveniences consumers but does not defraud them. For example, they will not intervene if an auto repair shop is merely slow in repairing your car, though they may intervene if the repair was grossly unsatisfactory or if the charges exceeded the written estimate. They will not intervene if a collection agency is rude to you, but they will take your complaint if the agency has violated the specific laws governing its practices.

- complaints against other government agencies—federal, state, or local. Because the attorney general represents some of these agencies or coordinates or cooperates with them, taking action against them would constitute clear conflict of interest.

- complaints involving race, age, sex, or other types of discrimination (although as the state's attorney, the attorney general may represent the state's human rights commission or other agency in its attempt to correct the problem).

- employee-employer disputes about wages or work conditions.

- landlord-tenant disputes. These are usually handled by another state or municipal office, to which the attorney general may refer the complaint.

An active state consumer protection division is primarily interested in monitoring the marketplace to ensure that it provides a level playing field: that it is honest and sufficiently competitive to allow your dollar to go to the supplier that provides you with the best goods or services at the lowest prices. By actively policing the marketplace with these criteria in mind, the consumer protection division not only punishes offending firms within the state but creates an environment that discourages other dishonest firms from moving into the state or even trying to solicit telemarketing business with the state's residents.

Because the consumer protection division can't possibly oversee every transaction, the essential data for this monitoring process consist of consumer complaints that accuse a firm—or an entire industry—of not "playing fair." Hence, the consumer protection division invites complaints (from businesses as well as from individual consumers) not merely in order to resolve them through mediation but, more important, to detect persistent patterns of consumer abuse, deceptive practices, and outright fraud. Once such a pattern is discovered, what originated as a private dispute between buyer and seller becomes a matter of broad public interest and thus warrants the attorney general's intervention under the state's consumer protection laws.

When you file a complaint, you are primarily concerned, of course, with getting it resolved and obtaining restitution of some kind. But whether or not it gets immediate resolution, your complaint may serve one of two additional purposes. It may, if it is sufficiently serious, provide the consumer protection division with an early warning of what promises to become a pervasive scam. Or it may function as a "last straw." A single complaint against a used-car dealer's sale of a seriously defective vehicle may go unresolved because by itself it doesn't warrant action by the consumer protection division's limited legal staff. But if the data bank reveals that this complaint is the fifth or sixth charging the same dealer with the same deceptive practice, the legal staff is more likely to take action.

An example of the "early warning" complaint involved an enterprise calling itself "Foreclosure Solutions," which offered homeowners who were threatened with foreclosure a "method" of avoiding loss of their homes for a fee of $450. After receiving the fee, the "counselor" simply advised the beleaguered homeowner either to borrow money from friends and family or to file a bogus lawsuit against the lender in order to delay foreclosure until such a loan could be obtained. Although only eight victims of this scam filed complaints, all received full refunds and the company was put out of business.

Not all investigated complaints center on small or fly-by-night companies. In a nationwide case, a television cable company provided a "free" subscription to a new channel, indicating in inconspicuous print that unless the subscriber actively rejected the service after one month by notifying the cable company, a monthly charge would be imposed. Because this "negative option" was a clear violation of the state's fair practices laws, the attorney general put a stop to the practice by obtaining a preliminary injunction and coordinating with other state attorneys general to stop the practice.

The Minnesota attorney general forced Spiegel's, which had set illegal interest rates on its charge accounts, to refund $750,000 to its card holders. Similarly, when Budget Rent-A-Car charged a renter who had had an accident not only for repairs to the car but an additional $4,000 that it stood to lose because it could not resell the car to the manufacturer, the attorney general recovered the money and referred the case to other state and federal authorities for further investigation.

Examples of "last straw" complaints, against a single company or against an industry as a whole, are numerous. Complaints against health clubs, for example, have generated state laws governing cancellation rights and the duration of memberships. And the attorney general of Florida, concerned by a mounting number of complaints about unsatisfactory transmission repairs, conducted a sting operation by making a minor misadjustment in the transmission of an expensive automobile and presenting it for estimates to several repair shops, every one of which misdiagnosed the problem and claimed that repairs would cost several thousand dollars. The prosecution of these firms served as a clear warning to every other shop in the state.

In some cases, the attorneys general of several states share complaint data and take joint action. For example, a consortium of attorneys general took punitive action against the Chrysler Corporation for disconnecting the odometers on "executive cars" and selling them as new.

In view of these successes, you should recognize that your complaint, whether or not it gets immediate resolution, can play an important role in cleaning up the marketplace.

FILING A COMPLAINT

Before filing a complaint, you should make a serious effort to resolve the problem with the seller (see Chapter 10). In a surprising number of cases processed by consumer protection divisions, the seller resolves the problem promptly and points out that it would have been resolved amicably and more quickly had the consumer first approached the seller.

A complaint against an out-of-state firm should be filed in your own state (because the attorney general will be interested to know whether a number of state residents are being victimized) but it should also be filed in the state where the offending firm is located, since that state's attorney general may carry more clout and get prompter action.

Your complaint may be filed in letter form, but many consumer protection divisions provide complaint forms, which can be processed somewhat more efficiently. The complaint should be legible, objective, and as concise as possible without omitting significant detail, and it should be supported by copies of whatever documents are available: contracts, receipts, logs of telephone calls, canceled checks, and so on. (The originals should, of course, be retained in case you need to take your case to small-claims court.)

Your complaint should also specify precisely the settlement you expect: a refund, a replacement of the product, or a reduction of the charges billed. Because the complaint will typically be sent on to the party accused, it should avoid hostility, sarcasm, name-calling, and other offensive language.

Complaint Processing

If your local consumer protection unit is adequately budgeted and staffed, its business/consumer mediation section will send the complaint to the accused firm and ask for a response or a rebuttal. At this point, there are four possible outcomes: (1) the firm makes the full adjustment requested or offers a compromise; (2) the rebuttal states convincingly that the complaint is not justified (in fact, the customer is *not* always right); (3) the firm does not respond; or (4) the firm refuses to adjust a legitimate complaint.

When the firm does not respond, the business/consumer mediation section usually follows up with a somewhat stronger letter and, if necessary, with a telephone call. Often this gets results because most firms that are concerned about their reputation in the marketplace take seriously a letter from the attorney general's office. But if there is no response, the business/consumer mediation section, because it has no legal enforcement power, may "send it upstairs" for further action.

Some Outcomes

Whether or not further action is taken on your complaint depends on a number of factors that may have little to do with its validity. As we've noted, some consumer protection divisions are so meagerly funded that a single attorney must operate largely by empty threat because there is no funding or staff for vigorous enforcement. Other consumer protection divisions choose for legal action those cases that promise the biggest bang for their legal staff's buck. Still others are hampered by the views of the legislature and the lobbyists that influence it.

If the behavior you complain about is truly outrageous, the attorney general may get actively involved in your dispute, especially if the problem, once resolved, would be a good precedent for educating consumers or businesses about prohibited practices. Thus, for example, the used-car dealer who sold an impoverished Hispanic a seriously defective vehicle, having failed to display the Spanish-language version of the Federal Trade Commission "as is" window sticker and having conducted the transaction in a mixture of English, Spanish, and pidgin, was forced by a strong letter from the attorney general's office to refund the customer's money and return his trade-in. The same action was taken against a dealer who sold a defective vehicle to a dyslexic customer who obviously did not understand the implications of a complicated written "as is" disclaimer form that was handed to him minutes before the dealership closed for the day. Both these cases, along with others, provided strong anecdotal evidence for the need for a used-car lemon law and brought home the attorney general's position on warranty problems with these dealers and with the industry as a whole.

But even if your complaint is totally valid and is one of many against the same firm, the consumer protection division may not be able to take legal action. For example, if a fraudulent mail-order firm appears on the market, its first defrauded customers are likely to wait at least a month before filing a complaint about undelivered or shoddy merchandise. Further complaints (in sufficient numbers to reveal a clear pattern of fraud) may not arrive for another two or three months. At this time, the firm, having cashed all the customers' checks and "slam-dunked" their credit card slips, goes out of business, leaving no traceable address. When this occurs, the consumer protection division can recover nothing, and the embittered complainants are likely to conclude that it is a political bureaucracy that serves no purpose.

Legal Action

Legal action by the attorney general, when it is practical, can take several forms. It may begin with an investigation, followed by an enforcement conference, which may result in an agreement by the offending firm to cease the offensive practice, to offer full or partial restitution to the abused complainants, to pay a civil penalty, and to reimburse the attorney general's office for its legal costs. Although, like all lawyers, the attorney general's office prefers to settle out of court, it will, in the face of a stubborn defendant, go to court. A favorable verdict can result in full or partial refunds for all the abused customers and can define for all businesses the margins between acceptable and unacceptable practices.

IS FILING A COMPLAINT RIGHT FOR YOU?

Because the entire complaint process—from filing to final outcome—may take four to six weeks or longer, it's not practical if your complaint involves the repair of a car that you need for the daily trip to work, or uncompleted work by a contractor. In situations in which time is of the essence, a sharply worded letter from a private attorney or filing suit in small-claims court may be the more effective tactic.

TABLE 11.1

The following list of state consumer protection divisions indicates the main office only. Many states have numerous branches, but a complaint filed with the main office will be transferred to a branch if necessary. The toll-free (800) numbers are usable only within the respective states.

ALABAMA
Consumer
  Protection
  Division
Office of Attorney
  General
11 S. Union St.
Montgomery, AL
  36130
(800) 392-5658/
  (205) 242-7334

ALASKA
Consumer
  Protection Unit
Attorney General's
  Office
1301 W. 4th St.,
  Suite 200
Anchorage, AK
  99501
(907) 269-5100

ARIZONA
Consumer
  Protection
Office of Attorney
  General
1275 W.
  Washington St.,
  Rm. 259
Phoenix, AZ 85007
(800) 352-8431/
  (602) 542-5763

ARKANSAS
Consumer
  Protection
  Division
Office of Attorney
  General
200 Tower Bldg.
323 Center St.
Little Rock, AR
  72201
(800) 482-8982/
  (501) 682-2341

CALIFORNIA
Dept. of Consumer
  Affairs
400 R St., Suite
  1040
Sacramento, CA
  95814
(800) 344-9940/
  (916) 445-0660

COLORADO
Consumer
  Protection Unit
Office of Attorney
  General
110 16 St., 10th fl.
Denver, CO 80202
(303) 620-4500

CONNECTICUT
Dept. of Consumer
  Protection

State Office Building
165 Capitol Ave.
Hartford, CT 06106
(800) 842-2649/
  (203) 566-4999

DELAWARE
Division of
  Consumer Affairs
820 N. French St.,
  4th fl.
Wilmington, DE
  19801
(302) 577-3250

**DISTRICT OF
COLUMBIA**
Department of
  Consumer and
  Regulatory Affairs
614 H St., NW
Washington, DC
  20001
(202) 727-7000

FLORIDA
Division of
  Consumer
  Services
218 Mayo Bldg.
Tallahassee, FL
  32399
(800) 327-3382/
  (904) 488-2226
For Lemon Law:
  (800) 321-5366

TABLE 11.1 (continued)

GEORGIA
Governor's Office of
Consumer Affairs
2 Martin Luther
King Jr. Dr., SE
Plaza Level—East
Tower
Atlanta, GA 30334
(800) 869-1123/
(404) 651-8600

HAWAII
Office of Consumer
Protection
828 Fort St. Mall,
Suite 600B
P.O. Box 3767
Honolulu, HI 96812
(808) 586-2630

IDAHO
Office of the
Attorney General
Consumer
Protection Unit
State House, Rm.
113A
Boise, ID 83720
(800) 432-3545/
(208) 334-2424

ILLINOIS
Consumer
Protection
Division
Office of Attorney
General
100 W. Randolph,
12th fl.
Chicago, IL 60601
(312) 814-3580

INDIANA
Consumer
Protection
Division
Office of Attorney
General
219 State House
Indianapolis, IN
46204
(800) 382-5516/
(317) 232-6330

IOWA
Consumer
Protection
Division
Office of Attorney
General
1300 E. Walnut St.,
2nd fl.
Des Moines, IA
50319
(515) 281-5926

KANSAS
Consumer
Protection
Division
Office of Attorney
General
301 W. 10th St.
Kansas Judicial
Center
Topeka, KS 66612
(800) 432-2310/
(913) 296-3751

KENTUCKY
Consumer
Protection
Division

Office of Attorney
General
209 St. Clair St.
Frankfort, KY
40601
(800) 432-9257/
(502) 564-2200

LOUISIANA
Consumer
Protection Section
Office of Attorney
General
State Capitol Bldg.
P.O. Box 94005
Baton Rouge, LA
70804
(504) 342-7373

MAINE
Consumer and
Antitrust Division
Office of Attorney
General
State House Station
No. 6
Augusta, ME 04333
(207) 289-3716
(9 A.M.–1 P.M.
EST)

MARYLAND
Consumer
Protection
Division
Office of Attorney
General
200 St. Paul Pl.
Baltimore, MD
21202
(800) 969-5766/
(301) 528-8662

TABLE 11.1 (continued)

MASSACHUSETTS
Consumer
   Protection
   Division
Department of
   Attorney General
131 Tremont St.
Boston, MA 02111
(617) 727-8400

MICHIGAN
Consumer
   Protection
   Division
Office of Attorney
   General
P.O. Box 30213
Lansing, MI 48909
(517) 373-1140

MINNESOTA
Office of Consumer
   Services
Office of Attorney
   General
117 University Ave.
St. Paul, MN 55155
(612) 296-2331

MISSISSIPPI
Consumer
   Protection
   Division
Office of Attorney
   General
P.O. Box 22947
Jackson, MS 39225
(601) 354-6018

MISSOURI
Trade Offense
   Division

Office of Attorney
   General
P.O. Box 899
Jefferson City, MO
   65102
(800) 392-8222/
   (314) 751-3321

MONTANA
Consumer Affairs
   Unit
Dept. of Commerce
1424 9th Ave.
Helena, MT 59620
(406) 444-4312

NEBRASKA
Consumer
   Protection
   Division
Dept. of Justice
2115 State Capitol
P.O. Box 98920
Lincoln, NE 68509
(402) 471-2682

NEVADA
Commissioner of
   Consumer Affairs
Dept. of Commerce
State Mail Room
   Complex
Las Vegas, NV
   89158
(800) 992-0900/
   (702) 486-7355

NEW HAMPSHIRE
Consumer
   Protection and
   Antitrust Bureau

Office of Attorney
   General
State House Annex
Concord, NH
   03301
(603) 271-3641

NEW JERSEY
Dept. of the Public
   Advocate
CN 850 Justice
   Complex
Trenton, NJ 08625
(800) 792-8600/
   (609) 292-7087

NEW MEXICO
Consumer
   Protection
   Division
Office of Attorney
   General
P.O. Drawer 1508
Santa Fe, NM
   87504
(800) 432-2070/
   (505) 827-6060

NEW YORK
Bureau of Consumer
   Frauds and
   Protection
Office of Attorney
   General
120 Broadway
New York, NY
   10271
(212) 341-2345

TABLE 11.1 (continued)

NORTH
  CAROLINA
Consumer
  Protection Section
Office of Attorney
  General
P.O. Box 629
Raleigh, NC 27602
(919) 733-7741

NORTH DAKOTA
Consumer Fraud
  Section
Office of Attorney
  General
600 East Blvd.
Bismarck, ND
  58505
(800) 472-2600/
  (701) 224-3404

OHIO
Consumer Frauds
  and Crimes
  Section
Office of Attorney
  General
30 E. Broad St.
State Office Tower,
  25th fl.
Columbus, OH
  43266
(800) 282-0515/
  (614) 466-4986

OKLAHOMA
Office of Attorney
  General
420 W. Main, Suite
  550

Oklahoma City, OK
  73102
(405) 521-4274

OREGON
Financial Fraud
  Section
Dept. of Justice
Justice Bldg.
Salem, OR 97310
(503) 378-4320

PENNSYLVANIA
Bureau of Consumer
  Protection
Office of Attorney
  General
Strawberry Square,
  14th fl.
Harrisburg, PA
  17120
(800) 441-2555/
  (717) 787-9707

RHODE ISLAND
Consumer
  Protection
  Division
Dept. of Attorney
  General
72 Pine St.
Providence, RI
  02903
(800) 852-7776/
  (401) 277-2104

SOUTH
  CAROLINA
Dept. of Consumer
  Affairs
P.O. Box 5757

Columbia, SC
  29250
(800) 922-1594/
  (803) 734-9452

SOUTH DAKOTA
Division of
  Consumer Affairs
Office of Attorney
  General
State Capitol Bldg.
Pierre, SD 57501
(605) 773-4400

TENNESSEE
Antitrust &
  Consumer
  Protection
  Division
Office of Attorney
  General
450 James
  Robertson Pkwy.
Nashville, TN
  37243
(800) 342-8385/
  (615) 741-2672
Health club hotline:
  (800) 422-CLUB

TEXAS
Consumer
  Protection
  Division
Office of Attorney
  General
Capitol Station P.O.
  Box 12548
Austin, TX 78711
(512) 463-2070

TABLE 11.1 (continued)

UTAH
Division of
   Consumer
   Protection
Dept. of Commerce
160 E. Third St.
P.O. Box 45802
Salt Lake City, UT
   84145
(801) 530-6601

VERMONT
Public Protection
   Division
Office of Attorney
   General
109 State St.
Montpelier, VT
   05609
(802) 828-3171

VIRGINIA
Division of
   Consumer Affairs

Dept. of Agriculture
   and Consumer
   Services
P.O. Box 1163
Richmond, VA
   23219
(800) 451-1525/
   (804) 786-2042

WASHINGTON
Consumer and
   Business Fair
   Practices Division
Office of the
   Attorney General
900 Fourth Ave.,
   Suite 2000
Seattle, WA 98164
(800) 551-4636/
   (206) 464-6811

WEST VIRGINIA
Consumer
   Protection
   Division

Office of Attorney
   General
812 Quarrier St.,
   6th fl.
Charleston, WV
   25301
(800) 368-8808/
   (304) 348-8986

WISCONSIN
Office of Consumer
   Protection and
   Citizen Advocacy
Dept. of Justice
P.O. Box 7856
Madison, WI 53707
(800) 362-8189/
   (608) 266-1852

WYOMING
Office of Attorney
   General
123 State Capitol
   Bldg.
Cheyenne, WY
   82002
(307) 777-7874

12

Small-Claims Courts

IN THEORY, THE small-claims court may offer abused consumers a swift, cheap, and efficient mechanism for resolving their disputes. In practice, it may prove completely unsatisfactory, highly frustrating, or simply not usable. The outcome will depend on the nature of the complaint, the care with which each party prepares his or her case, and the limitations that state law imposes on its small-claims courts.

The basic principles underlying small-claims courts are admirable. Instead of burdening the wronged party with legal fees, the long delays caused by crowded court calendars, and the intimidating formalities of a full-blown jury trial, the small-claims court offers a swift, inexpensive, and less formal hearing that results in an immediate verdict.

Although each state sets its own rules for small-claims courts (see Table 12.1, page 244), and they vary considerably, in general, small-claims courts:

- are designed to be user-friendly and much less intimidating or formal than higher courts;
- charge a moderate fee for filing a suit—a fee that will

frequently be assessed against the defendant if the plaintiff wins the case;

- prefer that neither party uses a lawyer but do permit the use of exhibits and witnesses by either party;
- will automatically decide in favor of the plaintiff by default if the defendant fails to appear after receiving proper notice of the complaint and the time, date, and place of the trial;
- may schedule court calendars during evening and weekend hours to accommodate plaintiffs who can't appear during the working day;
- may award the plaintiff penalties or multiple damages if the defendant is shown to have violated the state's business-practices or consumer protection laws.

The small-claims trial itself is a fairly simple procedure. If you fail to appear when scheduled, your case may be either continued or dismissed "with prejudice," in which case it cannot be reinstated. If the defendant fails to appear, you will be awarded the judgment "by default" if you can prove the basic elements of your claim for damages.

Once the trial gets under way, each side is invited to present his or her version of the dispute, supporting it with documents (such as bills or receipts), exhibits (such as damaged or defective merchandise or photographs of it), and witnesses—either in person or by a sworn statement of fact. In addition, plaintiffs may be able to bring to the court evidence (from Better Business Bureau records or through filing a public-disclosure request with the attorney general) of the defendant's prior history of similar consumer abuses.

Each party is permitted to question and challenge the other without the strict adherence to procedural or evidentiary rules that are part of more formal courtroom practice. Nevertheless, plaintiffs should bear in mind that the most convincing evidence is that which cannot be refuted (or is admitted) by the defendant and has been carefully prepared to ensure maximum credibility.

TABLE 12.1
State Small-Claims Court Analysis

Explanatory Note

Filing fee: Where a range of fees is shown, the fee is usually based on the amount of the claim.

Service of Process: C = certified mail at regular postal rate unless otherwise noted; M = regular mail; P = personal service by court through sheriff's office or personal service by third party with an affidavit of service filed with the court (P + denotes an additional charge per mile); N = published notice. Service by certified mail is regarded as valid even if the defendant refuses delivery. Service by regular mail is regarded as valid unless the process is returned by the post office as undeliverable. Publication is used if the defendant has no mail address.

Damages: All courts award general damages; some award punitive damages (P) or damages for pain and suffering (PS).

Schedule: All courts operate on weekdays; some conduct evening (E) or Saturday (S) sessions.

Representation by Attorney: Some courts permit either side to be represented by an attorney; others do not.

Alternative Dispute Resolution: Some courts transfer cases to mediation or arbitration by an alternative dispute resolution organization. O = judge's option; V = voluntary by disputing parties; M = mandatory.

State	Maximum Claim	Typical Filing Fee	Process Service	Damages	Court Schedule	Attorney Permitted	Alternative Dispute Resolution
Alabama	$1,500	$25[1]	C, P, N			Yes	None
Alaska	$5,000	$25	C($10), P($35)	P PS		Yes	Being considered
Arizona	$1,500	$13–15	C($4), P($10+)			Yes[2]/No[3]	Criminal cases

Arkansas	$3,000	$18–38	C($6), P($15)			No	None
California	$5,000	$8[4]	C($5), P($20)	P PS	E, S[5]	No	O[5]
Colorado	$3,500	$9–26	C($4), P($15+)		E, S[5]	No	O
Connecticut	$2,000	$30	M, P($30+)			Yes	None
Delaware	$5,000	$30	C, P			Yes	None
District of Columbia	$2,000	$1	C, P($2+)	P PS	S	Yes	O
Florida	$2,500	$10–25[5]	C, P($12)	Local rules vary	E	Yes	M, O, V[6]
Georgia	$5,000	$20–25	P ($25)			Yes	O
Hawaii	$3,500	$10	C($3–5), P($15+)			Yes[7]	M
Idaho	$3,000	$25	C, P			No	None

[1] Includes service
[2] If dollar value greater than $1,500
[3] If dollar value less than $1,500
[4] Increases to $16 for each claim in excess of 12 filed in calendar year
[5] Varies by county
[6] Mandatory in some cases, optional in others, voluntary also available
[7] Except in security deposit disputes

TABLE 12.1 (continued)

State	Maximum Claim	Typical Filing Fee	Process Service	Damages	Court Schedule	Attorney Permitted	Alternative Dispute Resolution
Illinois	$2,500	$27–42	C($5.50), P($20)	P PS		Yes	None
Indiana	$6,000	$28	C($6), P($8)	P PS	E[5], S[5]	Yes	None
Iowa	$2,000	$30	C, P($15–25)	P PS		Yes	O
Kansas	$1,000	$18–38	C, P[8]	*[9]		No	O[5]
Kentucky	$1,500	$15	C, P($10)			Yes	None
Louisiana	$2,000	$35[1,5]	C, P	P PS		Yes	O
Maine	$1,400	$30–40	C($4.75), M[10], P($20–40)[11]			Yes	O
Maryland	$2,500	$5–10	C($5), P($30)	P PS		Yes	None
Massachusetts	$1,500	$14–19	C, P($20–30)			Yes	O
Michigan	$1,750	$12–22	C($4.70), P($10+)			No	O

Minnesota	$5,000 $6,000[12] $7,500[13]	$13[14]	M[15], P($20–25+)	P PS		Yes[16]	V
Mississippi	$1,000	$34–40[1]	P	P		Yes	In development
Missouri	$1,500	$8–13	C($4.79), P($20+)			Yes	O/V[17]
Montana	$3,000	$10	P($24)		S[18]	No	None
Nebraska	$1,800	$6	C, P($15)			No	None
Nevada	$2,500	$10–30	C, P($11–21+)			Yes	O

[8] May be accomplished by process server or party
[9] Statutory damages allowed for worthless checks
[10] Only allowed if defendant signs acknowledgment of service form
[11] Plaintiff may serve
[12] Effective 7/1/93
[13] Effective 7/1/94
[14] Plus local law library fee ($1–$10)
[15] $35 for Secretary of State to serve nonresident corporations by mail
[16] Minneapolis and St. Paul judges may limit participation, all others by court permission—seldom granted
[17] In limited jurisdictions
[18] Limited to initial appearance but no trials

TABLE 12.1 (continued)

State	Maximum Claim	Typical Filing Fee	Process Service	Damages	Court Schedule	Attorney Permitted	Alternative Dispute Resolution
New Hampshire	$2,500	$25	C, P($17)	P PS		Yes	O[19]
New Jersey	$1,000	$12	C($3), M($3)[20]	P PS	S[21]	Yes	M or O[1]
New Mexico	$5,000	$37	C, P($15–20)	Local rules vary		Yes	O
New York	$2,000	$3[22]	M, C($2.58)[23], P($10)	*[24]	E	Yes	None
North Carolina	$2,000	$34	C($3), P($5)	P PS		Yes	None[25]
North Dakota	$3,000	$10–13	C, P(varies)	P PS		No[26]	None
Ohio	$2,000	$19[1]	C, P($20)			Yes	V
Oklahoma	$2,500	$37–64	C($5), P($20)		E, S[5]	Yes	O
Oregon	$2,500	$34–68	M, N, C(2.75)[27], P($20)			No	M[5]
Pennsylvania	$4,000	$11–34	C, P($16)		E[5]	Yes	None

Rhode Island	$1,500	$14	C, P($45)		*28	Yes	None
South Carolina	$2,500	$35	P	P PS	E, S	Yes	O—ltd
South Dakota	$4,000	$9–25	C, P(varies)	P PS		Yes	None
Tennessee[29]	$10,000	$51	P	P PS		Yes	None
Texas	$5,000	$10	C, P($30)		*5	Yes	O[5]
Utah	$2,000	$20	P($6+)		No daily E—3 days	Yes	O

[19]Mediation program in one county

[20]Mailed by court

[21]Middlesex County one Saturday each month except June, July, August, and December

[22]Plus mail service

[23]If C fails then plaintiff must effect personal service (cost varies)

[24]Triple damages if defendant has at least 2 other unsatisfied judgments

[25]Unless case removed to district court then mandatory arbitration program in 26 counties

[26]Attorney may be present but may not argue your case. Notice to the other party that you will have your attorney present is required.

[27]Permitted if amount claimed is less than $50

[28]Court sessions limited to 1 or 2 days per week

[29]No statewide small-claims court system; courts of limited jurisdiction available in some counties, no statewide statistics collected

TABLE 12.1 (continued)

State	Maximum Claim	Typical Filing Fee	Process Service	Damages	Court Schedule	Attorney Permitted	Alternative Dispute Resolution
Vermont	$2,000	$25–35[30]	M, P(15)[31]		E[32]	Yes	O[5]
Virginia[33]	$10,000	$12–18	P	P PS		Yes	O
Washington	$2,500	$10[34]	C, P($11+)		E[35]	No	O[5]
West Virginia	$3,000	$20–40	P[36], C($7)[37]	P	E[5], S[5]	Yes	None
Wisconsin	$2,000	$27	M, P	P, PS	E[5]	Yes	None
Wyoming	$2,000	$10	P($3.30)			Yes	None

[30]Includes 1st class mail service, if no return acknowledgment to court then personal service necessary
[31]Court will mail certified to out-of-state defendants
[32]Experimental in one county
[33]2 urban judicial districts have separate small-claims procedures for amounts of $1,000 or less with no ADR; this system is in addition to the one described
[34]Some counties add $15 surcharge to fund ADR centers
[35]In 1 of 39 counties
[36]Included in fee unless plaintiff elects to use private process server
[37]Only if personal service fails. Garnishments handled separately ranging from $9–$29.

The judge will often question both parties, and a decision may be rendered within a few minutes or a few days. The decision will either dismiss the claim or award the plaintiff part or all of what was asked for.

Although many aggrieved consumers have found the small-claims court an inexpensive and relatively speedy route to redress, it is by no means a panacea, and filing a suit, no matter how meritorious, is no guarantee of ultimate satisfaction. Hence, before deciding to use the small-claims court, you need to decide whether any of the following limitations make it inadvisable in your case.

Filing the Suit

A major limitation to the use of small-claims court is the nearly universal requirement that suit be brought in the court nearest to the defendant's residence or place of business. This presents no obstacle if the defendant is a local dry cleaner or an antiques dealer in a neighboring county. But if you live in North Carolina and are suing a department store based in New York City, the process is likely to prove uneconomical. Even if the amount of the claim is large enough to justify your travel expenses, there is no certainty of a favorable verdict or that these expenses will be reimbursed even if you win.

As the table on page 244 indicates, small-claims courts differ not only in the fee charged for filing but also in the procedures and costs involved in initiating a suit by serving your opponent with a complaint and a summons—that is, a demand to appear in court to respond to your lawsuit. Some courts permit you to file and serve notice of your suit by mail; others, however, require you to file your suit in person and arrange for personal service (hand delivery) of the summons—again a problem for plaintiffs suing in a distant court.

Once you've filed a claim, you'll be assigned a date for the trial, but this date can be moved ahead if for some reason you cannot appear on the date assigned. How soon your case will come up depends, of course, on the court calendar, and delays of three months or more are not uncommon. At the time of filing, the court clerk will be able to answer questions about the court calendar.

Serving the Defendant

The procedure of serving the defendant with the papers ordering a court appearance also differs from one state to another. In some states, you or the clerk of court will serve the defendant by certified mail, and in such cases the summons is considered served even if the defendant refuses to accept the certified letter. Other states, however, require personal service and leave this responsibility (and its costs) to the plaintiff. Some of these states prohibit or discourage the plaintiff from serving the defendant in person (perhaps as a safeguard against the risk of personal injury or to avoid controversy as to whether the service was properly carried out).

Depending on the court rules in such situations, the plaintiff can either delegate the responsibility to anyone over the age of eighteen who is not involved in the case or hire the services of a sheriff or a legal messenger service. (If the plaintiff wins a favorable verdict, the costs of this service will be included in the judgment against the defendant.)

Some Further Limitations

As the dollar limit placed on small-claims court cases suggests, the small-claims court deals only in financial reimbursement—not in requiring or prohibiting behavior. It cannot, for example, direct your neighbor to keep her dog out of your garden, but it can order her to pay for the plants you had to replace as a result of the dog's trespassing. It cannot force your auto mechanic to fix your car properly, although it may order him to compensate you for his unsatisfactory work.

In the case of the auto mechanic who botched the job through substandard workmanship, you may need to have his work redone by another mechanic and then sue the first one for your reasonable costs. Similarly, if you are suing a dry cleaner for damaging your suede coat, a leather expert's estimate of the damage may not be sufficient: you may have to prove that you have actually paid for the repair or replacement. In both these instances, there is always the risk that you may lose the verdict and be left bearing the total cost.

Although some courts will award money for injury or serious inconvenience if the damage can be demonstrated objectively (if, for example, the defendant's actions caused you to be absent from work), few will award money for "pain and suffering," "emotional distress," or other subjective damages that are difficult to prove. But documented out-of-pocket costs, such as loss of a day's work or reasonable rental costs for a replacement vehicle, may be awarded.

Perhaps the most serious limitation of small-claims courts is the possibility that the defendant, before trial, may be able to raise the stakes by having the case moved to a higher court—a tactic that may persuade the plaintiff to hire a lawyer, even though this is not strictly necessary.

Appeals

If the verdict is hotly contested, either side can appeal to a higher court, although some states allow an appeal only if the amount involved exceeds a specified sum or for very narrow reasons. If the case goes to a higher court, both parties will probably need to hire an attorney and suffer additional delay, thus losing the major advantages of the small-claims court. Hence, both parties may be induced to forgo the appeal and settle the case.

Collecting the Judgment

Another serious limitation of the small-claims court is the difficulty of collecting your claim once you have won a verdict. If your defendant is a well-established business—a corporation, for example, or a solvent chain store, department store, or insurance company—you are likely to collect easily. In most such cases, you will receive a check upon presentation of the final judgment, perhaps on the spot or within a few days.

But if you are dealing with a small business or a financially unstable individual, you may have serious difficulty in collecting on the judgment. The small business may simply ignore the court's order, and the individual (especially if you won the verdict because he did not appear for trial) may be difficult to locate or, if found, prove to be indigent. Estimates on the actual collection of small-claims awards vary considerably, but the most optimistic is 50 percent and some run as low as 25 percent.

In such a situation, it helps to obtain an enforceable judgment from a higher court. (Sometimes this involves nothing more than filing your lower-court judgment and paying the filing fee.) With this judgment in hand, you can write a letter demanding payment from the plaintiff. If your letter gets no results, you can pursue enforcement by preparing a writ of execution (perhaps with the help of the court clerk or a private attorney) and, working through the sheriff's office, attach or seize some of the defendant's property (a vehicle or a boat, for example) and sell it to satisfy the judgment.

Alternatively, again with the help of an attorney, you may prepare a writ of garnishment, which entitles you to satisfy the judgment through deductions from the defendant's bank account or wages. Another possibility is to file a lien against the defendant's property—a home, a motor vehicle, or a boat, for example—which prohibits the defendant from selling the property without paying you.

Lastly, you can turn the judgment over to a collection agency, which will buy the account from you at a price substantially discounted from the face amount.

All these tactics will have associated costs. Some, but not all, of an attorney's charges may be collected from the defendant along with the judgment. And a collection agency is entitled to keep from one-third to half of what it manages to collect. Hence, unless the amount of the judgment is substantial, none of these tactics may prove worthwhile and your only satisfaction from the entire outcome may be the verdict's assurance that your suit was justified in principle—and perhaps that you caused the defendant some discomfort and anxiety.

IS SMALL-CLAIMS COURT RIGHT FOR YOU?

Before filing suit in small-claims court, you might consider the following questions:

Is your case, when viewed objectively, really airtight? Which of your arguments is the defendant likely to rebut successfully? In short, how sure are you of winning your case? Try taking the role of the defendant and think about the counterarguments he or she is likely to present.

Is your suit based largely or entirely on emotion, frustration, or resentment, or is it grounded on unbiased evidence, including documentable facts? To answer this question, you might present the case to a friend whose objectivity you trust and heed any advice and criticism.

Where is the court in which you will have to bring suit? If it's at a distance, are the time and cost of travel worthwhile even if you are not reimbursed?

Is the defendant "collectible"? If it is an established business, it probably is. But if the defendant is unlocatable, unservable, unemployed, poor, or otherwise judgmentproof, you may win the case but never collect a cent. Is "the principle of the thing" worth your effort?

If you find the answers to these questions reassuring, then the small-claims court is clearly worth using. But if the answers make you dubious, perhaps the better plan is, depending on the nature of your claim, to consult an attorney (who can sometimes get you restitution merely by writing a pithy letter) or to file a claim with your state's consumer protection agency, a cost-free procedure that involves much less time and may be just as effective. Lastly, if the plaintiff will agree to participate, you can use one of the alternative dispute-resolution services described in Chapter 13.

13

Alternative Dispute Resolution

A LTHOUGH MOST ABUSED consumers think first of a regulatory agency or a court as a mechanism for resolving their problem, another very useful resource may be one of the many nonjudicial organizations set up to resolve disputes. What with crowded court calendars and high attorney's fees, alternative dispute resolution has, in recent years, become increasingly popular. Indeed, some courts, instead of delivering a verdict, order the disputants to settle their differences through arbitration, mediation, or reconciliation—a policy that reduces overcrowding of the courts and thus benefits both the judicial process and the disputants. A superior court in one state, for example, refers to arbitration all cases involving less than $35,000. By doing so, it has reduced its case load by 90 percent and shortened the waiting period for trial from four years or more to 18 months.

In addition, many commercial contracts—those between stockbrokers and their customers, for example—stipulate that any differences between the signatories are to be settled by arbitration rather than formal court litigation. Similarly, some contracts between members of the Better Business Bureau and their customers stipulate that disputes are to be resolved by BBB arbitration.

Alternative dispute resolution can take the form of arbitration, mediation, or reconciliation. Arbitration is generally used to resolve more complex legal issues, such as the meaning of a contract or whether one party fulfilled its obligations when differing interpretations are the cause of the dispute. It can also be used to settle conflicting factual issues. It may involve a single, neutral arbitrator or a panel of arbitrators—typically three, one selected by each side, the third by mutual agreement. In many cases, the arbitrators' decision is binding on both parties, but in some cases either party can appeal to the courts.

Mediation is somewhat less formal than arbitration. It is less adversarial and typically nonbinding. Whereas arbitration usually results in a "you're right, he's wrong" decision, mediation attempts to settle disputes by compromise. Generally speaking, when mediation is effective, neither party emerges as the winner, but both parties come away feeling that whatever concessions they made were less costly than litigation would have been.

Reconciliation is the least formal and least coercive type of dispute resolution. It involves little more than a meeting (or a telephone conversation) between the disputants, arranged by a third party who suggests, in effect, "Why don't you two people get together and see whether you can't iron out your difficulties?" This third party need not participate in the meeting but may serve as a "facilitator," offering no legal advice and playing no part in the process other than convening the parties and suggesting a format.

Arbitration is generally directed by professional arbitrators and almost invariably involves costs, which are borne by both disputants. Some arbitrators are lawyers; others are judges who work on their own time in what have been called "rent-a-judge" organizations; still others are specialists in their field—in labor relations, for example. Mediation, on the other hand, is often provided by community organizations staffed by volunteers—some of them highly trained, others well-meaning amateurs. Some mediation centers, supported by grants or philanthropic gifts, do not charge the disputants; others impose a nominal fee or ask for a donation.

Despite their differences, arbitration and mediation have similar advantages and limitations. Both are informal and economical in terms of both time and money. If court calendars are crowded, as is normally the case, the dispute is likely to be settled weeks, months—and sometimes years—earlier than through litigation. And the fees charged by arbitrators or by those dispute-settlement centers that impose a fee are significantly lower than the costs incurred by taking the dispute to trial in a court of law.

Although the decisions reached by arbitrators are likely to be binding on both parties, in mediation one or both parties may resort to the courts if either is dissatisfied with the proposed settlement—although penalties may be imposed on the appealing party if the appeal is unsuccessful.

On the other hand, unless they are specified in a contract or by court rule, both arbitration and mediation require voluntary participation by both parties. Hence, neither can be used if one of the disputants intransigently refuses to participate, preferring to settle in a "real" court. Moreover, as the term *mediation* implies, each party must be prepared to compromise instead of stubbornly maintaining an absolute position.

Lastly, because in some situations the mediators are required to maintain strict neutrality, they may not be able to offer either of the disputants advice about available legal remedies. When neutrality is imposed on them, mediators have sometimes had to stand by in silence as the less assertive disputant accepted a grossly inequitable compromise that was clearly not in accord with the law and with the provable facts.

Nevertheless, despite these limitations, the growing trend toward nonjudicial or alternative dispute resolution would seem to indicate that it is an increasingly useful alternative to a lawsuit.

When arbitration is not ordered by a court or stipulated in a contract, the choice of an arbitration or mediation organization depends on the nature of the dispute, the amount it involves, and the acceptability of the arbitrators or mediators to both disputants. In addition to professional arbitrators, various public and private dispute-resolution programs are to be found in every major community. The American Arbitration Association, for example, resolves a wide range of commercial and industrial disputes; the American Automobile Association arbitrates auto-repair disputes involving their certified repair shops. Some branches of the Better Business Bureau offer mediation services. The state Lemon Law programs (see p. 45) arbitrate warranty disputes on new (and in some states on used) vehicles.

The typical community dispute-resolution center handles the following issues, often at no charge to the disputants:

- small claims involving money, personal property, and real estate;
- landlord-tenant disputes over deposits, damage, etc.;
- nuisances, such as noise, harassment, and similar neighborhood problems;
- merchant-customer disputes about refunds, exchanges, etc.;
- employer-employee disputes where there is no union;
- school problems involving staff, students, and parents.

Few community dispute-resolution centers will mediate disputes in which violence or physical abuse is involved, or when one or more of the parties is involved with drugs or alcohol or cannot adequately speak for him- or herself. The centers do not impose a settlement, and disputants unable to reach an agreement are free to pursue other options for settling their differences, including filing a lawsuit. These centers do not provide legal advice or services but will refer disputants to appropriate community resources.

The number and variety of local arbitration and mediation facilities are far too great to permit listing here. They can be found in the *Yellow Pages* under the headings "Arbitration" and "Mediation" in the disputants' community or in a nearby metropolitan area.

14

Filing a Lawsuit

IF YOUR CLAIM exceeds the limit set by the small-claims court (see Chapter 12), and if the other regulatory agencies have not been able to get your dispute resolved, your only alternative is to consult a lawyer about filing a suit against the offending party.

Before taking this step, however, you need to do some calm and careful thinking. To begin with, if the firm you are planning to sue is located in another state, suing may be impractical because your lawyer will either have to travel to that state or hire a lawyer who is licensed to practice there. Even if the firm is located in your own state, court costs and lawyer's fees can easily amount to more than you can hope to recover—unless the court awards punitive damages and your costs in bringing the action. In short, your indignation and your desire to "sue the bastards" may cost you much more than taking the loss and forgetting about it.

Finding a Lawyer

If, on the other hand, you decide that your case is worthwhile, your first task is to find a suitable lawyer. Although some people talk about "my lawyer," implying that they have an attorney on annual retainer, most people have little or no contact with attorneys except for such routine matters as will preparation or real estate closing. Such lawyers may not be suitable for the kind of action you are contemplating. What you need is a lawyer well versed in business and consumer law, and the will preparers and real estate closers may not be experienced or comfortable practicing in this relatively new and specialized area. But, in the absence of reliable word-of-mouth recommendations, they can refer you to a specialist who is better able to advise or represent you.

If you cannot get a reliable recommendation, you can consult the lawyer referral service provided by most state and county bar associations. Once you describe your problem specifically, the referral service is likely to suggest a competent lawyer with relevant experience who practices in your vicinity. Usually an initial consultation is offered at no charge or at nominal cost.

Whether you find the recommended lawyer satisfactory depends largely on your expectations. As a layperson, you have no way of assessing a lawyer's competence—just as patients have no way of assessing the competence of a new physician. Hence, like many patients, you may use personality and deskside manner as criteria. Bear in mind, however, that lawyerly competence is not always related to personal charm. The lawyer who strikes you as cold and unpleasant will presumably strike your opponent the same way. Roughly 75 percent of lawyers can be categorized as conciliators who prefer a reasonable settlement to the risks of a courtroom battle. The other 25 percent are known as "mad dogs" who flourish in the adversarial arena of the courtroom. Both groups have effective and ineffective members.

When you go to your first meeting with the lawyer, you should be fully prepared to give a clear account of the problem and bring all documents relating to it. Within half an hour or so, he or she should be able to advise you on whether you have a case and whether it is worth pursuing. No ethical lawyer would attempt to predict with certainty the outcome of every case, but by the same token, no ethical lawyer will encourage you to pursue a case that seems clearly hopeless.

Legal Fees

Because the question of fees and other costs can be sticky, you should not hesitate to discuss them frankly at the outset. Although no lawyer's estimate can be accurate to the last dollar, it should enable you to establish a comfort zone, especially if the lawyer agrees to notify you if unanticipated developments increase the costs significantly. At this stage, you should get a general notion of whether its estimated costs make the lawsuit worthwhile.

Contingency Fees

Some lawyers will offer to take your case on a contingency basis— that is, charging you nothing if you lose the case but taking a percentage of whatever you win. Such fees range from 20 to 50 percent depending on the nature and complexity of the case and on the limits set by state law.

The contingency basis has been widely praised as "the poor man's key to the courtroom," and there is no doubt that it makes possible lawsuits that could not have been initiated on a regular fee basis. On the other hand, it has some serious limitations.

To begin with, although the lawyer's *services* are "free," all other costs—for filing, fees for expert and lay witnesses, jury fees, transcripts, travel, and so on—will be charged to you, *win or lose*. Perhaps more important, if the lawyer is able to settle the case out of court simply by writing one or two letters, you may feel that the contingency basis results in gross overpayment.

Lastly, the contingency basis may influence the lawyer's advice to you about settling out of court. If your case is supported by admissible evidence and good-faith legal argument, your attorney is obligated to go to trial rather than accept a settlement that you haven't authorized, but it is possible, of course, for the attorney to distort your legal situation in the hope of avoiding the varied work involved in preparing for a trial by persuading you to accept a settlement.

Class Actions

Many abused consumers seek retribution through class actions, believing they are highly effective because of the considerable publicity they receive and the large damage awards they often win. In a class action, all individuals who claim to have suffered loss from the same company for similar reasons bring suit as a class, and all share in proportion to their losses any award, after attorney's fees and costs of the suit have been deducted if they have not been awarded by the court. Class actions, when they are successful, can win relief for each member of the class without any advance investment in attorney's fees.

In reality, however, a class action is very difficult and expensive to initiate. To begin with, the attorney—or, more probably, a large law firm—must discover whether the abused customer is in fact a member of a large class of consumers who have been similarly abused. If, for example, a woman's credit card company has injured her by violating some part of the federal Fair Credit Billing Act, is she a solitary victim or have thousands of other cardholders been injured by similar actions of the same company?

The attorney must first obtain court approval of the claim and certification by the court that a class of plaintiffs actually exists before being permitted to prosecute the case. To be recognized by a federal court, the class must consist of at least 100 members each with a claim of at least $25, and total damages must exceed $50,000.

Once the class is approved, the lawyer must make reasonable efforts to identify by name each member of the class, invite each of them to participate, and offer them the option of not participating and suing on their own. Only then can the suit be maintained on behalf of the class. Members of the class pay no attorney's fees in advance. These usually staggering fees are deducted from the final judgment or settlement with court oversight and approval, although some settlements may require that attorney's fees be paid by the defendant.

As is readily apparent, the preliminary procedures are both expensive and time-consuming and can usually be undertaken only by a major law firm that has sufficient capital to meet the initial costs. And such a firm is unlikely to take on a case unless the facts virtually ensure a favorable verdict. Furthermore, if the case is won, the amount of reimbursement to each member of the class may be quite small, even if it includes punitive damages against the defendant.

A class action does make sense when the amount of possible recovery for an individual plaintiff is too small to justify legal action other than a small-claims suit (see Chapter 12). In such circumstances, when a wronged plaintiff is joined by hundreds or thousands of others, the potential recovery and the efficiencies of a class action make it economically feasible.

All in all, however, a class action, although it may be appropriate for a very small number of consumer complaints, is not a practical alternative to an individual lawsuit.

15

State and Local Consumer Protection Resources

IN RESOLVING CONSUMER disputes, you are likely to get more effective help from state and local agencies, both private and public, than from the geographically and politically remote federal regulatory agencies. To begin with, they are more accessible—by telephone or personal visit. In addition, they are more likely to become aware of, to be concerned with, and to take action against local consumer abuses that are chronic or severe. Perhaps most important, because the state agencies are more politically accountable, they are far more likely than their federal counterparts to seek restitution for the individual consumer and to take punitive action against the offending firms.

Obviously, the effectiveness—and even the existence—of state and local agencies is not uniform throughout the country. Rural areas tend to be served less adequately than urban, and tax-poor states necessarily offer consumers less assistance than more affluent ones. The political climate, too, has a strong influence on consumer protection. Nevertheless, the following listing is likely to include at least some resources that can help you resolve almost any consumer dispute. The sequence in which they are listed is not intended to reflect their effectiveness. The list begins with organizations concerned with a very broad range of problems and ends with those that are more specialized.

NONGOVERNMENTAL AGENCIES

Action Line

One cost-free resource for abused consumers is "Action Line," a regular consumer protection feature of some metropolitan newspapers and, under a different designation, some local television stations. The Action Line editor or the television host invites written complaints from the public and sends them on to the supplier with the implicit threat that the response, positive or negative, may be displayed or broadcast for all to see. In addition, some Action Lines publish or broadcast early warnings of scams that have made their appearance in the area they serve.

Although the effectiveness of these programs varies widely (and few of them, if any, publish periodic scoreboards), some of them seem to avoid confrontations with local merchants, auto dealers or repair shops, or banks—presumably to avoid losing advertising revenues. And relatively few confront major corporations with serious and costly cases of consumer abuse. The bulk of the published complaints involve nondelivery of magazines bought through telephone subscriptions or of merchandise offered by the less reputable mail-order companies.

In addition, many of the cases submitted to such programs are resolved not by the newspaper or the television host but by the state attorney general's office or regulatory department to which they refer the problem.

Despite these limitations, however—and despite the fact that the number of Action Lines has decreased in recent years even more swiftly than the number of independent newspapers—filing an Action Line complaint is relatively easy, and it may be effective, especially if you notify the supplier that you are about to do so. Because Action Lines and television consumer programs reach a wide audience, they can generate a volume of complaints that can result in prompt identification and correction of the abuse.

Better Business Bureau

This agency, with almost two hundred offices throughout the United States and Canada, is supported entirely by contributions from its member businesses. It monitors marketplace ethics in several ways. Firms that belong to it commit themselves to fair business practices and to arbitration of any customer disputes. In addition, the Better Business Bureau maintains complaint records on both member and nonmember firms and, in cases of flagrant abuse, issues press releases about unethical actions of businesses.

Some branches provide alternative dispute-resolution services to settle disputes between nonmember businesses and customers. Usually both sides must agree to a binding arbitration, arrived at after hearings by volunteer arbitrators who have been trained by professionals. The most significant dispute-resolution program set up by the bureau—AUTOLINE—provides mediation as well as binding arbitration between complainants and automobile companies. Many automobile manufacturers (Chrysler, Ford, and Toyota are exceptions) participate in the AUTOLINE program. Critics have pointed out, however, that AUTOLINE arbitration decisions tend to favor the manufacturer and that state Lemon Law arbitration, when the decision is binding, generally provides greater consumer satisfaction.

Although the bureau won't provide legal advice or evaluate or endorse specific businesses, it does actively promote consumer education by publishing buying guides and pamphlets on a variety of topics. As a member of the National Advertising Review Council, it monitors national advertising and works toward the modification or discontinuance of misleading or false advertising. In addition, its *Annual Charity Index* provides information on some two hundred national charitable organizations.

There are, of course, some limitations to Better Business Bureau policies. One is that many member firms require customers to commit themselves to BBB arbitration in the event of a dispute, thus depriving them of seeking recourse through consumer protection alternatives. In addition, in response to consumer inquiries about a firm's history of complaints, the BBB will report only complaints that have been totally unresolved and not those that have been lodged but settled by arbitration. Since BBB members are committed to arbitration, their complaint histories are likely to look better than those of nonmembers.

The location of the nearest office of the BBB can be obtained from the Council of Better Business Bureaus, 4200 Wilson Blvd., Arlington, VA 22203, (703) 276-0100.

Legal Assistance and Lawyer Referral

Consumers who need legal advice—to determine either what their rights are or whether these rights are worth litigating—have several sources of help and referral. Many state bar associations make two kinds of referral. Indigent clients are referred to individual lawyers, law firms, and groups of lawyers who will take on their cases at no cost. Clients who do not meet the means test for pro bono service may be referred to lawyers who offer an initial consultation at no cost or for a nominal fee. One state bar association, for example, arranges a 30-minute consultation with one of its members for a nominal fee of $20, which goes to the association and not to the member.

Landlord-Tenant Disputes

In a number of areas, privately funded organizations under such names as the Tenants Union advise tenants about their legal rights and obligations and may mediate landlord-tenant disputes. These organizations tend to be more user-friendly than the government agencies that regulate residential rentals.

Professional Associations

A wide range of professionals and other skilled practitioners—for example, attorneys, physicians, dentists, optometrists, accountants, real estate brokers, funeral directors, and cosmetologists—belong to statewide organizations (usually called associations) that, among other functions, maintain professional standards and monitor professional practices. Because their members either control or strongly influence the licensing process, these professional associations have been accused of limiting competition within the profession. But they are also responsible for disciplining any member who is unethical or negligent.

These associations have also been charged with protecting their membership against the general public by dismissing consumer complaints or by delaying their investigation interminably. But such charges are difficult to prove because, since the complaints remain confidential, there is no way of knowing how many of them are valid and how many are dismissed because they are in fact groundless or because the association lacks the funds and staff necessary to investigate them fully.

However, although individual complaints may be groundless, these associations do have an interest in the reputation of their profession and in weeding out clearly unacceptable behavior. Hence, numerous complaints against an individual practitioner from unrelated individuals—especially if they are similar in nature—are likely to prove difficult for the association to ignore or dismiss.

In many cases, the consumer's threat to complain to the association is enough to persuade the practitioner to resolve the dispute. This is especially likely if the practitioner is aware that earlier complaints have been lodged against him or her.

These associations are usually located in the state capital or the state's largest city. Their addresses can be obtained from any member, from telephone directories, or through the reference section of the nearest library.

Consumer Credit Counseling Service

Sponsored by merchants and lenders who offer consumer credit, the Consumer Credit Counseling Service provides assistance to consumers who, through loss of employment or other financial emergency or through an uncontrolled use of credit cards, find themselves so overwhelmed by debt that they consider bankruptcy the only way out. Because the sponsoring creditors would stand to get nothing in the case of bankruptcy, they authorize the Consumer Counseling Service to work out a lower and therefore manageable schedule of payments, often suspending interest charges on the outstanding debt.

The location of the nearest CCCS office can be obtained from the National Foundation for Consumer Credit, Inc., 8611 Second Ave., Suite 100, Silver Spring, MD 20910, (301) 589-5600.

STATE GOVERNMENT AGENCIES

By far the most widely used—and most effective—state agency is the consumer protection division of the attorney general's office. This organization processes the widest range of consumer complaints, and it is discussed in detail in Chapter 11. The agencies described below deal with a narrower range of consumer problems.

Lemon Law

A steadily increasing number of states have adopted a Lemon Law to protect consumers who have warranty problems with *new* cars, and the Lemon Laws of some states apply also to *used* cars. The eligibility for such programs—that is, the determination of precisely what constitutes a "lemon"—varies from one state to another, but some states have achieved remarkable results in requiring automobile manufacturers to buy back a defective vehicle or to offer the owner substantial remuneration not only for repair costs but also for loss of time. For detailed information on state Lemon Laws, see Chapter 3.

Housing

Real estate transactions are regulated by a state board, which approves contracts between realtor and client, licenses realtors, and accepts complaints about them. Residential leasing is usually regulated by state laws, but individual communities may have municipal agencies that deal with such issues as eviction, mobile-home-park leases, rental increases, condominium rules, and discrimination. The latter is also dealt with by the U.S. Department of Housing and Urban Development.

Utilities

Every state has an agency—in some cases a free-standing commission, in others part of another state commission—that regulates the rates of such public utilities as electric, gas, water, and telephone service. Most of these commissions adjudicate complaints that the consumer cannot resolve with the utility itself. A substantial number of complaints may produce commission action on rates and services.

Banking and Investments

Although national banks and federally chartered credit unions and savings and loan associations are regulated by the federal government, state banks are under the control of the state banking commission. In addition, a state securities commission regulates locally issued securities and the behavior of local stockbrokers, financial advisers, and others involved in the sale of investment instruments.

Insurance

In every state, an official designated variously as the Insurance Commissioner or the Supervisor of Insurance is responsible for licensing insurance companies to do business within the state, for regulating premiums, and for monitoring the processing of claims, deceptive advertising, and other questionable practices.

As with other state agencies, the effectiveness of the commissioner depends in part on the state budget and in part on the ideology of the governor, the legislature, and the actual commissioner. Some commissioners are do-nothing political appointees who have little interest in or understanding of the industry. Others have been labeled as spokesmen for and defenders of the industry. But still others are strongly committed to the interests of the consumer and have published informative guidebooks listing the least expensive policies from the most reliable companies.

Because insurance companies that market policies through television commercials or mass mailings may be unreliable, overpriced, or unstable, you should check with the insurance commissioner to make certain that these companies are licensed to do business in the state and have a good record of paying claims. State licensing is no guarantee that an insurance company is sound, but any offer from an unlicensed company is totally unacceptable.

Any difficulties that you encounter with insurance—automobile, casualty, homeowner's, life, or health—should be referred to the commissioner rather than to the attorney general (who has no jurisdiction over insurance). Presumably in deference to the powerful insurance lobby, insurance commissioners are unlikely to offer any help in collecting a disputed claim. But a significant number of complaints against a specific company can lead to action. If the amount you claim exceeds the maximum permitted in small-claims court (see Chapter 12), your only recourse is a private attorney.

Professional and Occupational Licensing Boards

All states have licensing boards that regulate not only the professions but also a number of occupations: for example, banking, securities trading, mortuary service, automobile sales and repair,

TABLE 15.1
State Insurance Commissioners

ALABAMA
Insurance
  Commissioner
135 S. Union St.,
  Rm. 181
Montgomery, AL
  36130
(205) 269-3550

ALASKA
Director of
  Insurance
P.O. Box D
Juneau, AK 99811
(907) 465-2515

ARIZONA
Director of
  Insurance
3030 N. Third St.,
  Suite 1100
Phoenix, AZ 85012
(602) 255-5400

ARKANSAS
Insurance
  Commissioner
400 University
  Tower Bldg.
Little Rock, AR
  72204
(501) 371-1325

CALIFORNIA
Commissioner of
  Insurance
100 Van Ness Ave.
San Francisco, CA
  94102

San Francisco: (800)
  233-9045/(415)
  557-3245
Los Angeles: (800)
  927-HELP/(213)
  736-2551

COLORADO
Commissioner of
  Insurance
303 W. Colfax Ave.,
  Suite 500
Denver, CO 80204
(303) 866-6400

CONNECTICUT
Insurance
  Commissioner
P.O. Box 816
Hartford, CT 06142
(203) 297-3800

DELAWARE
Insurance
  Commissioner
841 Silver Lake
  Blvd.
Dover, DE 19901
(800) 282-8611/
  (302) 739-4251

DISTRICT OF
  COLUMBIA
Superintendent of
  Insurance
614 H St., NW,
  Suite 516
Washington, DC
  20001
(202) 727-7424

FLORIDA
Insurance
  Commissioner
Plaza Level 11—
  The Capitol
Tallahassee, FL
  32399
(800) 342-2762/
  (904) 488-3440

GEORGIA
Insurance
  Commissioner
2 Martin L. King,
  Jr., Dr.
Atlanta, GA 30334
(404) 656-2056

HAWAII
Insurance
  Commissioner
P.O. Box 3614
Honolulu, HI 96811
(808) 586-2790

IDAHO
Director of
  Insurance
500 S. 10 St.
Boise, ID 83720
(208) 334-2250

ILLINOIS
Director of
  Insurance
320 W. Washington
  St.
Springfield, IL
  62767
(217) 782-4515

INDIANA
Commissioner of
  Insurance
311 W. Washington
  St., Suite 300
Indianapolis, IN
  46204
(800) 622-4461/
  (317) 232-2385

IOWA
Insurance
  Commissioner
Lucas State Office
  Bldg., 6th fl.
Des Moines, IA
  50319
(515) 281-5705

KANSAS
Commissioner of
  Insurance
420 SW 9th St.
Topeka, KS 66612
(800) 432-2484/
  (913) 296-7801

KENTUCKY
Insurance
  Commissioner
229 W. Main St.
P.O. Box 517
Frankfort, KY
  40602
(502) 564-3630

LOUISIANA
Commissioner of
  Insurance
P.O. Box 94214

Baton Rouge, LA
  70804
(504) 342-5900

MAINE
Superintendent of
  Insurance
State House Station
  34
Augusta, ME 04333
(207) 582-8707

MARYLAND
Insurance
  Commissioner
501 St. Paul Pl., 7th
  fl. S.
Baltimore, MD
  21202
(800) 492-7521/
  (301) 333-2520

MASSACHUSETTS
Commissioner of
  Insurance
280 Friend St.
Boston, MA 02114
(617) 727-7189,
  ext. 300

MICHIGAN
Commissioner of
  Insurance
Insurance Bureau
P.O. Box 30220
Lansing, MI 48909
(517) 373-9273

MINNESOTA
Commissioner of
  Commerce

133 E. 7th St.
St. Paul, MN 51101
(612) 296-2594

MISSISSIPPI
Commissioner of
  Insurance
1804 Walter Sillers
  Bldg.
Jackson, MS 39201
(800) 562-2957/
  (601) 359-3569

MISSOURI
Director of
  Insurance
301 W. High St.,
  Rm. 630
P.O. Box 690
Jefferson City, MO
  65102
(800) 726-7390/
  (314) 751-4126

MONTANA
Commissioner of
  Insurance
P.O. Box 4009
Helena, MT 59604
(800) 332-6148/
  (406) 444-2040

NEBRASKA
Director of
  Insurance
941 "O" St., Suite
  400
Lincoln, NE 68508
(402) 471-2201

TABLE 15.1 (continued)

NEVADA
Commissioner of
  Insurance
1665 Hot Springs
  Rd.
Capitol Complex
  152
Carson City, NV
  89710
(800) 992-0900/
  (702) 687-4270

NEW HAMPSHIRE
Insurance
  Commissioner
169 Manchester St.
Concord, NH
  03301
(800) 852-3416/
  (603) 271-2261

NEW JERSEY
Commissioner
Department of
  Insurance
20 W. State St.
  CN325
Trenton, NJ 08625
(609) 292-5363

NEW MEXICO
Superintendent of
  Insurance
PERA Bldg., Rm.
  428
P.O. Drawer 1269
Santa Fe, NM
  87504
(505) 827-4500

NEW YORK
Superintendent of
  Insurance
160 W. Broadway
New York, NY
  10013
(800) 342-3736/
  (212) 602-0429

NORTH
  CAROLINA
Commissioner of
  Insurance
Dobbs Bldg.
P.O. Box 26387
Raleigh, NC 27611
(800) 662-7777/
  (919) 733-7343

NORTH DAKOTA
Commissioner of
  Insurance
Capitol Bldg., 5th fl.
600 East Boulevard
  Ave.
Bismarck, ND
  58505
(800) 247-0560/
  (701) 224-2440

OHIO
Director of
  Insurance
2100 Stella Ct.
Columbus, OH
  43266
(800) 585-1526/
  (614) 644-2651

OKLAHOMA
Insurance
  Commissioner

P.O. Box 53408
Oklahoma City, OK
  73152
(800) 522-0071/
  (405) 521-2828

OREGON
Insurance
  Commissioner
21 Labor &
  Industries Bldg.
Salem, OR 97310
(503) 378-4271

PENNSYLVANIA
Insurance
  Commissioner
Strawberry Sq., 13th
  fl.
Harrisburg, PA
  17120
(717) 787-5173

RHODE ISLAND
Insurance
  Commissioner
233 Richmond St.
Providence, RI
  02903
(401) 277-2246

SOUTH
  CAROLINA
Insurance
  Commissioner
P.O. Box 100105
Columbia, SC
  29202
(800) 768-3467/
  (803) 737-6617

TABLE 15.1 (continued)

SOUTH DAKOTA
Director of
 Insurance
910 E. Sioux Ave.
Pierre, SD 57501
(605) 773-3563

TENNESSEE
Commissioner of
 Insurance
500 James
 Robertson Pkwy.
Nashville, TN
 37243
(800) 342-4029/
 (615) 741-2241

TEXAS
Director
Claims and
 Compliance
 Division
State Board of
 Insurance
P.O. Box 149091
Austin, TX 78714
(800) 252-3439/
 (512) 463-6501

UTAH
Commissioner of
 Insurance

3110 State Office
 Bldg.
Salt Lake City, UT
 84114
(801) 530-6400

VERMONT
Commissioner of
 Banking and
 Insurance
120 State St.
Montpelier, VT
 05620
(802) 828-3301

VIRGINIA
Commissioner of
 Insurance
700 Jefferson Bldg.
P.O. Box 1157
Richmond, VA
 23209
(800) 552-7945/
 (804) 786-3741

WASHINGTON
Insurance
 Commissioner
Insurance Bldg.
 AQ21
Olympia, WA
 98504

(800) 562-6900/
 (206) 753-7301

WEST VIRGINIA
Insurance
 Commissioner
2019 Washington
 St. E.
Charleston, WV
 25305
(800) 642-9004/
 (304) 348-3394

WISCONSIN
Commissioner of
 Insurance
P.O. Box 7873
Madison, WI 53707
(800) 236-8517/
 (608) 266-3585

WYOMING
Commissioner of
 Insurance
Herschler Bldg.
122 W. 25 St.
Cheyenne, WY
 82002
(800) 442-4333/
 (307) 777-7401

building contractors, auctioneers, collection agencies, barbers, cosmetologists, and realtors. In some cases, licensure requires an examination that measures competence: in others the licensee must, in addition, show evidence of a bond that may be used to reimburse dissatisfied clients. Although most of these state boards are composed of practitioners, some of them include a "public member"—that is, a layperson appointed specifically to protect the interests of the occupation's clients or customers.

These boards generally accept consumer complaints, although, like the professional associations, they are likely to take action only if numerous complaints accumulate against one practitioner. Moreover, since their membership consists largely of practitioners, they may be biased against the consumer. Nevertheless, the threat of reporting a practitioner to the licensing board may be a useful weapon in resolving a dispute.

Household Moving

Most states regulate intrastate movers through a transportation commission or a branch of the utilities commission.

State Department of Revenue

This department can provide information about which goods and services, no matter where purchased, are subject to state sales tax.

Legislators

The attorney general's office (see Chapter 11), because it functions as the law firm for the state itself, cannot accept complaints against any governmental agency, state or local. But legislators at the state, county, or local level will often act on behalf of their constituents who experience difficulties with government bodies on such issues as property taxes, zoning, driver licensing, and others.

Legislators are an excellent resource for two reasons. First, because they depend on voter support at the next election, they tend to be zealous in providing "constituent services." Second, because the offending agency may depend on the legislator for budgetary and policy support, it is likely to respond more promptly to a call or a letter from him or her on behalf of an aggrieved constituent and to resolve the problem swiftly.

In addition to helping consumers resolve their disputes, conscientious legislators monitor these disputes to determine whether further regulation is needed to strengthen existing regulatory agencies or whether specific government agencies just need to "shape up."

Because legislators may in some cases be your last resort, they should be used only after the "Let me talk to your superior" tactic has reached the top of the bureaucratic hierarchy without resolving the problem.

OTHER REMEDIES

The great advantage of the resources described in this chapter is that they do not charge you for their services. The disadvantage is that, no matter how legitimate your complaint, they are not always effective because they lack the will, the enforcement authority, the budget, or the human resources necessary to pursue each individual complaint.

Hence, if you get no restitution through these agencies and if your complaint is sufficiently serious, you should consider taking legal action, beginning, if possible, with the small-claims court (see Chapter 12), or, if necessary, with a private attorney (see Chapter 14).

16

National and Federal Consumer Protection Resources

THE GREAT ADVANTAGE shared by the various national and federal consumer protection organizations and agencies is a nationwide perspective that enables them to spot emerging trends in consumer abuse and thus, through press releases and other publicity, warn the consumer against them. In addition, the federal agencies have enormous resources when prosecuting offenders. Whether or not they exploit these advantages most effectively is another matter. Both nongovernmental and federal agencies have, as we shall note, serious—at times disabling—limitations.

NONGOVERNMENTAL ORGANIZATIONS

Independent Consumer Protection Groups

Several national organizations, supported by subscriptions, membership dues, foundation grants, and other means, are dedicated entirely to the welfare of the consumer. Although few of them will undertake the processing of individual complaints, many of them use consumer information on current problems to guide policy and determine future activities.

American Automobile Association
1000 AAA Drive
Heathrow, FL 32746

The AAA's mediation service, AUTOSOLVE, may be useful for consumers who are ineligible for their state's Lemon Law and who cannot resolve the problem with the manufacturer. In addition, the AAA certifies service stations and mediates complaints against them.

Bankcard Corporation of America
560 Herndon Parkway
Herndon, VA 22070

Dedicated to the interests of credit card holders, this organization publishes lists of the fees and interest rates charged by card issuers and of banks that offer secured credit cards (see p. 143).

Center for Automotive Safety
2001 S St., SW
Washington, DC 20009

Although primarily concerned with automotive safety, this organization is a source of information about "secret warranties" on automobiles and problems about mobile homes. Complaints can alert this organization to imminent problems.

Center for Science in the Public Interest
1875 Connecticut Ave., #300
Washington, DC 20009

With a 250,000 membership consisting primarily of scientists, journalists, and lawyers, the center studies the effects of technology on society and monitors the effectiveness of the federal regulation of the safety and marketing of food products.

Consumer Credit Counseling Service
8611 Second Ave., Suite 100
Silver Spring, MD 20910

Supported by credit card issuers and other institutions that offer consumer credit, local branches of this organization attempt to mediate between the creditor and the overextended debtor by easing the payment schedule. It will not assist debtors who do not have a current source of income.

Consumer Federation of America
1424 16 St., NW, #604
Washington, DC 20036

With a membership consisting of national, state, and local consumer advocacy and protection groups, consumer cooperatives, and labor organizations, the federation gathers and disseminates information on consumer issues and represents the consumer before Congress, the regulatory agencies, and the courts.

Consumers Union of America
101 Truman Ave.
Yonkers, NY 10703

Best known as the publisher of *Consumer Reports,* this organization has a long-standing reputation as a staunch defender of consumer rights. Although it does not process individual complaints, it welcomes them as a source of information about current abuses. The April issue of *Consumer Reports* offers guidance on new and used car models, and a pricing service on new and used cars is available for a fee.

Council of Better Business Bureaus
4200 Wilson Blvd.
Arlington, VA 22203

This organization, which coordinates the activities of local BBB branches, can provide consumers with the address of the nearest local office (see Chapter 15). Its reports on deceptive advertising and charities are available to the public. It also sponsors

AUTOLINE, which arbitrates disputes between dealers and buyers of new cars.

National Consumers League
815 15 St., NW
Washington, DC 20005

Established in 1899 to fight against child labor, exploitative wage levels, and unsafe food and drug products, this membership organization continues its research, education, and advocacy on these issues but is also concerned with consumer protection in such areas as finances, telecommunications, and fraud. It cosponsors the National Fraud Information Center, which invites consumer inquiries at (800) 876-7060.

Public Citizen
P.O. Box 1904
Washington, DC 20036

Founded by Ralph Nader, this group's consumer advocacy agenda includes corporate and government accountability, fairness in the marketplace, and environmentally safe energy uses.

Public Citizen Health Research Group
2000 P St., NW, #700
Washington, DC 20036

Focusing on health care delivery, drug regulation, and environmental safety, this group monitors the enforcement of health regulations, testifies before Congress, and petitions or files suit against federal agencies on behalf of the consumer.

Public Interest Research Group
215 Pennsylvania Ave., SE
Washington, DC 20003

This group does research and lobbying on a broad range of consumer and environmental issues. Much of its activity occurs at the state level in such organizations as PIRGIM (Public Interest Research Group in Michigan) or PIRGWA (Public Interest Research Group in Washington).

Professional Organizations

National professional organizations such as the American Bar Association, the American Dental Association, and the American Medical Association do nothing to aid clients and patients, although the American Bar Association (1800 M St., NW, Washington, DC 20036) publishes a list of state and local alternative dispute-resolution programs. Generally, complaints against licensed professionals should be addressed to the state professional licensing agency or to the state or county professional organization. Presumably abuses that are widespread may reach the national organizations through their own membership.

Trade and Industry Associations

Most trade associations were initially established to promote and protect the interests of their members. But because a flood of unresolved consumer complaints would, of course, threaten their membership's image, they have taken some responsibility for adjusting or mediating these complaints, thus diverting them from possible litigation or broad public exposure.

One might assume that these organizations, because they are membership-supported, would, in mediating a dispute, tend to favor the accused member rather than the accusing consumer. Unfortunately, their impartiality is almost impossible to evaluate because statistics are not available. Nevertheless, where statistics on case disposition are available, they indicate that the arbitration panels set up by the automobile industry, for example, have been significantly less favorable to the consumer than the state-supervised arbitration mandated by state Lemon Laws.

The list of these associations is large, ranging from the American Apparel Manufacturers Association to the U.S. Tour Operators Association. Because of space limitations, the following list is limited to organizations that the consumer is most likely to use and that offer consumers direct assistance or referral to local agencies. The reader who does not find a relevant listing here should ask the manufacturer whether an association exists or should consult the well-indexed *Encyclopedia of Associations* (available in most public libraries) or the *Consumer's Resource Handbook* (published by the U.S. Office of Consumer Affairs and available free from the Consumer Information Center, Pueblo, CO 81009).

American Hotel and Motel Association
1201 New York Ave., NW, #600
Washington, DC 20005

American Newspaper Publishers Association
P.O. Box 17022
Washington, DC 20041

Investigates fraudulent advertising published in newspapers.

American Society of Travel Agents
P.O. Box 23992
Washington, DC 23992

Automotive Consumer Action Program
8400 Westpark Dr.
McLean, VA 22102

Provides third-party dispute resolution through the National Automobile Dealers Association.

Better Hearing Institute
P.O. Box 1840
Washington, DC 20013

Mediates complaints against suppliers of hearing aids.

Cemetery Consumer Service Council
P.O. Box 3574
Washington, DC 20007

Direct Marketing Association
6 East 43rd St.
New York, NY 10017

This organization handles complaints against mail-order firms that comprise its membership. It is unlikely to be effective against the less reputable firms that do not belong to it. In addition, the organization's Mail-Order Action Line will accept requests from consumers to have their names removed from catalogue-mailing or telephone-solicitation lists.

Funeral Service Consumer Arbitration Program
1614 Central St.
Evanston, IL 60201

Major Appliances Consumer Action Panel
20 N. Wacker Drive
Chicago, IL 60606

This organization offers third-party resolution of disputes involving such items as refrigerators and ranges.

National Association of Securities Dealers
33 Whitehall St., 10th fl.
New York, NY 10004

Offers third-party resolution of disputes concerning over-the-counter securities and corporate bonds.

North American Securities Administrators Association
555 New Jersey Ave., NW
Washington, DC 20001

This organization is concerned with protecting the interests of the small investor.

U.S. Tour Operators Association
211 E. 51st St., #12-B
New York, NY 10022

"Corporate Contacts"

Whether or not they belong to a trade or industry association, some major producers of consumer goods—ranging from chewing tobacco and breakfast cereals to computers and automobiles—have set up toll-free numbers for consumer inquiries and complaints. The *Consumer's Resource Handbook* (U.S. Office of Consumer Affairs) lists addresses and telephone numbers of several hundred such "corporate contacts."

An appeal to these organizations may be a simple step that the consumer might take when the supplier is unwilling to resolve a dispute. But unless the complaint is acknowledged promptly and an investigation promised, the consumer should not delay pursuing governmental channels such as small-claims court or the regulatory agencies.

FEDERAL AGENCIES

The federal regulatory agencies—the Food and Drug Administration, the Federal Communications Commission, the Federal Trade Commission, and others—are the subject of three distinct stereotypes. Some people see them as staunch defenders of the health and welfare of the American citizen. Others see them as toadies of the business interests and those members of Congress whose political campaigns are subsidized by business interests. Still others see them as bureaucratic behemoths bloated in their staffing, ponderous in their everyday routines, and operating on a geologic time scale.

Like all stereotypes, each of these contains an element of truth.

Slow and bureaucratic though its procedures may be (especially from the point of view of drug manufacturers eager to bring a new medication to market), the Food and Drug Administration has saved countless lives and millions of dollars by keeping unsafe or ineffective medications and medical devices off the market. And the Federal Trade Commission has done much to prohibit and prose-cute exploitative credit practices, deceptive advertising, fraudulent mail-order schemes, and abusive collection agency practices.

On the other hand, it is also true that effectiveness of these agencies is regularly blunted by pressures from industry and from industry-friendly legislators at several junctures. When consumer protective legislation is in the making, lobbyists of the affected industries are as active (and use the same tactics) as those em-ployed by the National Rifle Association. Even if the legislation is passed despite their efforts, the lobbyists don't abandon their cause because, although Congress has *authorized* the legislation, its precise *formulation* and *implementation* result only after months-long public hearings and "rule-making" sessions, and it is here that the lobbyists can be most effective in "gentling," if not emasculating, the regulations.

No matter how strong the legislation that emerges from this process, it can be enforced only by a large and well-trained staff, and the special interests can prevent this situation simply by urg-ing legislators to cut the offending agency's budget. Budgetary re-straints not only restrict the number and scope of investigations but often prevent the hiring or retention of thoroughly competent staffs. In much litigation, the government's lawyers are no match for the high-priced legal teams hired by the defendant, and govern-ment lawyers who perform brilliantly despite a lack of resources are often hired by the defending law firms for their experience in such litigation.

In addition to budgeting restraints, federal agencies often face other staffing problems. Many of their administrators come from (or are nominated by) the industry itself, since it is unlikely that anyone outside the industry would have the expertise necessary to regulate it. And many of these administrators tend to favor the industry, not necessarily because they are corrupt but simply because they understand the industry's problems better than those of its customers.

Even when an agency, having survived these difficulties, takes action in favor of the consumer, it can be reversed by the political process. When, for example, the Environmental Protection Agency published a pamphlet urging consumers to use environmentally friendly and inexpensive household products for cleaning instead of expensive and environment-damaging proprietary products, Procter and Gamble, leading a consortium of affected manufacturers, managed to have the pamphlet withdrawn from publication. When a federal agency published an extremely useful automobile-buying guide, the Reagan administration had its publication canceled because it threatened the domestic automobile industry. And the auto manufacturers incessantly and effectively opposed government regulations intended to improve fuel efficiency and reduce collision damage. Although the auto industry promotes its safety devices now, it steadfastly resisted the mandatory installation of seatbelts and turn signals as long as possible.

These limitations, however, should not inhibit the abused consumer from filing a complaint that could increase the number of complaints to the critical point necessary to launch an investigation and possible prosecution of the offending firm or industry.

The following list of regulatory agencies is ranked in terms of the range of complaints the agency will handle—from broad to specialized. Although they are centered in Washington, D.C., many of these agencies have regional branches. If these are not specified below, they can be obtained from the Federal Information Center, which maintains toll-free numbers in thirty-seven states. The telephone numbers listed for each agency are dedicated consumer hotlines. Where no telephone number appears, the agency deals with mail inquiries only.

Federal Trade Commission
6th & Pennsylvania Ave., NW, #130
Washington, DC 20580

One of the mandates of this large and powerful agency is the monitoring of the marketplace to prevent misleading and deceptive advertising, package labeling, credit practices, and other types of consumer fraud or abuse. Its Bureau of Consumer Protection (6th and Pennsylvania Ave., NW, Washington, DC 20580) publishes a series of highly informative, free pamphlets on a wide range of consumer problems.

In general, the FTC does for the country as a whole what state attorneys general do in their own jurisdictions except that it rarely attempts to resolve individual complaints. If, however, it receives a significant number of complaints about either an individual firm or a widespread consumer fraud, it will take enforcement action. For this reason, the consumer who has filed a complaint with the state attorney general should file it also with the nearest of the following branch offices:

1718 Peachtree St., NW,
   Rm. 1000
Atlanta, GA 30367
(404) 347-4836

10 Causeway St.
Boston, MA 02222
(617) 565-7240

55 E. Monroe St.,
   Suite 1437
Chicago, IL 60603
(312) 353-4423

668 Euclid Ave.,
   Suite 520-A
Cleveland, OH 44114
(216) 522-4207

100 N. Central
   Expressway, Suite 500
Dallas, TX 75201
(214) 767-5501

1405 Curtis St., Suite 2900
Denver, CO 80202
(303) 644-2271

11000 Wilshire Blvd.,
   Rm. 13209
Los Angeles, CA
   90024
(310) 575-7575

150 William St., 13th fl.
New York, NY 10038
(212) 264-1207

910 Market St.,
   Suite 570
San Francisco, CA
   94103
(415) 744-7920

915 Second Ave., 28th fl.
Seattle, WA 98174
(206) 553-4656

Office of Consumer Affairs
U.S. Department of Commerce
Washington, DC 20230

Although this agency is largely devoted to improving customer relations of businesses, it also offers to process consumer complaints or refer them to the appropriate agency. It has no enforcement powers and its efficacy under past administrations has been questioned. It processes far fewer consumer complaints annually than the more active state consumer protection agencies.

The OCA publishes a wide range of consumer information pamphlets and leaflets (some free, some not), which are listed in a catalogue available from the Consumer Information Center, P.O. Box 100, Pueblo, CO 81002. Whether as a result of industry pressures or internal bureaucratic incompetence, the quality of these pamphlets is low. They are addressed to a lowest-common-denominator reader, and the advice is generally obvious. The most useful publication is the *Consumer's Resource Handbook,* which can be ordered free, but consumers have reported so much difficulty in receiving copies that readers should consider requesting it through their congressional representative.

Food and Drug Administration
5600 Fishers Lane, Rm. 1685
Rockville, MD 20857
(Consult a telephone directory or the Federal Information
Center for regional telephone numbers.)

The FDA's extremely broad mandate includes ensuring that drugs and medical devices are effective as well as safe, eliminating quack medicines and "cures," and monitoring packaged foods for purity as well as accuracy of labeling.

Complaints about medical problems usually reach the FDA from physicians troubled about the effects of certain drugs and treatments on their patients. Complaints about hearing aids and other medical devices should be directed to the FDA as well as to the state attorney general.

Complaints about food labeling or purity should be addressed to the FDA, but complaints about the safety of meat and poultry products are best reported to the Department of Agriculture's hotline: (800) 535-4555.

Federal Communications Commission
2025 M St., NW
Washington, DC 20554
(202) 632-7000

The FCC regulates all forms of communication, from ham radio and telephone service to radio and television broadcasting. It issues licenses for all forms of broadcasting, and it regulates rates for (and accepts complaints about billing and service of) interstate companies and long-distance telephone services. Although the FCC does not act as a censor or interfere with the free-speech rights of broadcasters, it accepts public comments about the program quality of radio and television stations when their licenses come up for renewal. Recently, it has established policy guidelines for communities issuing franchises to television cable companies, although the rates are determined by the franchising communities.

The aggressiveness of the FCC on behalf of the consumer has been questioned. It has done little, for example, to restrict unsolicited telephone calls from telemarketers or to regulate the television cable industry beyond encouraging more competitive freedom. Moreover, it has reduced competition in broadcasting by substantially increasing the number of radio stations that a single corporation may own. Nevertheless, since all regulatory agencies eventually respond to a high volume of complaints, one should file all complaints with the commission.

Complaints about telephone billing and service and interference with the consumer's reception of radio and television broadcasts by amateur radio broadcasters, aircraft communications, or home electronics devices should be addressed to the Common Carrier Bureau at the address above. Complaints about indecency on radio or television programs, if the local station or the network is unresponsive, should be filed with the Mass Media Bureau at the same address.

U.S. Department of Transportation
Office of Intergovernmental and Consumer Affairs
Washington, DC 20590
(202) 366-2220

This agency handles complaints about airline service, ticketing, lost baggage, "bumping," and other consumer problems.

U.S. Postal Inspection Service

Compared to the Postal Service as a whole, the U.S. Postal Inspection Service is considerably consumer-friendly. In addition to its role as a kind of Internal Affairs Department for the Postal Service, it monitors mail transactions for fraud. Although it does not resolve individual consumer complaints on a per-case basis, it tabulates them and takes action against firms that attract a significant number.

This action can take several forms. The Postal Inspection Service can, for example, stop and return to the sender all mail addressed to the offending firm and take criminal action against it. Or, in the case of delayed mail orders, it can seize the firm's assets and release them only as orders are shipped. In such cases, of course, its actions may secure restitution for the individual consumer.

It's important to note that the Postal Inspection Service can act only if the transaction actually involves the U.S. Postal Service. Thus, credit card orders placed by telephone and delivered by United Parcel Service or some other common carrier are not protected. (This is why many fraudulent telemarketers avoid using the mail and work their scams by using United Parcel Service or Federal Express to pick up their victims' checks.)

Although you cannot determine in advance whether the Postal Inspection Service will be able to resolve your individual problem, you should nevertheless file a complaint. If your complaint, added to others, reveals a systematic pattern of fraud, the firm will be punished or put out of business, giving you some satisfaction even if your individual complaint was not resolved.

Complaints about unfulfilled mail orders or suspected mail fraud should be addressed to the Postal Inspector in Charge located at the address closest to the offending company:

Atlanta, GA 30321-0489

Baltimore, MD 21203-1856

Birmingham, AL
    35202-2767

Boston, MA 02205-2217

Buffalo, NY 14203-2545

Charlotte, NC 28228-3000

Chicago, IL 60669-2201

Cincinnati, OH 45201-2057

Cleveland, OH 44101-0726

Denver, CO 80201-0329

Des Moines, IA 50302-0566

Detroit, MI 44232-3201

Fort Worth, TX 76101-1230

Harrisburg, PA 17105-9000

Hartford, CT 06101-2169

Houston, TX 77001-0902

Indianapolis, IN 46222-1669

Kansas City, MO
    64141-1606

Memphis, TN 38173-0180

Miami, FL 33152-0772

Milwaukee, WI 53201-0788

Newark, NJ 07101-5901

New Orleans, LA 70151-
    1690

New York, NY 10016-7801

Oakland, CA 94623-1005

Pasadena, CA 91102-2000

Philadelphia, PA 19101-9000

Phoenix, AZ 85036-0666

Pittsburgh, PA 15290-9000

Portland, OR 97205-2898

Richmond, VA 23260-5009

St. Louis, MO 63199-2201

St. Paul, MN 55164-2201

San Diego, CA 92112-2110

San Francisco, CA
    94188-2000

San Juan, PR 00936-9614

Seattle, WA 98111-4000

Tampa, FL 33622-2526

Washington, DC
    20066-6096

Complaints about postal service (as distinct from mail-order transactions) should be addressed to the Consumer Advocate, U.S. Postal Service, Washington, DC 20260, (202) 268-4267.

U.S. Consumer Product Safety Commission
Washington, DC 20207
(800) 638-8270

This agency monitors the safety of consumer products (especially those involving children) by issuing recalls and accepting consumer complaints. It maintains a consumer hotline for inquiries about recalls and complaints about product safety: (800) 638-CPSC.

Federal Aviation Administration
Community and Consumer Liaison Division
FAA (APA200)
Washington, DC 20591
(800)FAA-SURE

The FAA responds only to consumer complaints involving safety or the noise created by flight paths. Complaints involving ticketing, bumping, and other aspects of service should be filed with the Department of Transportation.

Interstate Commerce Commission
Office of Compliance and Consumer Assistance,
Rm. 4133
Washington, DC 20432

Although the ICC regulates all forms of interstate surface transportation—railroads and trucking lines, parcel delivery services, and buses—its primary consumer protection activity centers on interstate household moves. It publishes periodic reports that rank interstate moving companies in terms of the complaints filed against them. Although it will not adjudicate a consumer complaint, it will record it and transmit it to the carrier. For this reason, the threat of reporting the carrier may bring about an adjustment. Complaints should be filed with the Complaint and Authority Center of the nearest regional office:

3535 Market St.,
Rm. 16400
Philadelphia, PA 19104

215 Main St., Suite 500
San Francisco, CA 94105

55 W. Monroe St., Suite 550
Chicago, IL 60603

National Highway Traffic Safety Administration
Department of Transportation
Washington, DC 20690
(800) 424-9393

Provides information on vehicle recalls and accepts consumer complaints about vehicle safety.

Comptroller of the Currency
250 E St., SW
Washington, DC 20219

(Check with the telephone directory or the Federal Information Center for the location of the closest regional office.)
Handles complaints about national banks only—that is, banks with the word "National" or "NA" in their names.

Federal Deposit Insurance Corporation
550 17 St., NW
Washington, DC 20429
(800) 424-5488

Handles inquiries and complaints about state banks that are not members of the Federal Reserve System.

Office of Thrift Supervision
1200 G St., NW
Washington, DC 20552
(800) 842-6929

Accepts complaints concerning savings and loan institutions and savings banks.

National Credit Union Administration
1776 G St., NW
Washington, DC 20456
(202) 682-9640

Accepts complaints against federally chartered credit unions.

Securities and Exchange Commission
450 Fifth Ave., NW (MS2-6)
Washington, DC 20549
(202) 272-4750

The SEC monitors both the issuing and the trading of stocks, bonds, and other types of securities. Although SEC approval does not protect the investor against market fluctuations of a security, or even bankruptcy of its issuer, securities that do not have SEC approval should be avoided. Complaints against stockbrokers, if they cannot be resolved by the compliance officer of the brokerage firm, should be filed with the SEC.

Federal Information Center

This service can help you find information about federal programs and regulations. It can tell you which agency is likely to deal with your problem and where its nearest branch office is located. States having toll-free numbers are listed here, but these numbers are accessible *only within the cities listed*. Consumers without access to toll-free numbers can call (301) 722-9098 or write to the service at P.O. Box 600, Cumberland, MD 21506. The hearing-impaired can use a nationwide toll-free TDD/TTI number: (800) 326-2985.

Alabama
Birmingham, Mobile
(800) 347-1997
(800) 366-2988

Alaska
Anchorage
(800) 729-8003

Arizona
Phoenix
(800) 359-3997

Arkansas
Little Rock
(800) 336-2998

California
Los Angeles, San Diego, San
    Francisco, Santa Ana
(800) 726-4995

Colorado
Colorado Springs, Denver,
    Pueblo
(800) 359-3007

Connecticut
Hartford, New Haven
(800) 347-1997

Florida
Ft. Lauderdale, Jacksonville,
   Miami, St. Petersburg,
   Tampa, West Palm Beach
(800) 347-1997

Georgia
Atlanta
(800) 347-1997

Hawaii
Honolulu
(800) 733-5996

Illinois
Chicago
(800) 366-2998

Indiana
Gary
(800) 366-2998
Indianapolis
(800) 347-1997

Iowa
All locations
(800) 735-8004

Kansas
All locations
(800) 735-8004

Kentucky
Louisville
(800) 347-1997

Louisiana
New Orleans
(800) 366-2998

Maryland
Baltimore
(800) 347-1997

Massachusetts
Boston
(800) 347-1997

Michigan
Detroit, Grand Rapids
(800) 347-1997

Minnesota
Minneapolis
(800) 366-2998

Missouri
St. Louis
(800) 266-2998
All other locations
(800) 735-8004

Nebraska
Omaha
(800) 366-2998
All other locations
(800) 735-8004

New Jersey
Newark, Trenton
(800) 347-1997

New Mexico
Albuquerque
(800) 359-3997

New York
Albany, Buffalo, New York,
   Rochester, Syracuse
(800) 347-1997

North Carolina
Charlotte
(800) 347-1997

Ohio
Akron, Cincinnati, Cleveland,
   Columbus, Dayton, Toledo
(800) 347-1997

Oklahoma
Oklahoma City, Tulsa
(800) 366-2998

Oregon
Portland
(800) 726-4995

Pennsylvania
Philadelphia, Pittsburgh
(800) 347-1997

Rhode Island
Providence
(800) 347-1997

Tennessee
Chattanooga
(800) 347-1997
Memphis, Nashville
(800) 366-2998

Texas
Austin, Dallas, Fort Worth,
   Houston, San Antonio
(800) 366-2998

Utah
Salt Lake City
(800) 359-3997

Virginia
Norfolk, Richmond, Roanoke
(800) 347-1997

Washington
Seattle, Tacoma
(800) 726-4995

Wisconsin
Milwaukee
(800) 366-2998

Congressional Representatives and Senators

Consumer problems and inquiries that involve federal agencies—
a mix-up in the payment of Social Security benefits or delays in
the disbursement of Veterans Administration pensions or insurance, for example—are not uncommon, and responses to complaints directed to these agencies are often painfully slow.

The consumer who has tried persistently to resolve a complaint, including efforts to appeal to higher levels within the bureaucracy, should attempt to enlist the help of his or her congressional representative or one of the state's senators. For obvious reasons, federal agencies are much quicker to respond to these legislators than to the general public, and a carefully presented problem is likely to get resolved promptly.

Legislators vary in their commitment to this kind of constituent service, but almost all of them are likely to respond if only because solving consumers' problems is an unexcelled way of earning votes in the next election and maybe even some undying loyalties. For this reason consumers should enlist the help of their representative rather than their senator, since the former is more likely to be concerned about reelection in the near future.

Epilogue

As we have seen, the abused consumer has a number of avenues for obtaining redress, though these avenues do not always lead to the hoped-for results. And though many consumers do get their disputes resolved, the fact remains that currently they are in a weak position relative to the abusing sellers of goods and services. The reasons for this are several.

To begin with, in the course of daily life, typical consumers are vulnerable to abuse from dozens of sources: slipshod manufacturers, unethical retailers, careless or inconsiderate financial institutions, deceptive advertisers, and inefficient government agencies, to name but a few. Consumers may well conclude, therefore, that if they were to complain to the supplier or to regulatory agencies about every instance of mistreatment, they would hardly have time for life's daily activities.

The providers, on the other hand, be they automobile manufacturers or bankers, have a single interest to pursue—that is, resistance to (or weakening of) any regulation that threatens the maximization of profit—and they have ample resources for pursuing it. Thus, the automobile manufacturers can spend significant amounts of money on political campaign contributions and lobbying efforts to defeat legislation on fuel efficiency, pollution control, design safety, or the enactment of Lemon Laws.

Similarly, the banks can effectively influence legislation on credit card interest rates and other issues in which their interests are clearly opposed to those of the consumer. The huge agricultural conglomerates, by stressing the plight of the mythical "family farm," can influence legislation on price supports. Large manufacturing enterprises can blackmail communities into egregious tax concessions with the threat of departing and thus increasing the level of local unemployment.

Deceptive airline advertising remains in place, despite reform efforts by a coalition of state attorneys general, because the federal regulatory agency has preempted regulation and is apparently more sensitive to the interests of the airlines than to those of the deceived consumers.

One cumulative effect of these lobbying efforts is the budgetary starvation of regulatory agencies, both state and federal. As a consequence, many thousands of thoroughly legitimate consumer complaints fail to get resolved by the state attorneys general or by the Federal Trade Commission, not because these agencies lack aggressiveness or are necessarily "probusiness" but because they lack the funding (and hence the staffs) necessary to pursue each and every complaint.

It is only when a large number of complaints are generated by a single source of abuse that the regulatory agencies can move into action. For example, the regulations governing the practice of airline overbooking came about only after the impact of consumer complaints outweighed the lobbying efforts of the airlines. The Federal Trade Commission adopted its consumer-friendly Funeral Rule only after many thousands of complaints about funeral directors' rapacious exploitation of the bereaved. Similarly, regulation of (900) numbers, which could conceivably have been put in place before they appeared on the market, did not get formulated until thousands of consumers had been bilked out of millions of dollars.

The implication is that the consumer *should* complain as often as necessary, even when the likelihood of personal restitution may be low. And the complaint should be targeted at every level—the local dealer, the corporation, and the local, state, and federal legislators and regulatory agencies. The recycling of glass and aluminum beverage containers did not become compulsory in some states until the outrage of consumers countervailed against the lobbying of the beverage industry. The strict usury laws in some states came about only when the exploited borrowers were able to overcome the concerted efforts of the lenders.

Similarly, if the small-claims courts, the consumer protection agency, or the Lemon Law in one state are significantly less effective than those in another, pressure on the state legislators may eventually reduce the disparity. And if the state's professional licensing boards do little or nothing to protect patients or clients, voter protest may persuade the legislature to follow the lead of more progressive states by adding to these boards a "public member"—that is, a lay person whose principal function is to protect the interests of the consumer.

Once in a long while the alleviation of a consumer problem results from the efforts of an individual muckraker, such as Ralph Nader, or the congressional testimony of expert witnesses. Far more often, however, it results from an increasing tide of consumer resentment that can no longer be stemmed by the lobbying efforts of manufacturers and suppliers.

In the short run, consumers who complain often and early may or may not get individual restitution, but in the long run each individual complaint can serve a vital role in enhancing the fairness of the marketplace.

Index